THE GOD WHO SPEAKS
HANS URS VON BALTHASAR'S THEOLOGY OF REVELATION

LARRY S. CHAPP

THE GOD WHO SPEAKS
HANS URS VON BALTHASAR'S
THEOLOGY OF REVELATION

LARRY S. CHAPP

International Scholars Publications
San Francisco - London - Bethesda
1996

Library of Congress Cataloging-in-Publication Data

Chapp, Larry S., 1958-
    The God who speaks : Hans Urs Von Balthasar's theology of
    revelation / Larry S. Chapp.
        p. cm. – (Catholic Scholars Press)
    Includes bibliographical references and index.
    ISBN 1-57309-111-1 (cloth : alk. paper) -- ISBN 1-57309-110-3
    (paper : alk. paper)
    1. Revelation—History of doctrines—20th century. 2. Balthasar,
    Hans Urs von, 1905—Contributions in doctrine of revelation.
    3. Catholic Church—Doctrines—History—20th century. I. Title.
    II. Series: Catholic Scholars Press (Series)
    BT126.5.C48   1996
    231.7'4'092—dc20   96-44893
                                                               CIP

                    Editorial Inquiries:
                    International Scholars Publications
                    7831 Woodmont Avenue, #345
                    Bethesda, MD 20814

                    To order: (800) 55-PUBLISH

Dedicated to my daughter Kelsey,
who has shown me the true face of God

TABLE OF CONTENTS

Larry Chapp's lucid and perceptive study of Hans Urs Von Balthasar's theology of revelation makes a significant contribution toward our understanding of twentieth century Catholic theology. For, although Balthasar -- along with Karl Rahner -- represents one of the two most important Catholic systematic theologians of our century, his theology remains relatively unknown outside circles of the *cogniscenti*. Chapp's carefully crafted but critical introduction to the salient points of Balthasar's rich thought promises to remedy this situation in short order by allowing Balthasar's distinctive theological voice to be clearly heard -- by many, for the first time.

One reason for Balthasar's relative obscurity lies in his very method of writing theology: more aesthetic than narrative, and more meditative than discursive, Balthasar's theology demands the *habitus* of reflection and contemplation -- virtues that must be developed rather than presumed in our culture, but that richly reward the reader when brought to Balthasar's epochal synthesis. Another reason for the neglect -- until recently -- of Balthasar's thought lies in his thorough-going critique of Enlightenment "rationality" and its naively reductionistic faith in "narrative reason." Well before post-modernist critiques of Enlightenment discourse came into vogue, Balthasar quite prophetically recognized and decried the *cul de sac* into which devotion to such rationality has led modern philosophy and theology. While the mainstream of Catholic theology in our century has sought to borrow and utilize the insights of post-Enlightenment epistemology and phenomenology for its own purposes, Balthasar sought to provide a totally different kind of "rationality" for understanding the "truth" of Christianity. Chapp has gone a long way toward making Balthasar's understanding of the "rationality" of this revelation accessible to a wide audience.

Chapp's own reflective but sharp-edged approach to this essentially aesthetic theology uncovers for the reader the possibilities that Balthasar's theological synthesis holds for the western theological project as it approaches its third millennium -- especially in light of current widespread doubts about the ability of Enlightenment modes of discourse to interpret and order the "real world."

Much like an "art appreciation text" introduces students to aesthetic classics while inviting them to encounter those classics for themselves, Chapp's study adumbrates and contextualizes Balthasar's thought while inviting readers to encounter that synthesis first-hand. Chapp deftly accomplishes this contextualization both *ad intra* -- that is, by reference to other parts of Balthasar's wide-ranging synthesis -- and *ad extra* -- by an impressive ability to situate Balthasar's thought within the modern theological and philosophical project. Utilizing the "epistemology of Revelation" as his main interpretive key to Balthasar's thought. Chapp introduces the reader to the startlingly new and rich world of meaning that the phrase "faith knowledge" has for Balthasar, while also uncovering the key role that trinitarian and christological categories have for Christian theology itself and for its ecumenical discussion with other world religions.

Chapp's fine study is a most-welcome addition to the Christian and Catholic theological discussion, heralding a new voice with much promise.

Mark S. Massa, S.J.
Fordham University

ADDITIONAL FOREWORD

The work of Hans Urs Von Balthasar has already long been a major source of European theology. Recent years have witnessed a blossoming of interest on the other side of the Atlantic as well -- as evidenced not only by the continued translation, publication, and reissuing of his works, but also, for example, by the formation of a Balthasar Society at the Catholic Theological Society of America. The reasons for this somewhat belated American awakening to Balthasar are no doubt complex and varied. They probably include such factors as the obvious and acknowledged influence of his theology on Pope John Paul II (who cites him prominently, for example, in his encyclical "On the Dignity of Women"); the "postmodern" turn to intratextuality; the community of interest between Balthasar's project and the methods of the "cultural-linguistic" school influential in contemporary American Protestantism; a swing of the pendulum toward the interior, spiritual, and aesthetic connections of theology after the intellectualism and activism that followed the Second Vatican Council; a similar turn toward a reappropriation of the tradition and to *ad intra* theological discourse in reaction to the universalist and apologetic tendencies of transcendental theologies like Rahner's; and so on. Whatever the causes, the last decade has seen the publication of a spate of English-language books and dissertations introducing his theology or exploring various particular aspects of it.

The title of the present work might lead one to anticipate that it belongs to the second category. But what constitutes the originality of this study -- its focus on Balthasar's theology of revelation -- is also what gives it a wider relevance: for it makes a persuasive case for seeing the notion of "revelation" not merely as a significant theme, but as the hermeneutical key to the entirety of Balthasar's project. In his later life Balthasar complained about those who distorted the fundamental intent of his theology by misconstruing his sense of "aesthetics." This study, by contrast, understands the "aesthetic" nature of Balthasar's theology in the context of what for him was always central: the Word of God.

Balthasar's major theological writings are daunting in their volume, breadth, style, and complexity. The present study uncovers Balthasar's basic premises and method in a way that allows the reader not only to grasp the essential internal unity of these "systematic" theological works, but also to appreciate their intrinsic connection with Balthasar's more accessible short spiritual essays. In addition to presenting a sympathetic understanding of Balthasar's project, the author locates it critically in the context of contemporary Catholic thought. This book's logical organization, clear exposition, and careful analysis, will provide an excellent introduction to Balthasar's theology for those who are not acquainted with it, and a source of thought-provoking systematic insight for those who are.

Richard Viladesau
Associate Professor of Theology
Fordham University

PREFACE

Hans Urs Von Balthasar is one of the most important Catholic theologians of this century. However, his theology is exceptionally complex and is difficult to summarize or encapsulate. This complexity is due to the very nature of Balthasar's theological method which is a mystical, contemplative meditation on the overall aesthetic "wholeness" of God's revelation in Jesus. Unfortunately, this more "aesthetic" approach has the negative effect of rendering his theology somewhat diffuse and non systematic. This makes it extremely difficult to analyze and, importantly, to teach. Indeed, it is nearly impossible to teach to undergraduates which, I think, accounts for much of Balthasar's marginalization in the academy. Balthasar's is a theology to be savored, like a fine wine or good poetry. It is something, therefore, of an acquired taste that appeals largely to those who are already theologically literate and "seasoned." It is to be read slowly, by a theologically mature mind, and meditated upon over and over. This, then, is the first major point emphasized in my text -- that if one is to appreciate and understand Balthasar's theology one must first begin by taking it on its own terms and not to get frustrated when it does not engage in the kind of discursive, analytical, "critical," and systematic approach adopted by so much of modern theology. That is not to say that Balthasar never exhibits any of the above traits. However, it is a question of emphasis and Balthasar's theology is closer to a piano concerto than a philosophical treatise.

The problem with Balthasar's approach, from the perspective of the scholar who wishes to disseminate Balthasar's "ideas" more widely, is that, like good poetry, it loses a great deal in translation. There is no substitute, when one is

v

seeking an aesthetic experience, for an actual encounter with the artistic object itself -- works "about" the object, though useful, are a pale substitute at best. Therefore, there is a need for an analysis of his theology that attempts to identify the central controlling theme of his overall work so that the reader seeking an "experience" of Balthasar will have a "perspective" with which to approach the whole. Much as a text on "art appreciation" can aid one's understanding of a particular artist by providing an interpretive "key" with which to approach the artist's work, so too, the most important function served by my text on Balthasar is that it gives the reader a major interpretive key for the entire work. It makes no claim to be an exhaustive summary of all of the trajectories in Balthasar's theology. It is no substitute for reading Balthasar. However, I think that I have correctly identified the main controlling idea that animates Balthasar, the idea that puts "fire into his equations." That theme is his emphasis on the real "knowledge" that faith in God's Revelation brings. Thus, in my opinion, the task of analyzing this rather diffuse and complex theology must begin with an exploration of the manner in which Balthasar proceeds from his theology of "the epistemology of revelation" to his various theological conclusions. Such an analysis can shed light on his central determining theological motifs and the manner in which they control his entire theological enterprise.

Because of his emphasis upon Revelation Balthasar is frequently compared with Karl Barth. However, I believe this is a facile comparison. Most Christian theologians place some kind of emphasis upon Revelation as a starting point for doing theology. Clearly, some emphasize the inner integrity of Revelation and seek to analyze its categories without a great deal of "foundationalist" underpinnings. Barth and Balthasar share this approach. However, the similarities stop there. My text does not make an explicit Barth/Balthasar comparison, but the manner in which I analyze Balthasar's approach to Revelation should make the differences clear to anyone familiar with both thinkers. The main difference can be easily categorized as a Catholic-Protestant distinction. The early Barth rejected the doctrine of analogy and the late Barth was more accepting, but still extremely ambiguous as to the role it should play in theology. Balthasar's entire approach is predicated upon the doctrine of analogy -- the structure of finite reality, in all of its inner integrity precisely as the finite, can act as a vessel of divine self-communication. However, Balthasar defers to the epistemological priority of the act of faith and Revelation in his analysis of such analogies. This might seem like a fine distinction, but it is an important one.

The main question for Balthasar then, in his approach to Revelation, is: If Revelation and faith bring real "knowledge" to the believer, to what kind of "rationality" does it appeal? What is the best intramundane analogy in the realm of epistemology that we can use? Balthasar's answer is clear from the very structure of his overall work -- it is not the univocal, reductionistic, naturalistic, and overly "linear" rationality of the Enlightenment to which we must appeal, but the kind of rationality best typified by poets, playwrights, and mystics. Hence, we get the theological aesthetic and the theo-dramatic rather than a "summa" of systematized propositions. For Balthasar, rationality is important, but the epistemological priority is to the inner rationality of Revelation itself. It is a question of emphasis rather than a systematic rejection of foundationalism as in Barth. The anthropological tail of the Enlightenment must not be allowed to wag the revelational dog of the Church's kerygma. This is the fundamental point of chapter one and it sets the tone for the discussion in the rest of the text.

Before one proceeds to an elaboration of this idea, one has to first analyze the metaphysical underpinnings that Balthasar develops for the entire idea of Revelation as a possibility. This is what I try to accomplish in chapters two and three. The achievement of Balthasar's theological aesthetic is that he has attempted to develop a true "theology of the finite." What is the importance of finitude? Why did God create it? Can God use the finite to communicate the infinite? Can the finite act as a "vessel" for the infinite? My text contributes to an understanding of Balthasar in this area by developing Balthasar's metaphysical foundations for this whole approach. An analysis of the concept of "Being" leads to an intellectual cul de sac that drives us toward either a mythological dualism or a philosophical monism (either materialistic or "spiritual") without the insight brought by Christian Revelation in its doctrine of creation. Our experience of the "being" of the world must be viewed, fundamentally, as containing both a "real" existence in itself, as well as a recognition that the being of the world is non subsistent and is dependent upon a radically gratuitous, free communication from the "heart of Infinite Being." In other words, finite being, awaits a revelation of a divine love that alone can bridge the gulf between the finite and the infinite and satisfy the deep longing of finite being to achieve a full union with infinite Being while retaining its own integrity as "finite." My text explicates the close connection between Balthasar's metaphysics and his trinitarian theology -- only the unity within difference that is the trinitarian circumincession can act as the ground of possibility for a unity within difference in the God-world relationship. Balthasar's trinitarian metaphysics of love attempts to overcome the dualism of mythology and the monism of philosophy by developing the deep theological significance of "finitude" as part of the great Mystery of God's "relational" unity. Revelation, seen as an event within the finite horizon of our existence, finds its ground of possibility in God's trinitarian pattern of kenotic "going forth" in order to return to itself. God posits that which is "not God" (creation) while at the same time acting as the "bridge" that brings these two realms together into unity. The autonomy/heteronomy dialectic is thus overcome in the Mystery of God's trinitarian love. In many ways, this is the most unique contribution of Balthasar's theology which is why my text spends a full two chapters making this point. Revelation is possible because God is so "Wholly Other" (*Aliud*) that he can be the "Non Other" (*Non Aliud*).

Chapter four takes up the question of Balthasar's theological aesthetic as such. This analysis begins by pointing out that the central idea of Balthasar's theology of revelation is that God wills to be known by his creatures. Hence, the title of this work. The God of Jesus Christ is the God who would be known. The Christian God is a revealing God, a self-disclosing God, a "God Who Speaks." Thus, within Christian theology, apophatic theology must be viewed as simply an iconoclastic "corrective" within an overarching kataphatic framework. The fact that God accomplishes this task of self-communication through the finite and the visible -- e.g. the humanity of Jesus, the Scriptures, the Church, the "world," -- compels Balthasar to develop a theological aesthetic that sees in the earthly beauty (Gestalt) of the form of God's revelation in Jesus an analog to the divine "Glory." The central controlling theological idea that undergirds this method is Balthasar's assertion that the "form" of God's revelation is possessed of an infinite, inner "necessity" that is analogous to the aesthetic "necessity" of great works of art. Balthasar's development of his aesthetic is connected to his christology and vice versa. The "Ur" event of revelation is the Christ-event as such. It has an irreducible uniqueness. Therefore, Balthasar's theology of revelation runs directly counter to the current trend in theology to "abstract" from the historical particularity of revelation in order to better dialogue with other religious traditions. It is my hope that my text allows the reader to see that Balthasar's grounding of his Christology in his aesthetic is motivated by a genuine concern to preserve the integrity of historical finitude in the face of the infinite -- that finitude has as one of its constitutive properties its own inner integrity vis-a-vis the infinite.

One could, I suppose, read Balthasar's aesthetic christology, with all of its talk of "inner necessity" and "unique irreducibility," as a crafty way of reintroducing a triumphalistic view of Christianity vis-a-vis other world religions. However, one could also read it, as my text does, as a genuine attempt to preserve the importance of distinction and difference within our time-bound horizon. Indeed, it is the more "homogenizing" approach to the theology of world religions -- an approach that seeks some sort of Archemedean objectivity with which to judge all religions -- which is triumphalistic. Balthasar's "irreducible" and "incomparable" Christ affirms the importance of distinction and particularity and, therefore, by implication, the importance of real dialogue as well -- a real conversation between religious perspectives that are truly different. Thus, Balthasar's aesthetic approach to christology lays down the foundation stone for the entirety of his theology of revelation: God has spoken definitively and visibly in Jesus. This actually gives the Christian theologian something specifically Christian to say in interreligious dialogue.

This emphasis upon the aesthetic means that any "epistemology" of Revelation must emphasize that the best way to approach the Christ figure is with the eyes of faith. Only those who have been granted such "eyes" can truly "see" Revelation. Much as someone raised on "heavy metal" music probably does not have the "ear" to truly here Mozart, even if one has physically listened to all of the "notes," so too with God's Revelation in Jesus. Genuine Christian Christology, therefore, cannot be accomplished from a purely secular and "neutral" vantage point that "brackets" faith in an attempt to analyze the significance of Christ from within the categories of "comparative" religion. Christ cannot be reduced, Enlightenment style (Lessing), to a mere "type" of a more generic "savior figure" archetype drawn from the history of religions school of thought. Here, as elsewhere, the significance of my text is to point out this not so hidden attack upon the Enlightenment in Balthasar's theology. In everything that he writes in his aesthetic, Balthasar is engaging the Enlightenment.

Chapters five and six deal with the mediations of this Revelation in scripture and in the Church. Balthasar's theology of revelation centers around his attempt to counter the growing trend, mentioned above, to abstract from the particularity of

Revelation in favor of the rationalistic and reductionistic abstractions of the "history of religions" school of thought. By showing how God's self-revelation in Jesus is communicated to the believer through the normative mediations of Scripture and Church -- mediations which share in the original revelatory event and must be considered in conjunction with it, my text explicates Balthasar's development of Revelation's various finite mediations. Balthasar's approach to scriptural exegesis and ecclesiology can be summarized in a nutshell: God's revelation in Jesus posits its own field of interpretation that is itself, therefore, part of the original revelatory event itself. Revelation is not a static event, but an ongoing encounter. In order for the "Ur-event" of God's revelation in Christ to be ontologically contemporaneous with the believer, this originating event must be "mediated" in such a fashion that the believer is granted access to the same Christ to which St. Paul had access.

In biblical exegesis one has to begin with an analysis, yet again, of what Balthasar refers to as the "naive realism" of the Enlightenment. What my text attempts to do in this chapter on exegesis is to point out the many ways in which Balthasar's approach finds its inner motivation in its repudiation of the Enlightenment project in theology and philosophy as well as the facile post-modernism that is its stepchild. Firmly rooted in the classical and neo-Thomistic traditions, Balthasar does an excellent job of showing their continued vitality and fruitfulness as an antidote to the continued mechanism, reductionism, and dualism inherent within the modern project. His analysis makes it abundantly clear that the current confusion and loss of identity in Christian intellectual circles is a direct result of the loss of nerve created by the philosophical *cul de sac* into which we have been led. Beginning with the empiricist's denial that the mind knows the object of knowledge in itself, philosophy has increasingly driven a wedge between empirical fact and the inner "representation" of the object in the knowing, conscious mind. All that the mind can truly know is this internal representation -- not the object in itself. Thus, mind does not transcend itself through its knowledge of empirical objects. Whereas the medievals viewed the finite as a vehicle of a transcendence that could be apprehended by the mind, the empiricists denied the ability of the mind to transcend itself in this manner. Kant drives this point home in his distinction between what he calls the "sublime" and the finite form that mediates it.

The implications of this view for theology are clear and immediate: The shapely, finite fact of Christ cannot carry transcendent deity. Thus, the direction of Christian theology since the Enlightenment has been in the direction of a deistic doctrine of God and a form of biblical exegesis that makes overly neat "critical" distinctions between the historical "facts" that undergird the biblical narratives and the "noumenal" meaning given to the narratives by the biblical authors -- a meaning that is largely "detachable" from the actual events and which bears little to no intrinsic orientation to the facts it purports to interpret. The Bible must be "demythologized" through a series of critical assumptions, the first of which is that the very coming together of the transcendent and finite realms that the biblical events purport to describe is stated to be impossible (or highly suspect) on a priori grounds. Such an approach renders miracles impossible, sees the resurrection narratives as dubious theological constructs, and views the Christology of the New Testament as a pious ecclesiastical fiction retrojected back onto the historical Jesus. What is left of the towering figure of Jesus presented by the Gospels once the Enlightenment exegetes have finished, depends upon the prevailing Zeitgeist -- first a deistic moralist, then a deluded "eschatological/apocalyptic" prophet, followed by an angst-filled existential hero, and finally, today, the political liberator and "cynic-sage" who sees "oppressors" everywhere. The figure of Christ becomes surprisingly plastic and is soon rendered meaningless as anything other than a theological Rorschach.

What is needed is to rescue "critical" exegesis from the hegemony of "historical critical" exegesis where "history" is defined naively as "what really happened" and is played off of the "distortions" of later "interpretation." Balthasar's concern here, once again, is the same as in his approach to the unified "Gestalt" of the Ur event of Revelation in Christ: to develop a different kind of "rationality" that can act as the basis for a new type of "critical" exegesis. Balthasar is not talking here of a naive return to the allegorizations of the Fathers, but of an approach to exegesis that emphasizes that it is the completed canonical text that is normative -- not the "reconstructed Jesus" behind the text. Some have called this kind of narrative approach a "second naiveté." I don't know if Balthasar would like that phrase or not. But one thing is certain, Balthasar's aesthetic and dramatic "rationality" prefers to see the *Endgestalt* of the canonical text as normative for theology. Historical critical exegesis has its place in this mix -- he does not reject it utterly -- but it must lose its naive pretensions to giving us access to the "real Jesus" as opposed to the "Christ of Faith" presented by the finished Gospel texts.

Finally, my text ends with a discussion of the personalistic (dramatic) categories in Balthasar's approach to ecclesiology. This chapter will focus on Balthasar's theological development of the Church as a transparent mediation of the form of God's revelation in Christ. Thus, the question arises as to how the Church is both identified and not identified with Christ, i.e. how the Church is both "Body" and "Bride" of the Lord. The thesis argued here is that Balthasar asserts that this paradox is overcome in the unity within difference imparted to the Church through the agency of the singular subjectivity of Christ. Balthasar develops a theological-trinitarian concept of "person" that guides this analysis. This chapter explores the manner in which Balthasar develops the idea of the Church as a mediation of the Christ-event through the engraced participation of all believers in the unique christological "subjectivity" of the Church.

Thus, although Balthasar has a "high christology" and, therefore, a "high ecclesiology," he cannot be viewed as a simple ecclesiastical conservative. He himself may have been conservative on certain issues, but his emphasis in ecclesiology is on the engraced "praxis" of the individual believer as the bedrock for any talk of the church as the "Body of Christ." This explains his fascination with the "saints" as a genuine locus for theological speculation on Revelation, and upon "holiness" as a prerequisite for doing good theology. It also explains his defection from the Jesuits in order to found a secular institute. Christian theology must be "ecclesial theology" since Revelation is only rendered contemporaneous to the theologian through the mediation of the whole body of believers, both living and dead, and the ongoing lived experience of the risen Christ in the life of the Church. The "real Jesus" is the resurrected Jesus who is present in his ongoing mediations.

It is my hope that this text will inspire more readers to examine the works of this important theologian. To the extent that what follows accomplishes this goal, then I will consider the project to have been worthwhile and successful.

Chapter One:
A Brief Introduction to Balthasar and his Theology

The late Swiss theologian Hans Urs von Balthasar has grown in popularity in the English speaking world in recent years due to the ever increasing number of his works that are appearing in translation. There is also a growing body of secondary literature on his works.[1]   However, for many people the theology of this eminent theologian remains something of a mystery -- few have the time or expertise to "wade through" the prodigious amount of material produced by Balthasar.   Thus, for many of those who have been exposed to Balthasar's theology there is something of a "fragmentary" quality to their knowledge. Therefore, the question to which the current work addresses itself is the question of the whole: what is the central theological idea at the core of Balthasar's vision? If such a central idea or insight exists, then it might be possible to understand Balthasar's theology even if one is exposed only to some of the "fragments." Furthermore, if one can discover this controlling idea then it should be possible to compare Balthasar with other theologians and to situate his theology in the broader context of his times. Thus, the goal of this book is twofold: 1) To explicate and make clear the central theological insight of Balthasar's "method"; and 2) To situate this theology within its proper historical context and to thereby assess its overall importance to contemporary theology.

---

[1]See, for example, Edward T. Oakes, S.J. *Pattern of Redemption: The Theology of Hans Urs Von Balthasar*, (New York: Continuum, 1994). This is one of the more noteworthy works in a growing field of Balthasar literature.

The key idea at the heart of Balthasar's theology is the centrality of God's revelation in Christ. Of course, an emphasis on "revelation" is nothing new in Christian theology. So how is Balthasar's approach to the theology of revelation distinctive? It is in his insistence that revelation possesses a "structure" or a "form" (Gestalt) that shines forth with an inner beauty and light. This "beauty" in God's historical revelation is in fact an expression of God's eternal "glory" and is, therefore, analogous to but not identical with, earthly concepts of beauty. Karl Rahner developed a similar idea in his famous dictum: the economic trinity is the immanent trinity and vice versa. Balthasar takes this idea a step further and develops a corollary to this Rahnerian principle: if God's revelation in history is a reflection of God's inner life, then it should be expressive of God's inner beauty (Glory). Just as an older theology meditated upon the propositional truths that could be gleaned from revelation, Balthasar's theology pursues that aspect of revelation that makes it "attractive" in the first place. In short, Balthasar attempts to "repristinate" revelation and to thereby show that theology need not subordinate revelation to various philosophical systems in order to make it "believable": revelation shines forth with an inner credibility that springs from the depths of a form that is expressive of divine glory.[2]

Such a strong emphasis on historical revelation as a vehicle for divine glory opens up a series of problems. How can the finite mediate the infinite? And once one has attempted an answer to that question, one must then ask how a past historical event that claims to be an irruption of divine glory into the world can mediate this event to later generations in a manner that preserves its original quality. The structure of this book reflects a concern with these two questions. The current chapter will offer some introductory remarks with regard to the biographical details of Balthasar's life and career, followed by a brief overview of the fundamental elements of Balthasar's theology of revelation. Chapters two and three will analyze the metaphysical foundations for Balthasar's theology of revelation. What is the

---

[2]What Balthasar is saying here could also be formulated as an attempt to analyze the unique type of "rationality" that Revelation bears within its own categories. Here Balthasar shares the post-modernist's critique of the Englightenment's univocal approach to rationality. Balthasar, as we shall see, in no way rejects the doctrine of analogy or "natural theology." However, he points out that we must not "box in" Revelation to a set of presuppositions that are in turn based on "foundationalist" approaches that presume this more univocal Enlightenment approach to rationality and "credibility." Revelation has "aesthetic" and "dramatic" elements that are a contitutive part of its "rationality." These must be examined from within their own inner dynamic.

metaphysical "ground of possibility" for a finite mediation of the infinite? This will lay the foundation for a discussion, in chapter four, of Balthasar's theological aesthetic and the concept of the "form" of revelation. Chapter five will begin a discussion of the way in which the "form" of revelation is mediated to later generations of believers through the Scriptures. This will require an analysis of Balthasar's approach to scriptural exegesis. Chapter six will extend this discussion of the mediation of the form of revelation by examining the ecclesial nature of theology. Finally, some brief concluding remarks on the overall significance of Balthasar's theology will be offered in chapter seven.

A. Historical and Biographical Details.

Henri de Lubac has referred to Hans Urs von Balthasar as "perhaps the most cultivated man of his time."[3] Louis Bouyer has described Balthasar's work *Prayer* [4] as "possibly the finest book on prayer that has appeared since the seventeenth century".[5] Aidan Nichols has referred to Balthasar as "this century's greatest Catholic theologian."[6] And finally, with the publication of *Herrlichkeit: Eine theologische Aesthetik,*[7] few would deny that Balthasar stands out as one of the more noteworthy Catholic theologians of this century. And yet, Balthasar's enormous theological output has been, until relatively recently, largely ignored by the English speaking theological community. One could argue, perhaps, that this anonymity in North America is due in large measure to the lack of English translations (once again, until very recently), for most of Balthasar's major theological enterprises. However, does this not beg the essential question of why his major works were not deemed worthy of translation before now?[8]

---

[3]Henri de Lubac, "A Witness of Christ in the Church: Hans Urs von Balthasar," *Communio,* (Fall, 1975), 230.

[4]Hans Urs von Balthasar, *Prayer,* (New York: Sheed and Ward, 1961).

[5]Quoted in. J.K. Riches, "The Theology of Hans Urs von Balthasar," *Theology,* (November, 1972), 562.

[6]Aidan Nichols, O.P., *From Newman to Congar: The Idea of Doctrinal Development from the Victorians to the Second Vatican Council,* (Edinburgh: T&T Clark, 1990), 16.

[7]Hans Urs von Balthasar, *Herrlichkeit: Eine theologische Aesthetik* , (Einsiedeln: Johannes Verlag, 1961).

[8]Unfortunately, the works of Balthasar which were translated in the sixties and early seventies were his more controversial and "polemical" works. For example, his *Cordula oder der*

Two major reasons are usually put forward as the explanation for this lack of influence. The one is theological, the other biographical. The primary reason is, of course, theological, and we will examine this at great length. However, Balthasar's theology, like any theology, is marked by the controversies of its age, and a nuanced understanding of its complexities can only be achieved through a preliminary historical analysis of its theological milieu. Before we begin analyzing the historical context of his theology we need to glance at some of the basic biographical details of his life. It is not my intention to engage in a lengthy discussion of all of the details of Balthasar's lengthy career. These details have been chronicled elsewhere and need not be repeated here.[9] However, it is necessary to highlight certain key moments in his life since his developing theological insights often led Balthasar into career moves which left his friends and associates puzzled, and led to his theological isolation during his important middle years.

In the opening paragraph of his excellent "portrait" of Balthasar's life, Medard Kehl, S.J. gives a succinct chronology:

> Hans Urs von Balthasar was born in Lucerne on August 4, 1905. After attending the grammar school and the Gymnasium of the Benedictines in Engelberg and of the Jesuits in Feldkirch, he went on to the universities of Vienna, Berlin, and finally Zurich where, on October 27, 1928, he completed his doctoral examinations in Germanistics and philosophy. The title of his dissertation was: "The History of the Eschatological Problem in Modern German Literature." On October 31, 1929, he entered the Society of Jesus.

Ernstfall which came out in 1966 (Basel: Johannes Verlag) was widely perceived as Balthasar's criticism of Rahner's theology of the "supernatural existential" and the "anonymous Christian." Its tone is negative and contentious. However, as early as 1969 it was translated into English under the title *The Moment of Christian Witness* (New York: Newman Press) and became something of a "cult" book among those opposed to Rahner's theology. Contrast this with the delay in translation which greeted the first volume of his programmatic theological masterpiece *Herrlichkeit: Eine theologische Aesthetik*. Originally published in 1961 by Johannes Verlag, its English translation did not appear until 1982 under the joint efforts of the Scottish publishing house of T. & T. Clark and Ignatius Press in San Francisco. It is noteworthy once again that Ignatius Press has the reputation of being a "conservative" publishing company. This underscores the perception that many North Americans have of Balthasar that he too is a "conservative."

[9]For what follows I am indebted to two excellent secondary sources which deal with Balthasar's biography directly, and two primary sources in which Balthasar describes the close interconncection between his theology and the various people who have influenced his life: Hans Urs von Balthasar, *First Glance at Adrienne von Speyr*, O.C.D., (San Francisco: Ignatius Press. 1981).; Balthasar, "In Retrospect,"*Communio*, (Fall, 1975), 197-220.; Peter Henrici, "Hans Urs von Balthasar: A Sketch of His Life,"; Medard Kehl, S.J. and Werner Loser, S.J. (eds.), *The von Balthasar Reader*, (New York, Crossroad, 1982), 3-54.

4

After his two year novitiate in Feldkirch, he studied philosophy from 1931 to 1933 at the Jesuit philosophical faculty, ... in Pullach and then theology in Lyons (Fourviere) from 1933 to 1937. He was ordained to the priesthood on July 26, 1936. From the Autumn of 1937 to the Summer of 1939 he served as an associate editor of the journal *Stimmen der Zeit* in Munich. ... From the beginning of 1940 he worked in the university student chaplaincy in Basel. Since 1950, after leaving the Society of Jesus, he has been living in Basel as the spiritual leader of the *Johannesgemeinschaft* ... , publisher (the *Johannesverlag*), and theological writer. After the Second Vatican Council he became a member of the Papal Theological Commission, all the while continuing his varied activity as a lecturer and retreat director.[10]

There are two salient features of this biographical summary which are important for our present discussion. First, it often comes as a shock to many people when they realize that Balthasar, by his own choice, never taught theology in a major university or college on a full-time basis. Instead, he concentrated on retreat work and other forms of spiritual direction. That is not to say that Balthasar's theology is unscholarly or lacking in academic rigor. However, it is more than a mere suspicion that the emphasis in his theology on the role of prayer, contemplation, and general asceticism is somehow influenced by the absence of a formal "academic" setting for his theological career.

This absence of an "academic" setting for his theological career could also account for Balthasar's relative lack of interest in "apologetic" or "fundamental" theology. Apologetic theology, according to David Tracy, is the preferred theology of the academy since the need for evidentiary rebuttal is required in the argumentative forum of the university.[11] Balthasar's theology had no such "argumentative" context and often seems impatient with anyone who wants to waste time trying to "prove" Christianity to the rational skeptic. Balthasar's theology begins and ends with a concern to draw out the deep spiritual richness of revelation

---

[10]Medard Kehl, S.J., *The Von Balthasar Reader*, 3.

[11]David Tracy, *The Analogical Imagination: Christian Theology and the Culture of Pluralism*, (New York: Crossroad, 1989), 14-21. It should be noted here that I am using the term "argumentative" in a technical sense: theology is not only the systematic reflection upon the experience of faith, but must also engage in rational argumentation in order to justify its claims. I would agree with the assessment of Aidan Nichols, O.P. that theology, like any habit of study, must be argumentative, retentive, and imaginative. Aidan Nichols, O.P., *The Shape of Catholic Theology: An Introduction to its Sources, Principles, and History*, (Collegeville, Minnesota: The Liturgical Press, 1991), 14.

and the tradition it created as its own "field" of interpretation. Indeed, Balthasar states quite clearly that his theological "mission" is incomprehensible without reference to the secular institute he founded in conjunction with the mystic Adrienne von Speyr.[12] Thus, Balthasar's theological career is self-consciously oriented away from the concerns of the academy and toward those who, in some sense, already "believe." And the question of whether his theology influenced his career or his career his theology is of little importance.

What is clear is that Balthasar's method and his life both evince a concern for the presence of Spirit-given sanctity, and the desire to remain "open" to God's will in whatever form the divine self-communication may take place. Throughout his life Balthasar remained committed to the vision later articulated by Vatican II as the "universal call to holiness."[13] The task of theology, therefore, is to aid the Church in the promotion of this goal.[14]

Ironically, despite this new emphasis on holiness from the Council, the bifurcation between dogmatic and "spiritual" theology that began in the post-Tridentine Church perdured. Thus, an approach such as Balthasar's that sought to structure theology methodologically around the categories of christological *mission* and ecclesial *vocation*, was misunderstood as dealing with "spirituality." It was, therefore, seen as of little importance to "critical" theology. Any theology which forges too close a link between the "witness" of sanctity and dogmatics will run the risk of being accused of romanticism, and of a false mixing of subjective "piety" and objective, "scientific" theology. Such an emphasis can also lead to marginalization insofar as the demand for a connection between sanctity and

---

[12]*First Glance at Adrienne Von Speyr*, 13. Balthasar states: "On the whole I received far more from her, theologically, than she from me. ... I not only made some of the most difficult decisions of my life - including my leaving the Jesuit Order - following her advice, but I also strove to bring my way of looking at Christian revelation into conformity with hers. ... Today, after her death, her work appears far more important to me than mine." Also see, Balthasar, "In Retrospect," *Communio*, (Fall, 1975), 219. Balthasar states here: "Her work [von Speyr's] and mine are neither psychologically nor philologically to be separated: two halves of a single whole, which has as its center a unique foundation."

[13]Cf. Balthasar, *The Christian State of Life*, (San Francisco: Ignatius Press, 1983). Here Balthasar outlines his profound theology of Christian vocation seen as an imitation of the *via apostolica* . Christian life is seen as an imitation of the divine mission granted to Christ and passed on to the Church. Thus, the living of the three evangelical counsels is grounded, not in the artificial categories of post-tridentine scholasticism, but in an analysis of the *structura amoris* as revealed by Christ.

[14]Cf. Balthasar, "Theology and Holiness," *Communio*, (Winter, 1987), 341-350.

theology exposes the theologian making this claim to charges of spiritual arrogance: "are you claiming that *you* possess such holiness and that *we* do not?"[15]

This leads us to the second salient feature of Balthasar's biography. I have already mentioned Balthasar's involvement with the mystic Adrienne von Speyr and the secular institute (*Johannesgemeinschaft*) which they co-founded. Balthasar sought to integrate his Jesuit vocation with this new-found desire to found a secular institute. But after his petition for such an integration failed, Balthasar was forced into the most difficult decision of his life - leaving the Jesuits.[16] That the pain of leaving his Jesuit "home" never left him can be seen in his petition (the year he died) for readmission to the Jesuits along with his secular institute. Sadly, it was his departure from the Jesuit "family" to pursue an independent venture with an obscure mystic that probably, more than any other factor, had the net effect of marginalizing his theology at one of the most decisive junctures in the history of Catholic theology.

Balthasar also seems to have raised the suspicions of those who saw little value in anything that departed from post-tridentine scholasticism.[17] Although

---

[15]Cf. Paul Imhof and Hubert Biallowons, (eds.) *Karl Rahner in Dialogue: Conversations and Interviews 1965-1982*, (New York: Crossroad, 1986),124-126. Such an attitude toward Balthasar can be seen, at least partially I think, in Rahner's insinuation that Balthasar's theological involvement with Von Speyr led Balthasar into a kind of theological gnosticism. Inherent in Rahner's criticism is the idea that any theological elaboration of "private revelations" is questionable if such revelations lead the theologian to speculations which cannot be independently confirmed through a direct appeal to revelation itself. However, as anyone with any familiarity with Balthasar's theology knows (and Rahner would certainly fall into this category), the use of the "witness" of the saints and of their various charisms in order to open up theology to new Spirit-given insights into revelation for contemporary people, is, for Balthasar, far from a dabbling in esoteric revelations. Rather, it is one of the primary ways through which the Spirit speaks *in the Church's dogmatic tradition*. Furthermore, how could anyone seriously accuse Balthasar's theology of ignoring the Church's dogmatic tradition in favor of elitist private revelations? Rahner seems to be doing just that in regard to Balthasar's theology of the cross. One has to wonder if Rahner is not motivated here more by an anxiety over the (then) increasing fusion between "spirituality" and dogmatics in Balthasar's theology.

[16]The close connection between Balthasar's concern for the secular institute and his decision to leave the Jesuits can be seen in his admission that even this decision was made in dialogue with the advice of von Speyr. Cf. *First Glance at Adrienne von Speyr*. 13.

[17]Indeed, Balthasar's disgust with the narrow ossification of theology in the post-tridentine Church led him to publish (1952) his now famous *Schleifung der Bastionen. Von der Kirche in dieser Zeit*. Many see in this call for a greater openness in the Church a different Balthasar than the post-Conciliar "polemical" Balthasar. Kung, for example, states that this book of Balthasar's "came at the time like a loud, impatient trumpet blast, calling for the Church to drop its defensive posture toward the world - a position that Balthasar, admittedly, seems to have left far behind him." Hans Kung, *Theology for the Third Millennium: an Ecumenical View*, (New York: Doubleday, 1988), 266.

7

Balthasar's theology is heavily influenced by the neo-scholasticism of the early part of the century, he was never satisfied with its lifeless formalisms and the stiff, legalistic categories of its thought patterns. Indeed, Balthasar referred to his time studying philosophy as a "languishing in the desert of neo-scholasticism."[18] Balthasar puts it as follows:

> My entire period of study in the Society was a grim struggle with the dreariness of theology, with what men had made out of the glory of revelation. I could not endure this presentation of the Word of God. I could have lashed out with the fury of a Sampson. ... I ... was living in a state of unbounded indignation.[19]

Thus, Balthasar did not receive an enthusiastic hearing from either the theologians of the academy or of the Roman Curia. Fortunately, he found kindred spirits in neo-Augustinian[20] theologians like Henri de Lubac, S.J. and Jean Danielou who were on the cutting edge of the *nouvelle theologie* and were opening up the forgotten and profound riches of the Church's wider, pre-Tridentine tradition.[21] However, as we have seen, at this stage in his career Balthasar was more interested in pastoral work than strict academic theology per se, and was therefore never as influential in the preconciliar Church as were theologians like de Lubac, Rahner, Danielou, Grillmeier, Guardini, and Congar. That is not to say that Balthasar was not producing substantive theology during this time period. Nevertheless, the aim and scope of his theology was oriented toward the internal

---

[18]Hans Urs von Balthasar, *Rechenschaft 1965*, (Einsiedeln: 1965), 34. Quoted in, Peter Henrici, "A Sketch of Balthasar's Life," *Communio*, (Fall, 1989) 306-350.

[19]Adrienne von Speyr, *Erde und Himmel. Ein Tagebuch: Zweiter Teil, Die Zeit der grossen Diktate*, ed. and with an introduction by Hans Urs Von Balthasar, (Einsiedeln: 1975), 195 ff. Quoted in Peter Henrici, "A Sketch of Balthasar's Life, " 313.

[20]I borrow the use of this term to describe the general tenor of these theologians from Avery Dulles, S.J. Cf. "A Half Century of Ecclesiology," *Theological Studies*, 50, 1989, 439-440. Dulles uses it primarily in reference to a theological "school" of the post-conciliar Church (e.g., Ratzinger, de Lubac, Balthasar). Nevertheless, the pre-conciliar emphasis found in these theologians differs little from the post-conciliar and so I retain the use of the term "neo-Augustinian" for this time period. The term can be somewhat misleading if one is to understand it as indicating that these theologians were strict Augustinians in the traditional sense of that word. However, it is a good descriptive term insofar as theologians like Balthasar definitely interject a Platonizing and Augustinian element into their interpretation of Thomas and the entire pre-tridentine tradition.

[21]For a good assessment of Balthasar's opinion of de Lubac's theology see: Hans Urs von Balthasar, "The Achievement of Henri de Lubac," *Thought*, 51, 1976, 7-49.

spiritual renewal of the Church's life rather than a systematic concern for a "new" structure for dogmatic theology.[22]

This more systematic effort was not really begun until the 1960's with the publication of the initial volumes of *Herrlichkeit* . The delay in publishing his more systematic efforts meant that Balthasar was never the direct target of what he referred to as the "Roman-scalp hunters" as were his friends de Lubac and Rahner.[23] There was some question about the "soundness" of the works he was publishing, which were transcriptions of "dictated" visions from Adrienne von Speyr, as well as the danger that was seen in his theological aesthetic and his closeness to Barth.[24] However, they apparently did not constitute enough of a threat to bring down upon Balthasar's head the same sort of problems which befell De Lubac and Rahner.[25] Nevertheless, his theology remained "suspect" and his stock did not begin to rise among theologians with a more magisterial emphasis until after the Council with the publication of the first volumes of his theological aesthetic. The aesthetic represented something of a watershed in Balthasar's career since its main purpose - to "repristinate" revelation through a radical christocentric recentering of the Church's teachings - coincided with the postconciliar concern to reenergize Catholic theology by returning to a more holistic theology devoid of the polemics and "proof texting" of the manuals.[26]

---

[22]It is precisely the concern for the internal spiritual renewal of the Church (reform) that Balthasar sees as the primary thrust of the Council, rather than the more popular idea that the Council sought a "revolution" in theology that would lead to a complete revamping of dogmatic structures (aggiornamento). Cf. Balthasar, *Test Everything : Hold Fast to What is Good. An Interview with Hans Urs Von Balthasar by Angelo Scola*, (San Francisco: Ignatius Press, 1989) 23. Also: *"Reform oder aggiornamento ?" Civitas*, 21 (July 10, 1966), 679-689. And no less a light than de Lubac saw great promise in Balthasar's theology for a proper interpretation of the Council: "When later the time comes to exploit this treasure [Vatican II] it will be seen that for the accomplishing of this task no work will be as helpful and full of resource as that of von Balthasar." "A Witness of Christ in the Church, " 229.

[23]Cf. Peter Henrici, "A Sketch of Balthasar's Life," 344.

[24]"A Sketch of Balthasar's Life," 320-323.

[25]For a good synopsis of the history of the *nouvelle theologie* and the problems it encountered with the Holy Office see: Joseph A. Komonchak, "Theology and Culture at Mid-Century: The example of Henri de Lubac," *Theological Studies*, 51, 4, (December, 1990), 579-602.

[26]Peter Henrici, "A Sketch of Balthasar's Life," 340-341. Evidence of his acceptance in magisterial circles after the Council came quickly. One example should suffice: Paul VI appointed him in 1969 to the newly established International Theological Commission - an appointment he most certainly would not have received if he were in official disfavor.

9

Therefore, we must acknowledge that Balthasar, despite his earlier marginalization, most certainly did not die in theological obscurity. Balthasar's fame only grew after the Council - - a Council he did not attend (he was not invited!) and for which he, admittedly, had little emotional enthusiasm.[27] That is not to say that he "rejected" the Council and its reforms: the Conciliar reforms, seen in their true light, were viewed by Balthasar as a vindication of all that he had been saying before the Council.[28] However, it must be frankly acknowledged that he never seemed to share in the same emotional attachment to the Council's "spirit" that seemed to give other theologians such an overwhelming sense of "liberation" from an overbearing ecclesiastical regime. Indeed, for Balthasar, the greatest threat to theological discourse in the post-conciliar Church does not come from an "imperial papacy" (a reality which he thought no longer existed), but from a new "secular infallibility" that is more intolerant and elitist than the old papal version. Balthasar puts it as follows:

> The choice is between a papacy in the Church that understands the nature and limits of the *Civitas terrena* and a new, secular infallibility that claims to transform the miraculous grace of the *Civitas Dei* into manipulative economic miracles which will change human beings and the world. Moreover, it is passe' and pointless for Christians to attempt to weaken First Rome by shooting at her over their shoulders; such sniping always misses its mark, even when it is aimed at a real but long past form of the papacy.[29]

It is because of statements such as this that Balthasar's influence after the Council began to grow among "conservatives" who were all too eager to seize Balthasar's theology and to appropriate its emphasis on a patristic *ressourcement* for their own, more narrow agenda. One can see evidence of this "conservative" appropriation in a variety of sources. In the English speaking world, the best example can be seen in the ideological orientation of the publishing company (Ignatius Press) that has translated most of Balthasar's works into English. Headed by the "restorationist" conservative Joseph Fessio S.J., this publishing company is

---

[27]Cf. Balthasar, *Test Everything*, , 22. Balthasar states here: "You know that I did not attend the Council and therefore did not share in experiencing the enthusiasm of its participants."

[28]*Test Everything*, 23-24. Balthasar states that the primary concern of the Council was the internal spiritual reform of the Church rather than a revolutionary new dogmatics. This coincides with the primary thrust of Balthasar's theology.

[29]Balthasar, *The Office of Peter and the Structure of the Church*, (San Francisco: Ignatius Press, 1986), 349.

10

not only responsible for the translation and publication of numerous *ressourcement* theologians (Ratzinger, de Lubac, Danielou, Balthasar, Bouyer), but is also busy publishing books from the American "right wing" that are somewhat inflammatory and of dubious intellectual quality.[30] And it has only been recently, with the English publication of Balthasar's book on Christian hope (*Dare We Hope "That All Men Be Saved "*),[31] that many American conservatives began to question Balthasar's credentials as an "orthodox" theologian.[32] However, despite this misgiving about his views on Christian hope and salvation, the conservative appropriation of Balthasar in American circles continues.

We cannot maintain, however, that Balthasar's emergence from relative obscurity is due solely to his appropriation by conservative restorationists. Balthasar himself was certainly no restorationist, and his theological writings are far too complex to classify simplistically as "conservative."[33] A far more important reason for the increase of his importance since the Council is the fact that the popes who have occupied the Chair of Peter since the death of John XXIII have been more sympathetic to the theology of *ressourcement* as an interpretive key for the

---

[30]For example: Gene Antonio, *The Aids Cover-Up? The Real and Alarming Facts about Aids.*; Bryce Christensen, *Utopia Against the Family*; Congressman William Dannemeyer, *Shadow in the Land: Homosexuality in America.* All of these books are representative of the general "conservative" tone of many of the books published by Ignatius Press.

[31]Balthasar, *Dare We Hope "That All Men Be Saved? "* (San Francisco: Ignatius Press, 1988).

[32]The vitriolic response to this book by such conservative publications as *The Wanderer* caused Balthasar to quip that he was now hated by both the right and the left: "So be it; if I have been cast aside as a hopeless conservative by the tribe of the left, then I now know what sort of dung-heap I have been dumped upon by the right." *Dare We Hope?* 19-20.

[33]Balthasar's theology has a deep and profound respect for the Tradition as the fundamental locus for theological reflection on revelation. Furthermore, Balthasar has adopted positions on certain ecclesiastical issues of our time, e.g. women's ordination, clerical celibacy, and artificial contraception, that are "conservative" in the journalistic sense of that word. However, Balthasar bases his conclusions on these issues upon a form of theological rationality that reasons deductively from a radically christocentric interpretation of revelation. And such theological deduction does not always lead to such "conservative" conclusions. For example, as already noted, Balthasar asserts that we must at least hope that God's mercy is stronger than human sin and that, therefore, all may be saved. Also, Balthasar refers to the practice of infant baptism as one of the gravest mistakes in the history of the Church. Cf. Balthasar, *The Glory of the Lord: A Theological Aesthetics: I. Seeing the Form,* (San Francisco: Ignatius Press, 1982), 579-580. His positions on various issues, therefore, do not appear to be based upon the typical restorationist premise that the form of "Catholic culture" that existed in the post-Tridentine Church is, in some vague sense, normative for today. Indeed, Balthasar routinely rejects the use of all sociological arguments for how the Church ought to be structured in the modern world - be they arguments from the "left" or from the "right." Church structure and discipline must be based on the "constellation" of ecclesiastical paradigms that surround Christ in the New Testament. Cf. Balthasar, *The Office of Peter*, 131-172.

11

Council's texts than they have been toward the theologians who emphasized a more radical theology of *aggiornamento* . Thus, Balthasar, who was not even invited to the Vatican Council as a theological consultant, was now appointed by Paul VI to the newly formed International Theological Commission - a Commission which soon established itself as a strong voice in favor of interpreting the Conciliar texts along *ressourcement* lines.[34] It was during a meeting of this Commission in 1970 that Balthasar, de Lubac, Danielou, Bouyer and Ratzinger discussed the possibility of launching a theological journal that would interpret the Conciliar renewal from within the perspective of *ressourcement* theology.[35] It was out of this meeting that the international theological review *Communio* was to come into existence - a theological journal which has since become the primary journal for *ressourcement* theology in Europe and the United States. Balthasar was pressed into service as the leader of this undertaking.[36] Finally, at the very end of his life, John Paul II invited Balthasar to join the ranks of the College of Cardinals - an honor which he agreed to very reluctantly and at the urging of the Pope. However, he died two days before he was to be officially "elevated" to the cardinalate - a fact which serves as a fitting symbol for the general course of his life: he always seemed two steps away from the "mainstream" of both institutional ecclesiastical office and of theological academia.

What conclusions can be drawn from all of the twists and turns of Balthasar's theological career with regard to his theology? We have already noted that his association with von Speyr and his decision to leave the Jesuits meant that he lived in relative obscurity during his important middle years. Furthermore, and perhaps more significantly, it meant that he was not to attend the Vatican Council.

---

[34]Cf. *International Theological Commission: Texts and Documents, 1969-1985,* (San Francisco: Ignatius Press, 1988).

[35]Cf. David Schindler, "Introduction," *Communio,* (Fall, 1989), 304.

[36]Balthasar himself was somewhat reluctant to take on this added responsibility late in his life when he was still engaged in finalizing his own theological trilogy. Nevertheless, the journal became one of the chief vehicles for disseminating his views before his more substantive works were fully translated. This was both a blessing and a curse: although his theology was now to be made available to a much wider public, the general tone of many of his short articles was polemical and could, at times, be somewhat mean-spirited. Thus, the general impression that many people had of Balthasar's theology was often fairly negative and caused many to ignore his more substantive works once they were translated. Cf. Henrici, "A Sketch of Balthasar's life," 346-347. It should also be pointed out that John Paul II, while still Archbishop of Krakow, was closely associated with the Polish edition of the journal and had frequent contacts with Balthasar. Cf. John Saward, "The Promotion of *Communio* in Britain," *Communio,* (Spring, 1991), 135.

These two biographical facts had two fundamental consequences for Balthasar's theology, one practical and the other intellectual. First, while most other Catholic theologians of any note were engaged in preparing for and participating in the Council, Balthasar was busy writing the first volumes of his theological aesthetic. Thus, on a purely practical note, Balthasar's marginalization had the net effect of allowing him to produce a theology that was ready for widespread debate immediately upon the closing of the Council. Furthermore, since the Church after the Council was immediately polarized into rather superficial groupings of "liberals" and "conservatives," it was only a matter of time before Balthasar's theology, with its emphasis on the "objectivity" of revelation and the importance of the Tradition, would be appropriated by "conservatives" for polemical purposes.

The second consequence of his relative anonymity during the years of the Council was more directly theological. It meant that Balthasar's theology evolved during this time period in a rather organic manner from his own theological antecedents. Most of the theologians attending the Council were engaged in producing the "occasional" theology required by the conciliar process and the questions it raised - both inside the Council and out. And even though such "occasional" theology also flowed from antecedent theological roots, it was marked by a much stronger interest in apologetics, fundamental theology, and the new dialogue with the "world," i.e., it was marked by a concern for *aggiornamento* .[37] Balthasar's theology, being more organically related to his theological roots in pre-conciliar *ressourcement* theology, had much more in common with an earlier theology than with the new *aggiornamento* theologies that were beginning to take shape during and after the Council. It could be said, therefore, that Balthasar's theology is more representative of a kind of pre-Vatican II liberalism than with post-Vatican II conservatism. The former was more concerned with the theological criteria for "reform," while the latter was often more interested in preserving a cultural, rather than theological, reality. This description, of course, is not meant to imply that Balthasar's theology is "out of date" or did not change at all after the

---

[37]Yves Congar, O.P., *A History of Theology*, (Garden City, New York: Doubleday, 1968), 14. Congar, already in 1968 recognizes that a shift had taken place in Catholic theology characterized by a movement away from dogmatic, "conclusion-centered theology" toward fundamental and apologetic theology: "I cannot exaggerate the importance of the new consciousness which theologians have acquired of their responsibility to the Church and to the internal credibility of the faith which the Church must offer mankind. There is less question today of technical details derived from standard theological systems."

Council. In fact, the present work is an attempt to show that Balthasar's theology is, in fact, one of the most original and unique theologies to emerge out of the conciliar and post-conciliar era. However, Balthasar accomplishes this task precisely by constantly returning to his roots in the patristic *ressourcement* theology that was largely responsible for preparing the way for the Council in the first place.[38]

B. Theological Overview

Joseph Ratzinger, in his book *Introduction to Christianity*, compares the state of modern theology to the story of "Lucky Jack" who had a lump of gold that was so heavy he found it bothersome to carry around. Therefore, in succession, he traded the lump of gold for a horse, a cow, a goose, and a whetstone, which he finally ended up simply discarding. What he gained psychologically from this process was a feeling of freedom and liberation. What he "gained" in reality was the loss of something extremely valuable. Ratzinger uses this story to describe the crucial question facing modern theology: How do we reconcile the need for faithfulness to the revelation of God manifested historically in Christ and mediated to us in the faithful witness of the Church, with the need to translate or "transpose" that historical revelation into the language and conceptual categories of our contemporary situation? Ratzinger fears that all too often the modern theologian has erred in the direction of "Lucky Jack." The modern reaction against the ultramontane authoritarianism of the past has led many into a false and illusory liberation from "authority" of any kind. This in turn has led to a diminution of the authoritative role of "revelation" as a point of departure for theology. For Ratzinger, what we are left with is a cacophony so deafening that the legitimate voice of "authentic" theological reflection is never heard.[39]

---

[38]The question of which interpretive key is best suited to the Council, or whether any single interpretive key is to be preferred, will be left to others to decide. However, it seems evident that Balthasar's importance resides in his status as one of the principal architects in the post-conciliar Church of a theology that has its roots deep in the *nouvelle theologie* and *ressourcement* theology of the pre-conciliar Church.

[39]Joseph Ratzinger, *Introduction to Christianity*, (New York: Herder & Herder, 1970), 11. Cf. Hans Urs Von Balthasar, *Convergences: to the Source of Christian Mystery*, (San Francisco: Ignatius Press, 1983). Balthasar makes a similar point to the one Ratzinger is making in the above story of "Lucky Jack": "Today we are on the way back - so much so that in many places it looks like confused flight. To save the foundering ship, things are thrown overboard

14

This metaphor of Ratzinger's can be restated in more hermeneutical categories: How does the modern theologian allow the meaning "in front of" the biblical text (and the tradition) to speak on its own terms, to work its power of transformation and interpretation on the theologian? How can the theologian allow revelation to manifest the disclosive power of its own inner truth, while at the same time retrieving the text for a modern situation through "critical" reason? David Tracy summarizes this point as follows:

> The future of serious Catholic theology lies with its ability to recover [the] classic resources of the mystical tradition without forfeiting the need to retrieve them critically. Hermeneutical thought, with its grounding in the notion of truth as manifestation, provides one promising way to achieve this necessary substantive rethinking of Catholic theology.[40]

Balthasar's theology revolves around a theology of revelation that emphasizes the disclosive power of truth as as a "manifestation" of God. Thus, one could be led to the conclusion that Balthasar is a "hermeneutical" theologian such as Tracy describes. However, it is not as easy as it first appears to characterize Balthasar's approach as a type of "systematic hermeneutical theology."[41] Most hermeneutical theologians concern themselves almost

---

blindly and at random. It is thought that liberating unity is achieved by ridding oneself of superfluous amassed goods. Not only churches are emptied out until they stand there naked and bare - ... but so too are dogmatics." 11-12.

[40]David Tracy, "The Uneasy Alliance Reconceived: Catholic Theological Method, Modernity, and Postmodernity," *Theological Studies*, (1989), 565.

[41]Cf. David Tracy, *The Analogical Imagination.* See especially the chapters dealing with the "Christian Classic," 233-338. Tracy defines the "hermeneutical" theologian as one who is concerned with the disclosive power of the tradition in itself - i.e., concerned with the truth manifested "in front of the text" rather than the quest of modernism to peel away the layers in order to find the truth "behind the text." The implicit assumption of modernist approaches is that the tradition (even within the Scriptures themselves) distorts the original event to such an extent that an ever more sophisticated "retrieval" of the original event, now seen as hiding "behind" the tradition, has to be undertaken by theology. Thus, the task of theology is to submit the tradition to various types of "criticisms" which expose its distortions and to restore the original. Theologians like Balthasar resist the positivistic, Enlightenment biases of this approach and are therefore characterized by Tracy as hermeneutical theologians. However, even though this model of Tracy's has much to commend it, it is overly simplistic since it does not deal with Balthasar's theology from within its own theological grounds: Balthasar does not believe in the "disclosive power" of the tradition because it is a type of "religious classic." Rather, he sees the tradition as the "bearer of truth" because of the self-authenticating power of God's trinitarian self-manifestation. The disclosive power of revelation is analogous to the disclosive power of the artistic classic, but it is not ultimately "explained" by this metaphor. To say otherwise would be to make an intra-mundane anthropological category the measure of revelation. The concept of the self-authenticating nature of God's self-revelation will be dealt with more substantively in chapter three. However, it is important to offer here a brief definition of what Balthasar means by this

exclusively with intratextual associations and the development of a theological "grammar."[42] Balthasar is also deeply concerned with the internal "symmetry" and "Gestalt" of revelation itself. However, he differs markedly in his deep concern for the metaphysical underpinnings of the hermeneutical task. Thus, Balthasar is not easily characterized in neat stereotypes; he is more "intratextual" than Rahner, but more metaphysical than Barth.

Fortunately, although Balthasar never gives us what we could term a highly systematized methodology, he does outline the formal principles of his theology on numerous occasions.[43] Balthasar's entire theological corpus is animated throughout by a constant concern to return theology to its proper sources and thereby to maintain the Christ-event as the sole formal and material principle for all Christian theology. The question which runs like a thread throughout the unbelievable variety of his work is a simple one: what is specifically Christian about Christianity? A simple question perhaps, but one which, phrased slightly differently, poses us with a distinctly methodological problem: what is the proper object of a specifically Christian theology and how should a Christian theologian approach this object in order to bring out its uniqueness and to preserve its

---

term. By "self-authenticating" Balthasar is attempting to express something of the quality of what the Old Testament refers to as God's "Glory." Human analogies are possible in order to help us to "perceive" this Glory. However, no human category can exhaust the infinite dimensions of the divine mystery that permeates each and every epiphany of God. Such mystery imparts to each epiphany that quality of the "something more" that the human soul gropes after but can never quite "attain." The experience is analogous to the human mind's perception of the "something more" that we perceive in our knowledge of finite beings and to which we ascribe the universal metaphysical phrase, "Being as such." Likewise, the divine epiphany can be seen as analogous to the "religious classic" as Tracy defines it. However, the divine "something more" in each epiphany is ultimately its own justification, its own *apologia* . In short, Balthasar is simply asserting that we must never allow the anthropological tail to wag the theological dog, i.e., the relationship between God and world must be presented in such a way that the divine Glory is never in any danger of being "swallowed up" in intramundane categories.

[42]E.g. George Lindbeck, *The Nature of Doctrine: Religion and Theology in a Postliberal Age*, (Philadelphia: The Westminster Press, 1984).

[43] For example, the volumes in *Herrlichkeit* dealing with "theological style" are one of the many ways that he deals with the issue of theological method. However, these volumes are not so much an analysis of method *per se* as they are descriptions of theologians that Balthasar thinks exhibit the proper "contemplative" approach to the heart of theology. Here, as elsewhere in Balthasar's theology, one can glean a "method" from these descriptions but they are not a critical treatise on methodology. Cf. Hans Urs Von Balthasar, *The Glory of the Lord: A Theological Aesthetics. II: Studies in Theological Style: Clerical Styles*, (San Francisco: Ignatius Press, 1984); *III: Studies in Theological Style: Lay Styles*, (1986). For a good sysopsis of the formal principles of his theology see: *Love Alone: The Way of Revelation*, (London: Sheed and Ward, 1968). [Henceforth, all volumes of *The Glory of the Lord* shall be designated as *GL* followed by the volume number.]

16

Christian integrity? For Balthasar the answer is as simple as the original question. What is specifically Christian about Christianity is Christ himself. It is Balthasar's contention that in the mad rush to update Christian theology since the Council, many theologians have adopted operative principles in their theology which are borrowed from modern philosophical systems that have had the net effect of displacing the Christ-form from its central position in Christian theology.[44]

Of course, one could counter this accusation by pointing out that it is more correct to say that God is the central object of Christian theology and not Christ. After all, did not Christ himself point us in this direction? Is it not true that the theologian, in order to avoid falling into a narrow, particularistic, Christomonism, must place his Christology within the larger and more universalistic context of a monotheistic doctrine of God? For as David Tracy points out, theology is nothing more than the deliberate attempt to reflect on *God* as such, and must therefore be radically theocentric. All theology, insofar as it is theology, and regardless of whatever "secular" sciences are being utilized (e.g., psychology or sociology), must be theocentric in order to contribute to the dialogue with the broader world.[45]

Balthasar would not disagree with the fundamental assertion that theology must be theocentric. However, he would question why such an assertion is being posed in the first place in the form of a relation of opposition between Christ and God: either Christ *or* God, either a christocentric theology *or* a theocentric theology. For Balthasar, the assertion that Christian theology must be theocentric still has told us nothing about what is specifically Christian about Christianity. Presumably, even Jewish and Islamic theology is theocentric. According to Balthasar, there is often an over- exaggeration upon the apophatic aspects of theology in a misguided attempt to develop a theology of world religions that reduces all revelation to unfathomable mystery. This leads to a diminution of the role of the positive and particular aspects of revelation and eventually turns all revelation based religion into a glorified religious philosophy. Therefore, and this is crucial to an understanding of Balthasar's theology, if we are to know anything about God at all, (beyond his incomprehensibility in a "negative" theology), it is absolutely necessary to affirm *a priori* that it is possible for the transient finite

---

[44]Cf. Balthasar, "From the Theology of God to Theology in the Church," *Communio: International Catholic Review*, (Fall, 1982), 215-216.

[45]David Tracy, *The Analogical Imagination*, 51.

forms of this world to be suitable and adequate vehicles for the self-revelation of the Infinite Other.[46] In other words, the *via negativa* , despite its absolute necessity for reminding us that God is the "ever greater," must nevertheless be seen within an antecedent *via positiva*: The "dark night of the soul" is not the darkness of the void but the blinding infinite light itself. The "stillness" of the mystic is not the rest of death but the composure of infinite life.[47]

The implications of this position are easy to discern. If the finite categorical forms of this world can be suitable and adequate vehicles of the divine self-revelation, then the importance of the historical Christ-form takes on added significance for theology. Suddenly, it becomes possible to affirm that, for the Christian theologian, the theocentric *is* the christocentric.[48] The Christ-form, now seen as the definitive historical self-revelation of God, must be seen as the *divinely willed* center of theology. Jesus is the archetypal "theo-logian," because he is God's word about himself. Theology is not primarily, as David Tracy states, "*logos* about *theos* " spoken from a purely human perspective. Theology is primarily a reflection on, and a contemplation of, the original "*logos* by *theos* about *theos*."[49] The theologian, through faithful prayer and reflection, enters into a contemporaneous relationship with this historically once given revelation through immersion into the dually conditioning mediations granted by the Spirit's witness: Scripture and the living ecclesial tradition. Therefore, theology, precisely because it is christocentric, must be ecclesial. There is no such thing as a "private" Christian theology.[50]

Thus, Balthasar's theology does exhibit a fairly consistent recentering of theology in a strongly christological theology of revelation. Historically speaking,

---

[46]*GL I*, 155. Balthasar states: "If there were no such thing as the resurrection of the flesh, then the truth would lie with gnosticism and every form of idealism ... for whom the finite must literally perish if it is to become spiritual and infinite. But the resurrection of the flesh vindicates the poets in a definitive sense: the aesthetic scheme of things, which allows us to possess the infinite within the finitude of form ... is right. The decision, therefore, lies between the conflicting parties of myth and revelation."

[47]*GL I*, 186-187.

[48]*GL I*, 463-525. Balthasar states: "Christian thought has always known that Jesus Christ is the central form of revelation, around which all other elements in the revelation of our salvation crystallize and are grouped. ... In the one Christ the Father renders witness to himself through the Holy Spirit, and the one Christ, in the indivisible form he sets before us, witnesses to the Father in the Holy Spirit. Here, too, content and form are inseparable." 154.

[49]Balthasar, "From the Theology of God," 195-196.

[50]"From the Theology of God," 202-216. Also see: *GL I*, 527-604.

this approach of Balthasar's finds its proper "home" in the pre-conciliar theological movement known as the *nouvelle theologie* and which we might today refer to as *ressourcement* theology.[51] Walter Kasper refers to this approach as a "theological theology" which sees in a "return to the sources" (*ressourcement*) the only valid and fruitful way forward toward real "*aggiornamento*."[52] He summarizes this as follows:

> For finding the new direction, concepts such as postmodern, postliberal, and post critical are certainly no more than preliminary. ... This is not only a disadvantage, but also an advantage: after the shipwreck of all possible theologies in the genitive (theology of the world, of development, of revolution, of liberation, and the like), it gives to theologians the possibility, and imposes upon them the duty, of contributing to the shaping of the future with a "theological theology" that springs from its own proper sources.[53]

Similarly, what we see in Balthasar's theology is a concern for Christian theology's true "object" or "center." This concept of theology's "center" is paramount for Balthasar: like the spokes of a giant wagon wheel all theological roads eventually "converge" on the one unifying hub that holds the entire apparatus together. And for Christian theology the unifying center must be the revelation of God in Christ. All theology, insofar as it is rooted in its dually conditioning and normative sources (Scripture and tradition), will always find its way back to Christ. Balthasar states:

> The expression the "center of the form of revelation" does not refer to a particular section of this form however central which, in order to be read as form, would then essentially need to be filled out by

---

[51]Balthasar was deeply influenced by Henri de Lubac and remained his lifelong friend. Balthasar, although heavily influenced by the thought forms of neo-scholasticism, was a resolute foe of the preconciliar "school theology" and argued loudly for a return to the more neo-platonic Fathers as a necessary corrective to the overly narrow focus on the post-tridentine tradition in the theology of the "manuals." However, it is important to notice here that Balthasar should be considered a pre-conciliar liberal rather than a radical: his constant call is to a greater immersion into all of the riches of the tradition rather than the restorationist's fixation on Trent or the radical's flirtations with systems of modern philosophy spawned by protest atheism. Cf. Hans Urs Von Balthasar, "The Achievement of Henri de Lubac," *Thought,* 51, (1976), 7-49; also, *Schleifung der Bastionem,* (Einsiedeln: Johannes Verlag, 1952).

[52]For a good summary of the relationship between theologies of *ressourcement* and theologies of *aggiornamento* see: J.A. DiNoia, O.P., "American Catholic Theology at Century's End: Postconciliar, Postmodern, Post-Thomistic," *The Thomist,* (July, 1990), 499-518. Also see, Balthasar, "*Reform oder Aggiornamento,* " 679-689.

[53]Walter Kasper, "Postmodern Dogmatics: Toward a Renewed Discussion of Foundations in North America," *Communio,* (Summer, 1990), 190-191.

other more peripheral aspects. What the phrase is intended to denote is, rather, the reality which lends the form its total coherence and comprehensibility, the "wherefore" to which all particular aspects have to be referred if they are to be understood. The fact that Christ is this center - and not, for instance, merely the beginning, the initiator of an historical form which then develops autonomously - is rooted in the particular character of the Christian religion and in its difference from all other religions. ... Christ .... is the form because he is the content. ... If for a single moment we were to look away from him and attempt to consider and understand the Church as an autonomous form, the Church would not have the slightest plausibility.[54]

The relationship between this central reality and its mediations is quite clear for Balthasar: the Scriptures and the Church are the central loci of the Spirit's mission of interpreting for humanity this central revelation. However, they must not be monistically equated with this revelation in a relationship of identity. There is no second "hypostatic union" in either the Scriptures or the Tradition - to say otherwise would be to risk a kind of idolatry of the Church or of the Bible. To be sure, the Scriptures are the word of God and are inextricably bound up within the total movement of the divine economy of salvation. As such they bear an intrinsic teleology (carried by the Spirit) toward the Christ event. Indeed, as Balthasar points out: "Part of what the form [Christ] *is* is provided by its attestation, and this attestation ... belongs to the very structure of the form itself."[55] However, like Barth, Balthasar asserts that the Scriptures are the Word of God only in a secondary and derivative sense.[56] The Scriptures are the Spirit's inspired witness to the Ur-Word who is Christ. As Balthasar states: "Scripture is the word of God that bears witness to God's Word. The one Word therefore makes its appearance as though dividing into a word that testifies and into a Word to whom testimony is given."[57]

---

[54]*GL 1*, 463. See also: Balthasar, *In the Fullness of Faith: On The Centrality of the Distinctively Catholic*, (San Francisco: Ignatius Press, 1988). Here Balthasar restates this central theme as follows: "Here, initially, we are concerned to show that a ("hierarchically") superordinate reality can so inform a subordinate plurality that the latter is lifted up into the former's unity without being robbed of its distinctive character. Thus a formative principle seizes on matter and provides itself a shape. (We must also realize that it may no longer be possible for some people to appreciate this.)" 15.

[55] *GL 1*, 527. For a detailed examination of this entire topic see pp. 527-677.

[56]Karl Barth, *Evangelical Theology: An Introduction*, (Garden City, New York: Doubleday & Company, Inc., 1964), 11-30.

[57]Hans Urs Von Balthasar, *Explorations in Theology: I: The Word Made Flesh*, "The Word, Scripture and Tradition," (San Francisco: Ignatius Press, 1989), 11. [Henceforth, all references to this work will be referred to as *Explorations* followed by a volume number.]

Thus, the point to Balthasar's insistence on a return to the sources is not the restorationist's yearning for a simplistic positivism of either the Church or the Bible. It is, rather, a simple concern for the christocentric center of all Christian theology. And this approach of Balthasar's is just as critical toward any "liberal" theology which seeks to get beyond the scandal of Christian particularity by placing Christ within a broader philosophical "system" that subordinates God's unique self-revelation to an intra mundane *a priori* . For example, Balthasar objects to the attempt to minimalize the uniqueness of the Christ-event on the basis of a universalist philosophy that has no room for the "truth claims" of a theological particularity. Such theologies run the risk, as Balthasar points out, of falling into a non-theological rationalism:[58]

> Theology cannot maintain that God's Covenant with Israel was only one of the many ways in which God has had communion with man, for the Covenant with Israel is a unique election which led to the uniqueness of Christ. Theology must sustain the *skandalon* entailed in the truth that Jesus is the concrete universal (*universale concretum*).[59]

For Balthasar, theology (or any science for that matter) must be appropriate to the object being studied. In other words, one's "method" will be determined in large measure by the inherent qualities of the object under scrutiny and not vice versa. The "object" of theological research is the revelation of God in Jesus Christ, and it is this object which must be granted its full normative power before any talk of "hermeneutical filters" and "transcendental categories" are entertained. In short, the "hermeneutical tail" must not be allowed to wag the "christological dog."[60]

---

[58]"From the Theology of God," Balthasar states: "By concentrating on the formal element of the contents of the faith, the inquirer will be prevented from falling into a non-theological rationalism, such as that practiced, for example, in decadent scholasticism, and today by enlightenment theology." 213.

[59]"From the Theology of God," 216.

[60]Hans Urs Von Balthasar, *A Short Primer for Unsettled Laymen*, (San Francisco: Ignatius Press, 1985), 54. Balthasar states: "The simple basic rule of all science [is] that the object determines the method appropriate to it and that only the method determined in this way can be considered adequate and 'scientific'. Here the object is Jesus Christ, certainly in human form but with the claim of proclaiming God's final word to the world. No purely worldly method can be the one demanded by this object unless it subordinates itself as a humble instrument to the only appropriate response to the Word: the faith of the Church."

At this juncture a cautionary flag must be raised. We are engaged here in a brief summary of Balthasar's central theological insight. Care must be taken, as with all theological summaries, not to eliminate all of the nuance and "texture" in a theology as complex as Balthasar's. Thus, we are not speaking here of a theology which is naively "objective" and "positive" any more than one would characterize, say, Rahner's theology as naively "subjective" and "negative". It is a question of emphasis and where one chooses to place it in doing theology. For Balthasar, the greatest theological trap that one can fall into is to allow one's theology to become overdetermined methodologically and to thereby mute the full force of God's Word in Christ with the shallow but deafening noise of one's own chatter.[61]

The centrality of the Christ-event as the guiding norm and formal principle for all Christian theology in Balthasar's approach causes us to pause for a moment and ask an important question: What is so new about such an affirmation? Do not such theologians as Karl Rahner, Paul Tillich, and Jurgen Moltmann, among others, all claim the same thing? What is unique in Balthasar's approach? Let us return for a moment to David Tracy. Tracy contends that Balthasar's theology exhibits a method which he refers to as anti-correlational, i.e., he categorizes Balthasar as a kind of neo-Barthian who rejects the use of intra-mundane categories as an intrinsic moment within the act of theologizing itself. The authenticity of revelation can only be established by the power of the revelation itself - not by the appeal of apologetic theology to "external" yardsticks and categories of thought which modern society finds easy to grasp. Tracy puts it as follows:

> "For ... Balthasar and Ratzinger, ... Catholic theology, above all, needs to clarify and affirm its own unique identity as **such** and not in correlation with the ever-shifting and dangerous contours of the contemporary situation. Such theology can make great use of any extraecclesial thought: as Bonaventure clearly did with Neoplatonism; as Balthasar and Ratzinger clearly do with German idealism. But such correlations should be present only in an **ad hoc**, not systematically correlational manner. The effect should not

---

[61] This congruence of theology and method is no accident as we shall see. Balthasar sees such a congruence in the theology of the Fathers. Cf. Balthasar, *GL I*, 39: "For the reasons mentioned, the Fathers regarded beauty as a transcendental and did theology accordingly. This presupposition left a most profound imprint on the manner and content of their theologizing, since a theology of beauty may be elaborated only in a beautiful manner. .... The happy congruence of subject-matter and methdology is particularly true of the Fathers' doctrine of contemplation..."

22

be any attempt to correlate systematically a Catholic self-understanding with that of modernity.[62]

It is important to understand here what Tracy means by "anti-correlational." What this term does not mean is that theologians like Balthasar are unconcerned with the "signs of the times" or the question of how the gospel message can be preached most fruitfully in the modern situation. In fact, it can be easily shown that Balthasar does show an explicit concern with the question of how the faith is to be rendered credible ("*glaubhaft* ") in our modern situation.[63] Furthermore, Balthasar does not reject the use of secular sciences as vehicles for illuminating the message of the gospel. When God became a human being he did not come as the heteronomous "Other" imposing his will on our autonomy and thus "violating" human nature. Balthasar states this quite clearly:

> ... it is essential to examine fearlessly the supernatural revealed truths of Christianity in the light of the sciences that have man as their object; these include philology, sociology and psychology. God, in becoming man and taking man into his trinitarian life, did no violence to human nature; in founding a new community centered on his incarnation it was not in spite of the laws of sociology, and religious sociology in particular. Consequently it cannot be disputed that the "religion" we contend to be the only true one is in one of its aspects on the same sociological plane as "other' religions.[64]

It is absolutely crucial for a proper understanding of Balthasar to understand that he does not "compartamentalize" history into two distinct areas: the one worldly and inferior, and the second supernatural and superior. Many of his polemical writings can lead one to this erroneous conclusion. But even his polemics must be kept in the historical context of Balthasar's battles with what he perceived to be post-conciliar theological radicalism. However, despite his polemics, it is quite clear that Balthasar's theological anthropology affirms a strong

---

[62]Tracy, "The Uneasy Alliance," 554-555, (emphasis his). Tracy also notes here the close similarity between this type of Catholic theology and the anti-correlational neo-Barthians among Protestants in the United States. He specifically mentions Lindbeck's contention that theology must be "intratextual" rather than correlational.

[63]For an excellent discussion of Balthasar's concerns for the "inculturation" of theology see: Marc Ouellet, "Hans Urs Von Balthasar: Witness to the Integration of Faith and Culture," *Communio*, (Spring, 1991), 111-126.

[64]*Explorations I*, "God Speaks as Man," 69.

relationship between general human history and salvation history. As Balthasar puts it:

> We can no longer speak of various independent species of progress in universal history. The more we understand the implication of human reflection ... in the course of the sacred history of both the Old and New Testaments, of the synagogue and the Church, the more we perceive a convergence (never an identity) of "natural" and "supernatural" progress. There are not two but three modalities of progress: that of revelation (completed with the death of the last apostle), that of the development of doctrine..., and that of secular history.[65]

Where Balthasar parts company with transcendental "correlational" theologies is the issue of where this correlation is to receive its credibility: is the *chief* warrant for the credibility of God's revelation in Christ to be found in that revelation itself, or is it to be located someplace "outside" of this revelation? We can most certainly use modern thought patterns in order to illuminate the central meaning of revelation for a modern audience. However, theology must never make it appear as if the credibility of the gospel message is to be located within the overall matrix of an "external" system of philosophical thought. Balthasar, like Kierkegaard, saw in the rationalistic systematization of religion since the Enlightenment the very spirit of the Anti-Christ: devoid of soul and "personality," the modern era is characterized by the crushing depersonalization of various "systems" and totalitarianisms of the left and the right.[66] Everything must be made "to fit" - from "one size fits all" mass produced clothing to the central planning of the modern bureaucratic state. The great enemy of such systems is the unpredictability of the "personal." It is no surprise that theology too has "caught the bug" for systemization and has reduced the once towering "personal" figure of the gospels to the tamed plaything of an alienated rationality and of "critical exegesis."

Ultimately, the credibility of revelation must come from within revelation: the beauty of God's self-manifestation is in its utter gratuity, and any "apologetic"

---

[65] *Explorations I*, "God Speaks as Man," 89.

[66] *Cf. The Moment of Christian Witness*. In this short work Balthasar devotes an entire chapter to a description of "the system" (Kantian subjectivism) that has turned theology's gaze from the gratuity of God's personalizing self-manifestation and has therefore robbed theology of its proper center. It is within this context that Balthasar's objections to Rahner must be viewed. Furthermore, with regard to Kierkegaard, Balthasar develops the personalizing nature of Kierkegaard's dialogical theology beautifully in, *Love Alone*, 40ff.

theology which seeks to "explain" revelation by tying it to philosophical systems which are palatable to modern tastes is simply "smudging the lens" and blurring the image.[67] God is certainly the "term of our transcendence" and the ground of possibility for all knowing and loving. However, Christian theology must affirm that God is also much more than this - God is the "ever-greater" whose utter freedom is so shocking, whose love is so gratuitous, that we must not tie this divine "surprise" to any system which dulls the sharp edge of its newness. Balthasar states:

> Anyone who penetrates into the mysteries of God recognizes more and more that the world as a whole is created "for nothing", that is, out of a love that is free and has no other reason behind it; that is precisely what gives it its only plausible meaning. Recognizing or failing to recognize this relationship will constitute the core of the action in theo-drama.[68]

This is crucial for Balthasar since it lays the foundation for a theology that is concerned with the modern situation as a situation standing in need of judgment and salvation, rather than a theology which sets the situation up as the "measure" of revelation.[69] Here, Balthasar's theology bears some resemblance to the dialectical "crisis theology" of Karl Barth. Humanity stands in judgment before the gratuity of God's love. The more we penetrate into the mystery of the sheer gratuity of God's grace, the more we will understand the tremendous contradiction that stands between our sinfulness and God's holiness. A dialectical moment opens before our eyes that pushes us into a moment of "crisis"; we recognize for the first time the "nothingness" of the world in the face of God's "Being." This crisis compels us to utterly entrust ourselves in faith to God's grace as the sole sufficient ground for

---

[67]It is important to note at this juncture that Balthasar does not reject the concept of "natural theology." To cite just one example: Balthasar believes that the development, by the Greeks, of the concept of "Being" seems to be "one of the final 'prerequisites' of man if the incarnation is to take place." *Explorations I*, "God Speaks as Man," 90. There are many human thought patterns throughout history that constitute, for Balthasar, a *praeparatio evangelica* . Indeed, Balthasar's strong affirmation of analogy (both the analogy of being and of faith) is what differentiates him from other "anti-correlational" theologians such as Karl Barth.

[68]Balthasar, *Theo-Drama: Theological Dramatic Theory: II: Dramatis Personae: Man in God,* (San Francisco: Ignatius Press, 1990), 260. [Henceforth, all references to this work will be referred to as *Theo-Drama* followed by a volume number.]

[69]Balthasar's theology strongly emphasizes the fact that the "world" stands in judgment and in need of Christ's expiatory redemption. This is an extremely important point that must be kept in mind and to which we will return later. For a detailed examination of his theology of the cross see: Hans Urs Von Balthasar, *GL VII*, 202-235.

human salvation. The emphasis in theology, therefore, shifts from liberal Protestantism's emphasis on "pious feelings" and general "religious consciousness," toward a new emphasis on the sovereignty of God's word in revelation. Therefore, it is misleading to "bring to the Bible" modern religious consciousness in an attempt to "fit" the Bible within a broader schema of "religious feelings."[70] Instead, we go to the Bible in order to have our preconceived notions about God and religion judged by the word found therein. This approach of Barth's is summarized nicely by Hans Kung as follows:

> Barth's "theology of crisis," later called "dialectical theology," demanded, in the face of the collapse of society and culture, of institutions, traditions, and authorities, a paradigmatic shift: away from subjective experience and pious feelings, toward the Bible; away from history, toward God's revelation; away from religious discourse on the concept of God, toward proclamation of God's word; away from religion and religiosity, toward Christian faith; away from the religious needs of the individual, toward God, who is the "totally Other," manifest only in Jesus Christ.[71]

The exact relationship between Barth's theology and Balthasar's is too complex to deal with here. However, it is important to point out that despite the similarities between Barth and Balthasar, Balthasar disagrees sharply with the young Barth's rejection of "natural theology." The emphasis on the "objectivity" of revelation must not be used to eliminate the human side of the equation. The truly theandric quality of revelation is guaranteed in the doctrine of the "two natures" in the Incarnation. All Apollinarian tendencies must be avoided no matter how strong the dialectical moment between God and world is seen to be. Balthasar criticizes Barth's early dialectical period as overemphasizing a revelational "actualism" that absolutizes the dialectical moment of contradiction between God and world. It must never be forgotten, according to Balthasar, that dialectics is not theology itself, but merely a corrective moment within theology. To say otherwise would be to

---

[70]Cf. Hans Frei, *The Eclipse of Biblical Narrative: A Study in Eighteenth and Nineteenth Century Hermeneutics*, (New Haven: Yale University Press, 1974). Frei analyzes this shift in emphasis in theology with regard to scriptural exegesis. Frei is sympathetic to the Barthian critique of eighteenth and early nineteenth century liberal Protestantism. Frei refers to the "eclipse" of the biblical narrative as the attempt to make the Bible "fit" into our world rather than attempting to place our world within the ambit of the biblical worldview. The former, according to Frei, encourages the denuding of the real existential and *kerygmatic* force of the biblical narratives.

[71]Hans Kung, *Theology for the Third Millennium*. 189.

establish dialectics as an external principle which stands in judgment over revelation - the very thing Barth's theology wants to avoid.[72] It begins by wanting to do "pure theology" and ends up doing philosophy instead. Furthermore, creation is robbed of its true theological integrity; the creaturely realm either collapses into God (its origin and goal) or into the sheer void of nothingness (sin). Balthasar summarizes this as follows:

> Pure dialectics dissolves those subjects between whom the theological event takes place: God and creature. God's aseity is dissolved in the event of his revelation and abolishes itself. On the other hand, the creature has no self-subsistence of its own vis-`a-vis God. It either collapses into God ... or becomes pure contradiction to God (in sin) and dissolves into nothingness.[73]

We can summarize the foregoing by stating that Balthasar does indeed exhibit some of the characteristics of an "anti-correlational" theologian. However, this proposition must be nuanced by Balthasar's strong affirmation of natural theology, metaphysics, and the interrelationship between secular history and salvation history.[74] What emerges from this tension is a theology that integrates the analogy of being and the analogy of faith in a way that preserves the integrity of both while affirming their mutual interdependence. The two analogies converge in a trinitarian ontology that combines elements of classical philosophical metaphysics (analogy of being) and the "knowledge" about God gained from contemplative reflection on God's own self-manifestation in Christ (analogy of faith). We shall examine this topic at much greater length in a later section. For our purposes now it

---

[72]Balthasar, *The Theology of Karl Barth*, (San Francisco: Ignatius Press, 1992), 84. Balthasar states: "The irony is that at the very place Barth wants to do pure theology, where human thought has no more room for maneuver unless it be dialectical and 'superseded,' here we encounter the unexpected (but also unavoidable!) irruption of a very unbiblical philosophical pantheism (or more precisely, theopanism)."

[73]*Theology of Karl Barth*, 85.

[74]Cf. Hans Urs Von Balthasar, *A Theological Anthropology*, (New York: Sheed and Ward, 1967). 169 ff. Also: *A Theology of History*, (New York: Sheed and Ward, 1963). Balthasar states here: "This is why the hope of the Old Testament, insofar as it aims at a future kingdom of peace and at nothing else, has to be abrogated as something provisional and made to yield to a kingdom of God which intersects the direction of history, existing in hidden form and suddenly 'flaring up' from within it. ... In the end, therefore, only two things stand face to face: mankind as it struggles for order and justice, and God's deed in Christ, announcing the totality of salvation." 141. For Balthasar, the most theology can say on this issue is that the *kairos* which the incarnation represents in sacred history, is also a *kairos* for secular history even though this fact must remain hidden in God's mysteriousness until the end of time. However, the fact that God uses secular history as a vehicle for the progress of grace leaves an indelible (transformative) mark on this history. Christ thereby becomes the norm for judging all history. 133 ff.

is sufficient to point out that what Balthasar fears more than anything is theological reductionism in all of its forms - the systematic "leveling out" of the multi-layered, multi-faceted self-manifestation of God to a variety of boring, depersonalizing and bloodless monisms. He states this fear as follows:

> If God is not apparent as free and personal, then he is not, in the full sense, apparent, but remains hidden behind the symbols of a world-ground, and then there does not appear to be any eternal significance in a created human being. But if God is apparent as a free, personal being, then his appearance is in the manner of a free election, scandalous for all-leveling world-reason. In the center of the divine revelation stands Yahweh's covenant with Israel: here, abstracting man is trained in the fulfilling exclusivity of the relationship to God.[75]

Balthasar is not arguing here (as we have seen) against a theological anthropology or against the necessary anthropological reflections in theology. After all, Jesus was a human being and it is the structure of the human being that God assumed. Furthermore, the same holds true for the redemption of the cosmos as a whole. Therefore, certain types of cosmological reflection also have a place in theology. But none of these approaches (anthropological or cosmological), taken by themselves, have the internal dynamism or logic required to preserve themselves from the virus of rationalistic systemization. Theology can only preserve itself if it keeps its focus on the blindingly unique gratuity of God's self-revelation in Christ and how this same revelation transforms anthropological and cosmological categories from within. Rowan Williams, in an excellent essay on Balthasar's metaphysics, sums up this line of thought as follows:

> It has been said that to understand a philosopher you must understand what he is afraid of. Balthasar's dread is the inquisitorial claim to love humanity more than its maker does - the most comprehensible and sympathetic of all blasphemies - and that is why, for him, revelation is a radical assault on what we know of love, or of liberty, or of hope. If Rahner's Christ is an answer to the human question, a faintly but distinctly Tolstoyan figure, Balthasar's Christ remains a question to all human answers, and to all attempts at metaphysical or theological closure.[76]

---

[75]Balthasar, *Theological Anthropology*, 187-188.

[76]Rowan Williams, "Balthasar and Rahner," in *The Analogy of Beauty*. (ed.) John Riches, (Edinburgh: T. & T. Clark, 1986), 34.

This characterization of Balthasar also coincides with the distinction which David Tracy makes between a hermeneutical theology, concerned with the disclosive power of the "religious classic," and the technical, functional rationality that dominates the modern quest for "truth" in the public square. This could explain why he characterizes Balthasar as an "intratextual" theologian concerned with the truth claims inherent within the disclosive power of the received tradition rather than the various "isms" of modern society.[77] Tracy summarizes the judgment upon technical reason by hermeneutical theologians as follows:

> When technical rationality reigns, no recognition of the event-character of truth can occur. Any interpreter of the religious classics must early decide whether to impose some standards of technical rationality upon all classical expressions or risk exposing oneself to another mode of rationality: a mode proper to the thing itself as it discloses itself to consciousness. We cannot, in fact, verify or disprove the claims of classical religious expressions through empiricist methods. We cannot adequately adjudicate the world disclosed by Dante's *Divina Commedia* simply by bringing Dante's traditional metaphysics before the judgment seat of a more adequate contemporary metaphysics.[78]

It is precisely in his aversion to the hegemonic control of modern technocratic positivism, and its effects in an overly rationalistic theology, that Balthasar's development of the first part of his trilogy, the theological aesthetic, is to find its proper historical context. Balthasar's theology, as we have seen, is radically christocentric, and his primary concern is to render the image of Christ found in Scripture and Tradition "credible." However, Balthasar seeks to ground the credibility of the Christ image in the *self-authenticating* authority of this image itself.[79] Any recourse to the way of anthropological or cosmological "verification" for the credibility of this image must be strictly *ad hoc* to the primary authority of Christ's image itself. Balthasar refers to the dynamic interplay between the self-authenticating authority of the Christ-form, and the perception of this form on the part of the Spirit-filled subject as a theological aesthetic. It is aesthetic because it

---

[77]David Tracy, *The Analogical Imagination*, 380. Tracy states: "Other contemporary theologians, whose understanding of reason remains more traditionally speculative than modern-critical, ... turn for their sustenance not to modern critical, experiential and linguistic philosophies, but to the great *exitus-reditus* schemata of the Christian neo-Platonic traditions as does von Balthasar ..." Also: Tracy, "The Uneasy Alliance," 564 ff.

[78]Tracy, *The Analogical Imagination*, 195.

[79] Cf. Hans Urs von Balthasar, *Love Alone*, esp. 7-50. Also: *The Moment of Christian Witness*, esp. 47-76.

29

deals with the human power for perceiving beauty within the limitations of finite form. It is theological because, in this case, both the objective form itself and the perception of the form by the subject are part of the same dynamic movement of the trinitarian God in the economy of salvation.[80] And Balthasar conceives of this approach to theology precisely as an antidote to the corrosive nihilism of modern "systems":

> Our situation today shows that beauty demands for itself at least as much courage and decision as do truth and goodness, and she will not allow herself to be separated and banned from her two sisters without taking them along with herself in an act of mysterious vengeance. ... nothing else remains, and yet *something* must be embraced, twentieth- century man is urged to enter this impossible marriage with matter, a union which finally spoils all man's taste for love. But man cannot bear to live with the object of his impotence, that which remains permanently unmastered. He must either deny it or conceal it in the silence of death. ... in such a world the good also loses its attractiveness, the self-evidence of why it must be carried out. ... In a world that no longer has enough confidence in itself to affirm the beautiful, the proofs of the truth have lost their cogency. In other words, syllogisms may still dutifully clatter away like rotary presses or computers which infallibly spew out an exact number of answers by the minute. But the logic of these answers is itself a mechanism which no longer captivates anyone.[81]

All of the foregoing has been simply a lengthy way of saying that Balthasar's theology must be seen against the backdrop of what he is reacting against. It is facile in the extreme to simply categorize Balthasar as a conservative reactionary intent on "restoring" the forms of the past. [82] It is equally facile to categorize him as an "anti-correlational" theologian and then be done with him. Rather, in order to understand all of this talk of "anti-correlational" and "hermeneutical" or "anti-foundational," we must first recognize that Balthasar's primary concern is to place Christian theology in a counter-cultural stance vis-`a-vis all of the depersonalizing "systems" of modern society.[83] Thus, Balthasar's

---

[80]Cf. *GL 1.* esp. 131-218, & 429-525.

[81]*GL 1,* 18-19.

[82]Cf. Tracy. *The Analogical Imagination,* 99. Tracy states: "The difference between the traditionalism of Archbishop Lefevbre's movement and the profound respect for tradition in Hans Urs Von Balthasar is a difference become a chasm."

[83]This concern for the counter-cultural nature of modern Christianity is one of the primary reasons he left the Jesuits in order to found a secular institute (the Community of St. John) with the mystic Adrienne von Speyr. Cf. Balthasar, *First Glance at Adrienne Von Speyr.*

theology stands in the tradition of Kierkegaard - a man who was also characterized by his contemporaries as an angry "naysayer" railing against a cultural ethos he could not change. And yet, if you look beyond the rhetoric and the polemics of both, what you find are two profoundly "cultured" men misunderstood by their contemporaries and accused of being "antimodern" when in many respects they are more deeply modern than the modernists themselves.[84]

Thus, despite the lack of an explicit methodology in Balthasar's work, one could say that Balthasar's overriding concern is methodological insofar as the central proposition of his theology is the absolute primacy of the Christ-event as the formal and material principle of all Christian theology. Balthasar sums this up as follows:

> ... A theological aesthetic in the dual sense of a study of perception, and a study of the objective self-expression of the divine glory ... will try to demonstrate that this theological approach, far from being a dispensable theological by-road, is in fact the one possible approach to the heart of theology - the cosmic world-historical approach, and the path of anthropological verification, being secondary aspects, complementary to it.[85]

Balthasar's "method" is in reality a strongly christological theology of revelation that seeks to diminish the importance of all human-made efforts to "systematize" and "explain" the christological image in strictly intra-mundane categories. The emphasis throughout is "contemplative" rather than "critical," more "aesthetic" than rationalistic. To use the modern parlance, Balthasar's theology resists "closure," and thus often finds itself relegated to the "marginalia" of modern academic theology.[86]

---

[84]Cf. Herman Haring, "Joseph Ratzinger's 'Nightmare Theology'," in *The Church in Anguish: Has the Vatican Betrayed Vatican II?* (ed.) Hans Kung, (San Francisco: Harper and Row, 1987). Haring comments: "A tragic aspect of his [Ratzinger's] development is that he has not been inspired by the breadth of vision of an Yves Congar but rather by the antimodern predisposition of a Hans Urs Von Balthasar." 87. And again: "every expansion of problems [for Balthasar] that might go beyond the perspective of patristic horizons is equated with heresy." 90.

[85]Cf. Hans Urs von Balthasar, *Love Alone*, 8; Also: *Explorations I*, "Revelation and the Beautiful," 95-126. These shorter works of Balthasar contain a good synopsis of his theological aesthetics.

[86]It is interesting to note at this juncture that Balthasar seriously contemplated leaving out part three of his theological trilogy (1. Theological aesthetics; 2. Theological Dramatics; 3. Theological Logic). The theological dramatic was closest to his heart followed by the aesthetic. But, as Peter Henrici points out, "The *Theologik* mattered to him less; indeed, he originally thought of not writing it at all." Peter Henrici, "Hans Urs Von Balthasar: A Sketch of His Life." Indeed, Joseph Cardinal Ratzinger finds this resistance to rational "closure" to be one of the

This contemplative and receptive stance toward the objective "Form" (*Gestalt*) of God's unique and gratuitous self-revelation is one of the chief characterizing features of Balthasar's approach to theology. The emphasis throughout is on the self-disclosive power of God -- both in terms of the objective form of revelation as such, and on the Spirit's imparting to the believer the new "spiritual eyes" necessary to "recognize" this form. The contemplative and receptive stance of the theologian toward the objective form of revelation is made possible by the utter simplicity of God's "speech."[87] The theologian simply needs to remove the artificial barriers to such speech in order to hear it in all of its beauty and simplicity. What the principle of analogy affirms in the abstract the Incarnation renders concrete,[88] i.e., this creation is radically "God's creation" and God is therefore certainly capable of using the exigencies of language and finite form in order to make himself known while still remaining God. "God", as Balthasar points out, "is his own exegete"[89] and there is nothing esoteric or difficult about this revelation - only those who are "wise" clutter the issue with their own "systems" and "explanations" and thus render the message "foolish."[90] Balthasar emphasizes the words of John 1:18 where the Son is referred to as abiding in the Father's bosom and as the one, therefore, who "makes the Father known." In other words, Jesus is the Father's own self-interpretation, his own "exegesis." In the same prologue to John's gospel Christ is referred to as the union of "grace" and "truth." Balthasar sees here an affirmation that:

---

primary strengths of Balthasar's theology vis-a-vis the tightly constructed "rationality" of Rahner's theology. Cf. Ratzinger, *Principles of Catholic Theology: Building Stones for a Fundamental Theology*, (San Francisco: Ignatius Press, 1987),162-171.

[87]Cf. "From the Theology of God." Balthasar states: "Observe how this God who speaks uses a language which man can understand perfectly. He does not impart unintelligible mysteries about himself. He does not engage, then, in a negative theology, but in a theology which is absolutely positive, intelligible to everyone, also and precisely when it expresses itself in human words. The only negative element in this theology is that people are quite able to understand it, but quite often, ... they refuse to do so. Moses did not break the tablets because their contents were too difficult for the Israelites to understand, but because the people preferred to dance around the golden calf." 195-196.

[88]*Theo-Drama II*, Balthasar states: "As we have said elsewhere, the divine Son who becomes man is 'the concrete analogia entis.'" 267.

[89]Hans Urs Von Balthasar, "God is His Own Exegete," *Communio*, (Winter, 1986), 280-287.

[90]Cf. Balthasar, *Does Jesus Know Us? Do We Know Him?*, (San Francisco: Ignatius Press, 1983), 5-6.

Grace and truth do not stand next to one another indifferently, they immediately form an indivisible unity. The introduction into the essence of the Father, which the Son *is*, will thus never be merely theoretical; there is in the Bible, insofar as it is God's revelation, no theoretical truth at all. Instead, Jesus, as interpreter, always actively reveals the Father.[91]

It is of crucial importance to take note here of what Balthasar means when he says the Son "reveals" the Father. What he does *not* mean is a static "unveiling" of propositional truths about the nature of the "divinity" which we can now codify in a book, thinking all the while that "here at last" we have the definitive "answer" to insoluble mysteries. To pursue this course is to fall back into the same rationalistic trap that Balthasar sees operative in the West since the Enlightenment. For Balthasar, the Cartesian demand for *indisputable* rational grounds for all cognitive enterprises has led to the death of true "Mystery" in theology and its eventual retreat, on the one hand, into "right-wing" pseudo-scholastic "proofs" and the use of dogmas as theological straight-jackets, and on the other hand, into "left-wing" historicism that questions the legitimacy of anything transcendent or universal.[92]

The key here to understanding the true nature of God's revelation in Christ is that Jesus does not simply "show us" what God is "like" through some sort of supernatural picture show. Revelation is not simply an epistemological event in the history of human consciousness, but a real historical-ontological event that effects a new reality. Something real, something dramatic *happens* during Jesus' "hour" on the cross, his "descent into hell," and in his resurrection that causes a new reality to come into existence: the reconciliation of the world to God. There is a "drama" that takes place on the stage of world history - a drama whose plot is thick with the tension between two types of freedom: the divine-infinite and the human-finite.[93] And this self-manifestation of God in the drama of world history, far from providing us with propositional certainties, opens us instead into the most fundamental Mystery properly so-called - the Mystery of God's inner triune life as it is offered on the stage of creation.[94]

---

[91]Balthasar, "God is His Own Exegete," 281.

[92]*GL I*, 70-79.

[93]*Theo-Drama II*, 189-334.

[94]*Theo-Drama II*, 260. Balthasar states: "For it is far more incomprehensible that the Eternal God, in his freedom, should set forth to come to us, caring for us by means of his

The central affirmation of Christian revelation is not to be conceived along the lines of static propositional models, but within the context of a dynamic (dramatic) interplay between human freedom and a divine freedom which "assumes the responsibility" for this human freedom while guaranteeing its integrity. The "tension" between divine and human freedom (heteronomy vs. autonomy) is bridged by God in the Incarnation precisely because God is already in himself a positing of that which is "other" through the "going-out and coming-back" of surrender and obediential return in the Trinitarian relations. This is the traditional doctrine of the circumincession taken to its conclusion. But it is a circumincession which is not conceived along the lines of a "closed circle": God's life *is* largesse, *is* excess, *is* a *complete* finding of self in the *complete* giving away to the "other."[95] Therefore, the world is able to find its "where" within God himself - not as an "emanation" from God, nor in a monistic "identity" with God - because God is already in himself an identity in difference that allows the other "to be" while remaining one with himself.[96] The differentiation between God and world has its ground of possibility therefore in the differentiation within God himself. Balthasar summarizes all of this as follows:

> The "nothing-out-of-which" the world came into being can only be sought in infinite freedom itself: that is, in the realms of creatable being opened up by divine omnipotence and, at a deeper level, by the trinitarian "letting-be" of the hypostatic acts. The "not" which characterizes the creature - it is "not" God and cannot exist of itself - is by no means identical with the "not" found within the Godhead. However, the latter constitutes the deepest reason why the creaturely "not" does not cause the analogy of being between creature and God to break down. The infinite distance between the world and God is grounded in the other, prototypical distance between God and God.[97]

For Balthasar, this revelation of God's trinitarian mystery is the only possible "answer" to the question of "where" creation is to be situated if God is to be affirmed as "everything." Classical theism preserves God's immutability but cannot do justice to our "religious" sensibility that God is somehow "affected" by

---

Incarnation, Cross and Eucharist and opening up to his own realm of freedom so that, in it, we can attain the fulfillment of our own freedom. Now everything becomes mystery."

[95]Cf. *Theo-Drama II*, 256-267. Along these lines Balthasar says: "Here we must recall, however, that in the first place what the Father 'does' is nothing other than the Son himself." 267

[96]Cf. Balthasar, *Heart of the World*, (San Francisco: Ignatius Press, 1979).

[97]*Theo-Drama II*, 266.

his creation.[98] This leads inevitably to the "reification" of God as an object of my experience who "stands over against" my own autonomy as a heteronomous "other." The final step into protest atheism is a short one. And, as Balthasar points out to those critics who accuse his own trinitarian theology of anthropomorphism, nothing is more anthropomorphic than the heteronomy-autonomy polarity that conceives of God and humanity as being grounded in two utterly contrary realities.[99] Furthermore, there is no escape from the problem via a retreat into one of the many forms of process theology. These theologies may provide us with a God who can be affected by history, but always at the cost of robbing God of his divinity by placing God within the still broader matrix of the world-God interrelationship.

The only way out of this impasse, according to Balthasar, is by way of the trinitarian ontology outlined above.[100] For Balthasar, the fundamental cognitive reality of the human being is not the sense of one's own self-transcendence toward the infinite horizon of all acts of knowing and willing, but our radical sense of being part of an antecedent "world." And Balthasar sees in the human sense of participation in Being through participation in the world *vestigia trinitatis* .[101] From the very first moment of our existence we become aware of ourselves only because we have been antecedently engaged by the "others" - our parents, our friends, our language , our culture - who "impose" upon us an awareness of themselves which leads to our own self-awareness.[102] In short, the *dialogical* quality of human

---

[98]For an excellent overview of Balthasar's development of the concept of God's immutability see: Gerard F. O'Hanlon, *The Immutability of God in the Theology of Hans Urs Von Balthasar*, (Cambridge: Cambridge University Press, 1990)

[99]*Theo-Drama II*, 204-205. Balthasar states: "In the long run this '*monos pros monon* ' becomes untenable. It leads either to an escape from finitude into the unity of the divine or to the absolutizing of the intramundane unity - and the divine *polis* ('*Roma divina*') of late antiquity came too late to be credible; .... and where, as in Israel, God is imagined to be a person, there is no possibility whatsoever of this kind of escape, except to Manichaeism or atheism. The Old Testament notion of a personal, single God ... is essentially transitional and hence transitory. It can be dissolved by a return to a pagan philosophical idea of a superpersonal One .... or else it must go forward and be transcended into the idea of God found in the New Testament and the Church."

[100]*Theo-Drama II*, 9. "Thus the God of theo-dramatic action is neither 'mutable' ... nor 'immutable.' ... We shall have to see, as the drama unfolds, how it is impossible for him to be either the one or the other."

[101]*Theo-Drama II*, 209-210.

[102]*Love Alone*, 61-62. Also: *Theo-Drama II*. Here we see the influence of Heidegger. For Balthasar, the "others" are seen as an "imposition" in the sense that we perceive the world, not just as a "gift" (*gegeben*) which we affirm as good and as nonmerited by ourselves, but also as

nature is absolutely fundamental. Therefore, even though the bi-polar nature of human consciousness (self awareness and awareness of the "others") must always be seen as concurrent and interdependent, the priority must be given to the "objective" pole of consciousness because it is only through our affirmation of the goodness-in-itself and the unique freedom "to be" of the "other" that we can come to that same conclusion about our own self. When we affirm the freedom, uniqueness, and goodness of the "other" in itself, we achieve a level of disinterestedness and "indifference" toward the object's possible "use" for our own egoistic purposes. Thus, we affirm the "other" (and hence, ourselves) as being free and non-functional vis-`a-vis the world and as "good in itself."[103] It is this fundamentally dialogical character of human consciousness that causes Balthasar to give primacy to the "objective" pole of our subjectivity over the self-referential pole. This is stated by Balthasar as follows:

> Now the other pole of finite freedom comes into full view: if self-possession comes first, all that follows - the endeavor to acquire other good things, including God himself - could seem to be the egoistic attempt to remedy the originally imperfect self-possession by referring it back to oneself, totally, through absolute self-satisfaction. This could happen in the absence of that openness to Being in its totality that unveils this prime thing (myself) as only one being among others. We can put it this way: ... the "part" loves the whole more than itself. ... thus it is not just a mere striving [for the whole], and the gracious quality of the goal that thus discloses itself is brought out; only in this way is freedom fully realized.[104]

The affirmation of an indivisible "core" of freedom as the unique center of every contingent "other," should bring us to an awareness that this freedom must be grounded in the unbounded, infinite freedom of Being as such. Being is thus disclosed as free in itself from necessity and, therefore, gratuitous in how it chooses to manifest itself. Therefore, human nature is disclosed as radically

---

something which is "laid upon us" (*aufgegeben*) since it is, after all, a gift which none of us "asked for." In that sense it is a strange sort of "giftedness" because we become gradually aware as we mature that this "gift" also lays upon us certain "obligations" and requires from us commitment and duty. Balthasar refers to this sense of the world's "claim" upon our freedom as our "throwness" (*Geworfenheit*) into the world that requires an "answer" from us whether we like it or not.

[103]*Theo-Drama II*, 210-211. Balthasar points out that the foregoing analysis will only make sense to the person who has made this "breakthrough" to an awareness of the unique freedom of every contingent "other."

[104]*Theo-Drama II*, 211-212.

dialogical and open, not just to the possibility of dialogue with contingent "others," but also to the radical possibility of dialogue with an infinite "Other" - an "Other" that cannot be "explained" or "contained" by human reason but which can only be known if it freely chooses to reveal itself.[105] The self-disclosure of the trinitarian God reveals to us that "Being" and "love" are co-extensive and only such a revelation gives "plausibility" to the world's ultimate significance.

Here we see a theological development very close to Heidegger's assertion that our fundamental metaphysical awareness is one of "surprise" or "shock" that anything exists at all rather than nothing. However, as far as Balthasar is concerned, Heidegger does not take this awareness far enough: the sense of "shock" over the world's existence is, at its most fundamental root, our innate awareness of its sheer gratuity, i.e., that Being brings forth being out of the sheer largesse and "*excessus*" of its own freedom - a largesse that revelation manifests as trinitarian love. As Balthasar states: "For who could have dared describe God as love, without having first received the revelation of the Trinity in the acceptance of the cross by the Son?"[106] Here, we must concur with Walter Kasper's assessment that Balthasar's theology begins with a notion of being as a cause of "astonishment," and that, for Balthasar, "by its very non-necessity, love becomes the radically astonishing dimension of being. It is the answer to the question of why there is a world instead of no-world. ... The Christian answer to modern atheism is to prove not that God is necessary but that he is the ever-greater."[107]

In Balthasar's development of his trinitarian ontology in the theo-drama we see why his theological aesthetic emphasizes the self-authenticating nature of the revelation of God in Christ - it is self-authenticating because it is without worldly parallel. For Balthasar, the divine trinitarian love manifested on the world stage in the great drama of the tension and reconciliation of infinite and finite freedom, is certainly without parallel in the world. There can be no "other Christs" because the

---

[105]*Theo-Drama II*, 260. Balthasar summarizes this as follows: "For the realm of infinite freedom, now opened up, is always both things at once: it is both the realm of God's incomprehensible sovereignty - beyond our grasp at all points - and the realm of unlimited trinitarian communication of the inner-divine love. Thus everything can be both crystal-clear speech, a clarion summons to responsibility, and a fairy-tale gift; and each pole heightens the other and hence itself."

[106]Balthasar, "Current Trends in Catholic Theology and the Responsibility of the Christian," *Communio*, (Spring, 1978), 80.

[107]Walter Kasper, *The God of Jesus Christ*, (New York: Crossroad, 1984), 55.

final act of this play reveals a resolution from the side of infinite freedom - a resolution which must therefore be final in its significance for the whole world. In other words, God's drama is without parallel precisely because it is *God's* drama. Were it anything short of that it would be no real resolution at all. In one important sense therefore, God's theo-drama is unlike intramundane theater: it is not a "contrived" and "artificial" activity complete with "props" intended to "mimic" the tensions of human life (which is essentially what docetism was saying). Rather, it *is* the resolution of the divine-human tension and therefore the ultimate eschatological seriousness of this act should not be diminished by positing its "repeatability."[108]

The divine love revealed in Christ is beyond the wildest expectations of human reason because it surpasses what we could have anticipated based on an analysis of our "needs" as human beings.[109]   God's revelation, therefore, confronts us as something wholly gratuitous and yet, at the same time, as fulfilling the deepest longings of the human heart.   But this fulfillment should not be characterized along the lines of a transcendental theology that sees the *a posteriori* quality of God's revelation as a condition of possibility for the "coming to objectivity" of my antecedent experience of grace.   For Balthasar, the transcendental approach diminishes the importance of finite form as the locus of the revelation of a divine action which so exceeds our own inner "dynamism," that we have to say that it [revelation] can only be approached on its own terms, from within its own God-given categories in order to be fully appreciated in all of its force.   Anything short of this tends to "functionalize" the objective form of Christ, which is now seen as a means for mediating my own interiority to itself.   This functionalizing of the Christ-form runs the risk of reducing the dialogical encounter with God in revelation to the subjective pole only: the "objective" encounter with the kerygmatic Christ, once viewed as a call to *metanoia* and life in the ecclesial *communio*, now degenerates

---

[108]Balthasar himself affirms that the analogy between God's activity in history and the "activity" of human theatre should not be stretched too far. Cf. *Theo-Drama: II*, 17.

[109]"Current Trends in Catholic Theology," 80. Balthasar notes: "My main argument - not only against Rahner but against the entire transcendental school ... - is this: It might be true that from the very beginning man was created to be disposed toward God's revelation, so that with God's grace even the sinner can accept all revelation. *Gratia supponit naturam* . But when God sends his own living Word to his creatures, he does so, not to instruct them about the mysteries of the world, nor primarily to fill their deepest needs and yearnings. Rather he communicates and actively demonstrates such unheard-of-things that man feels not satisfied but awestruck by a love which he never could have hoped to experience."

into a solipsistic litany of my own felt needs. And the Christ-form, now robbed of its real existential and historical weight, becomes the increasingly "plastic" and impersonal symbol of an "emerging world consciousness." Such a "panchristic" religious philosophy paradoxically ends up rendering Christ superfluous in the face of a generically conceived universal "inner experience of God."[110]

Thus, according to Balthasar, God's self-revelation must be seen as self-authenticating . Revelation could in no way have been "guessed" or "anticipated" in its particulars in advance. However, once revealed, its unparalleled quality imposes upon the individual an awareness that, here at last, a pinnacle has been reached, a kind of theological-historical watershed: either this man is "truly the son of God" or he is that "stumbling block" of the Jews, the "foolishness" of the Greeks. One could rephrase this and say that, with Christ's advent, the world's self-consciousness is forever changed in the direction of a fundamental "Yes" or "No": either this man represents the final resolution of the divine-human tension, or, if he is not, then the world must pursue the antithesis of that proposition - the rejection of the heteronomous God in favor of human autonomy and the pursuit of a purely, intramundane "progress." The latter is, according to Balthasar, the path clearly chosen by the West in the last centuries.

The fact that the theo-drama is without worldly parallel shows us that theology should not pursue the dialogue with the modern world with an overemphasis on apologetic theology. Apologetics certainly has its place in theology, but Christian theology needs to spend at least as much time explicating the full ramifications of the revelation itself.[111] Only revelation forms the "bedrock" upon which all subsequent theologizing can proceed. Indeed, Balthasar is quick to point out that modern theologians seem to suffer from a kind of inferiority complex that causes them to short-change the ability of the nonchristian to appreciate the full significance of God's unparalleled act of revelation.[112]

---

[110]Cf. Balthasar, *The Moment of Christian Witness*, 60-68. Also, Balthasar, *Theodramtik: Anlage Des Gesamtwerkes, Band III: Die Handlung* , (Einsiedeln: Johannes Verlag, 1980), 253-263. Balthasar deals in these tightly packed pages with Rahner's soteriology.

[111]Cf. Edward T. Oakes, "Ethics and the Search for God's Will in the Thought of Hans Urs Von Balthasar," *Communio*, (Fall, 1990), 409-431. Oakes states: "...[the] counsel to admit the full force of modernity is by no means the last word. The task of both explicating the Christian message as well as shaping a new apologetics has, with this admission, barely begun. The very length of the Theodramtics shows this." 424-425.

[112]Hans Urs Von Balthasar, *Convergences: To the Source of Christian Mystery*, 65.

For Balthasar, apologetics finds its place within a unified theological structure which has three interrelated and interdependent "faces": the contemplative, the kerygmatic, and the dialogical.[113] Contemplative theology is characterized by a meditative "immersion" into the various aspects of salvation history, and the subsequent search for ever new relations between the individual aspects themselves as well as their relationship to the whole.[114] It forms the "root" out of which the other two branches grow and is "indispensable for all subsequent forms."[115]

Kerygmatic theology flows from the first insofar as contemplative meditation on revelation is not a neo-Gnostic exercise in self-fulfillment, but is intrinsically oriented to *praxis* . This theology is still, as Balthasar points out, a theology which operates, so to speak, from the "inside to the outside." The theologian, in seeking to "translate" the gospel into a modern idiom must constantly refer to the sources of revelation (Scripture and Tradition) in order to retain a vital contact with the very historical revelation that he or she is attempting to translate. The contemplative approach nourishes the kerygmatic, and the kerygmatic "enfleshes" the contemplative. As Balthasar puts it:

> The demand for translation which lies in the command to be understandable to all nations is not free to make concessions ("teach them to observe everything"); the translation, then, must proceed ever anew out of the vision of the whole (the "first" theology), and is to make use of the peoples' form of thought, in critical observation. The Spirit-inspired, definitive word of witness concerning God's act of salvation remains normative for proclamation, yet contains, not naked facts, but a presentation of the facts which is already "theologically" meditated in the people of God - the two are inseparable.[116]

Finally, dialogical theology reverses the order and operates from the "outside to the inside." Balthasar locates apologetic theology within the dialogical,

---

[113]*Convergences*, 60-67. Cf. Oakes, "Ethics and the Search for God's Will," 425, n. 33.

[114]An example of how Balthasar utilizes this type of theology can be seen in his analysis of how dogmatic formulas are to be approached: "In all 'definitions' one should remember above all that a segment is lifted out of a whole that belongs together and is examined, as it were, with the magnifying glass. For this reason a later view can order what has been 'defined' in this way into a larger context that does not really relativize it but 'relationalizes' it, so to speak, by placing it into a frame of reference." Hans Urs Von Balthasar, *A Short Primer For Unsettled Laymen*, 67-68.

[115]*Convergences*, 61.

[116]*Convergences*, 63-64.

but obviously considers it to be a pale shadow of true dialogue. "The apologist," according to Balthasar, "is engaged essentially in one-sided speech, or at best in the anticipatory refutation of possible objections."[117] The true goal of dialogical theology is to take on the form of a *theologia crucis* in which one "dies" to one's own perspective and allows the "other" the "space" within yourself out of which true dialogue is fostered. This is not a relativization of the gospel but a simple awareness that even God had to "descend" into the silence of death in order to "identify with" and "speak" to the world. Furthermore, lest the Christian grow smug in some pseudo-awareness that he or she "possesses" the truth of God's "unparalleled" revelation, dialogical theology reminds the believer that the same "unparalleled" quality of God's revelation is predicated upon its manifestation of the divine largesse, the divine ever-greater, which no single human being can ever grasp fully. Therefore, dialogue with other perspectives is theologically required of the Christian by the internal logic of the Christian revelation itself: all truth, all goodness, all beauty, no matter where it is found, is intrinsically ordered to its divine ground and is a manifestation of the depths within the trinitarian life of God. The mere fact that, in a certain metaphysical sense, all "truth" is contained in revelation should not lead the Christian to an arrogant assumption that he or she necessarily has grasped its deep and infinite significance:

> Yet the Christian must remain aware, not only that "there is something true" also in other points of view, but that the Christian truth is always greater than what he, in thinking, proclaiming, and indeed living, can capture; that he himself, then, precisely because he knows this, remains under the judgment of the Word he proclaims, and that this judgment can also meet him through his brother. Still less will he forget, next to the second form of the theology, the first form: the ever new immersion, in prayer and adoration, directly in the first truth, before striving for any kerygmatic and dialogical goals, in order to draw new power for proclamation and encounter by meditating on God's incomprehensible mystery of love. Thus the three forms of theology form a system of circulation. Or, rather, it is the same face in three-fold, changing expression.[118]

Finally, therefore, Balthasar's theology could be characterized as contemplative and synthetic rather than critical-analytical, as kerygmatic rather than

---

[117]*Convergences*, 65.
[118]*Convergences*, 67.

systematic, and as dialogical rather than dialectical-apologetic. And all of these elements, taken as a whole, seek to explicate the central mystery of Christian revelation in such a way that the Christ-form remains the formal and material object of all theologizing, a form that remains the "fulcrum" upon which all the various theological "faces" are balanced. And it must never be forgotten that this "object" of theology can never be eclipsed by any "system," nor fully grasped by rationalizing philosophy or science. In this sense, the Christ-event carries within itself an analogous "uniqueness" comparable to the uniqueness of any historical event or work of art. As Balthasar puts it: "An historical event as well as a great, 'unique' work of art can be an object of scientific research, - and thereby of progressive knowledge as well - without the object ever being really 'worked out'."[119]

C. Conclusion.

Balthasar's theology stands or falls with the integrity of the Christ-event as the definitive irruption of God's Kingdom into human history. It is, according to Balthasar, a dialogical event that involves a "dramatic" encounter between human freedom and the divine freedom. And this encounter carries within itself the most profound repercussions for the very depths of worldly being as such. The question, therefore, of the metaphysical grounding for such an event is of paramount importance. How does Balthasar define "freedom?" How does he conceive the relationship between creation and Creator? What are his grounds for asserting that the God-world relationship is dialogical rather than dialectical? And if this relationship is dialogical how does Balthasar avoid a heteronomous dualism between God and humanity, or a mythological doctrine of God? Furthermore, given his frequently repeated caveat against using metaphysical "systems" in an overly reductionistic manner in providing a "grounding" for revelation, how does he work out the relationship between metaphysics and theology? Finally, how does all of this help to illuminate the Christ-event as the central reality of human history? These are just some of the questions that will be dealt with in the next chapters.

---

[119]*Convergences*, 51.

Chapter Two:
Metaphysical Foundations: The Ambiguity of Antiquity

The task that is now before us is a formidable one: to show how the various "strands" of Balthasar's non-analytical theological corpus hang together as a unified whole as a result of the "Gestalt-giving" power of God's revelation in Christ.[1] This quest to ground all of theology in a unified christocentric foundation leads Balthasar to a discussion of the metaphysical concept of Being and how the Christ-form transcends and fulfills metaphysics. The definitive revelation of the Word in salvation history brings together within itself all of the many ways in which engraced nature already reflects the immanence of the Word in all of history.[2] If such a strongly universalistic concept of Christ's role in human history is to be taken seriously, then a study of the general human "thirst" for God is necessary. How have human beings expressed in outward form the deep inner longing of the human soul for God? All of history reflects something of the "restlessness" of humanity, the ambiguity of the human religious quest, and the frustration of the philosopher before the ultimate questions of existence. In short, if Christ is the "answer," what is the question?

Balthasar turns to the history of the dialectical interplay between mythological and metaphysical thought for clues concerning the real outlines of the

---

[1] I will be following the primary outline of three of Balthasar's main works on metaphysics and its relationship to revelation. They are as follows: *The Glory of the Lord: A Theological Aesthetics IV: The Realm of Metaphysics in Antiquity* ; *The Glory of the Lord V: The Realm of Metaphysics in the Modern Age* ; and *Theo-Drama II*, 189-334. *Glory of the Lord* will be designated by *GL* .

[2] *GL IV*, 32.

human longing for the divine.[3] He pursues an interpretation of Christian revelation as the manifestation of a divine freedom so utterly gratuitous that it is designated with the quality of "glory." However, this glory is also mediated to us through the metaphysical depths of Being.[4] This "glory," states Balthasar, "is a fundamental statement that leavens all of Scripture. God himself is glorious: in his appearing ... and in the whole cosmos irradiated by his glory."[5] However, this universality of the revelation of God's glory, precisely because he has imbued all of creation with this glory, "must confront that other universality, the universality of the human spirit, ... the spirit which of its nature is open to understand the being of all that is."[6] It is this universalizing quest of the human spirit to plumb the depths of being *qua* being that Balthasar gives the name "metaphysics." However, it must be noted that Balthasar does not limit this term to the dialectical world of the strictly philosophical: the dialogical world of myth and "natural" religion, in so far as they too attempt to interpret the "light" that shines forth from the center of being, are also an expression of the human metaphysical *eros* . Balthasar states this as follows:

> Christians in a period like our own (which cannot 'believe' any longer in a metaphysical glory) must not attempt to offer a biblical glory, without any continuity or mediation, to the world: rather, what they must offer to the world is, together with the biblical glory, the metaphysical depth of being, once thought lost and now again drawn forth anew from the scriptural revelation.[7]

---

[3]*GL IV*, 24. Balthasar states: "Metaphysics, in the breadth of myth, philosophy and religion already offers an interpretation of man that radically directs him to the 'divine'."

[4]In what follows I will use "Being" to denote the"absolute" or the "infinite" (*Sein*) and "being" to refer to the finite world of "things" (*Dasein*). Furthermore, Balthasar will make a twofold distinction (following Aristotle and Aquinas) with regard to infinite Being: 1) The infinite, wholly subsisting Being of God (thus, "Being" as such); and 2) The infinite but nonsubsisting Being of creation-as-a-whole which emerges from God's act of Being and participates in its "light" analogously. The latter reaches subsistence and self-possession only through its concretization in *Dasein* . This presupposes, however, a distinction within finite existents between essence and existence which, as shall be seen, forms the heart of Balthasar's phenomenological analysis of our "primal perception" of "Being" in "beings." Therefore, in all that follows, when referring to infinite Being I will use the qualifying terms "subsistent" or "nonsubsistent" to differentiate between God's Being and the Being of "creation-as-a-whole" where such a distinction is needed in order to maintain clarity. Otherwise, I will simply speak of "Being" and "being." This less nuanced distinction is especially appropriate when speaking of pre-Christian (or, at least, pre-Aristotelian) myth and philosophy in the West which rarely speaks of infinite Being in such a manner as to require a distinction between subsisting and nonsubsisting Being.

[5]*GL IV*, 11.

[6]*GL IV*, 11.

[7]*GL IV*, 14.

This chapter takes up these metaphysical/theological issues by examining the crucial relationship between Balthasar's theology of revelation and the philosophical underpinnings which ground the whole enterprise. It will be clear from the outset that Balthasar is concerned with "reviving" the classical world's emphasis on "Being" as the foundation of all philosophy and of all genuine theology. It will be shown that, for Balthasar, this "revival" of classical metaphysics is necessary in order to understand the unique, historical context within which Christian revelation was originally formulated. The modern world's flight from a transcendent metaphysics is really a flight from Being (Heidegger) and is, therefore, destructive of genuine Christian theology. Balthasar puts it as follows:

> [The] "popular", philosophically unrefined view of God is actually current in many places, as is shown by modern atheism. For when the latter protests against God ... it becomes clear "that every form of rejection of God is directed against a specific, distorted and grotesque notion of God", but also that in this process the last two centuries (roughly) have seen a gradual dissolution of the "common understanding". Here the adoption of the biblical events and affirmations as part of a total, humane, religio-philosophical world of thought ... is not even taken into consideration, mostly because all such reflection is rejected as superfluous and alienating. Consequently there is no awareness of the biblical paradox that God can be "everything" (Sir 43:27) and yet man can be "something"; and that God can be absolutely free without robbing man of his genuine freedom.[8]

The above mentioned "common understanding" is, in fact, the classical philosophical-religious tradition and its assimilation into Christian theology. The response of the Enlightenment to this tradition, according to Balthasar, was overly simplistic - it simply rejected this centuries old synthesis as an outdated, pre-critical, mythological "encrustation" on Christian revelation which could be scraped away like so many barnacles in order to retrieve "real" Christianity or the "real historical Jesus." The essential mistake in such an approach is the titanistic assumption that modern humanity had largely freed itself from the dynamic interplay between the three basic components in the history of metaphysics: myth, philosophy and natural religion.[9] But, according to Balthasar, it is only an anti-supernatural and

---

[8]*Theo-Drama II*, 192.
[9]*Theo-Drama II*, 420.

reductionistic bias which could naively miss the fact that these three dynamic components of metaphysics will always be with us because they are an essential aspect of our humanity (as is evident, according to Balthasar, from history).[10]

We shall therefore begin with a straightforward examination of how Balthasar summarizes and reconstructs the history of metaphysical thought around his controlling theme of "glory". From there we will proceed to an analysis of how this metaphysics points toward a fulfillment in Christian revelation. Finally, we will see how this relationship between metaphysics and theology helps to shape the direction of his theology of revelation.

Myth, Philosophy and Religion

Balthasar's central thesis is that the tension between the dialogical concept of Being expressed through myth and its negation in the dialectic of philosophy is transcended in the dialogical metaphysics of love expressed in the trinitarian Christian revelation.[11] Without a revelation from the heart of Being, metaphysics would remain in a state of constant tension and "oscillation" between the dialogical dualism of myth and the monistic, "monological" world of philosophical dialectic. Thus, revelation is the "guardian" of all genuine metaphysics, and metaphysics, through its probing of the depths of human existence, addresses Being with a question that can only be answered by a revelation from the heart of Being - a revelation which can only be the product of a sovereign freedom.[12]

Balthasar sees genuine philosophy as having an "advent-like" character *vis-`a-vis* Christian revelation, he often uses the term "philosophy" to mean simply classical, pre-Christian, Western philosophy. All post-Christian philosophy is influenced by Christian revelation.[13] Balthasar is interested in testing the limits of

---

[10]*GL IV*, 15-19.

[11]*GL V*, 629. It can also be concluded from all of this that one cannot understand the true depth of Christian revelation unless one engages in metaphysical analysis. Balthasar notes: "The dynamic interrelationship between classical theo-philosophy and the Christian theology of revelation is indissoluble, because the transcendental claim of reason and the universal claim of revelation will always sit uneasily together." *GL V*, 14.

[12]*GL V*, 636.

[13]*GL V*, 655. Balthasar states: "Pre-Christian thought in all its complexity preserved an advent-like openness of the coming of something greater than itself by which it could be

that philosophy which is uninfluenced by Christian revelation in order to build his case that, without revelation, philosophy is an incomplete "wisdom." This pre-Christian "incomplete" and "advent-like" philosophy is given a fairly positive evaluation as a necessary "anteroom" to the mansion of Christian revelation. However, the assessment is much more negative when Balthasar discusses those modern philosophies which are "forgetful of Being" and, therefore, of revelation: what we see in modern philosophy is, for Balthasar, a "decline" and a degeneration.[14] Thus, Balthasar tends in the direction summed up by Chesterton: "Paganism was the biggest thing in the world; and Christianity was bigger; and everything since has been comparatively small."[15] The bottom line is quite clear - Balthasar is not interested in a "dialogue" with those theologians who are "forgetful of Being" and who suppose that one can do Christian theology without entering into a conversation with the great metaphysical tradition of the West.[16]

A. Myth

Balthasar develops his metaphysic by outlining its evolution in the history of the transition from myth to philosophy and its culmination in revelation. The guiding thread in his analysis is the distinction and tension between the "dialogical" world of myth and the "dialectical" world of philosophy. The pre-Christian history of metaphysics oscillates between these two poles with no clear resolution possible. This is illustrated clearly in Plato's use of myth to express the soul's desire for participation in Being even though Plato, throughout his work, heaps scorn upon the mythic world of the poets. Thus, even though philosophy "supersedes" myth, it can never entirely replace it or do without it since philosophy discovers a "dialogical" moment within Being that cannot be expressed adequately through a

---

determined, and ... post-Christian thought, whether it will or not, has been determined by that which is greater than itself."

[14]*GL V*, 9-47.

[15]Quoted in, Peter Kreeft, *Back to Virtue*, (San Francisco: Ignatius Press 1992) 55.

[16]*GL V*, 628-656.

strict dialectic.[17] Myth, for Plato, "is to be found, and belongs, where the lines drawn by philosophical reflection stretch beyond its grasp."[18]

The essence of myth resides in its character as a kind of "primal address" from the very "limit" of our experience of the depths of Being. Myth brings us face to face with that deep suspicion of the human heart that we are not "alone" and that we are addressed by Being in a most personal way. At most, philosophy can simply point to the deep ambiguity of such an awareness: are we being addressed by Being or is this experience a mere projection of human transcendence onto Being? However, myth, as myth, is not concerned with such speculation and seeks to bring present something of the power of this dialogical experience of Being. Myth is not satisfied with "monological," monistic interpretations of Being and presses forward to the very limits of our "dialogue" with Being.[19]

Nobody, according to Balthasar, pushed the limits of human mythic consciousness more than Homer.[20] The Homeric world is fundamentally dialogical: born out of a preexisting and ancient canon of texts, Homer's myths are purged of their magical components and given an orientation toward an increasingly naked moral encounter between the "world" of divinity and the "world" of

---

[17]*GL IV*, 195-196. Balthasar states: "Philosophy remains in that situation where it must at once create myth as its own limit and yet critically take it back again: at the same time it must place things in the overflowing radiance of the inspiration of *eros*, which it cannot justify by rational consideration. The implications of this become palpable in the *Timaeus* -myth, where in response to mythical imagination a personal god is set above the gods of the cosmos and yet in accordance with philosophical considerations must be subordinated to the Idea of the Good."

[18]*GL IV*, 195.

[19]*GL V*, 629. Balthasar states: "Myth itself persists in indissoluble ambiguity: a spirit-like cry from the depths of Being - or projection of the human personality on to impersonal Being? The claim of metaphysics to critical self-responsibility through reason will necessarily tend towards the latter and will explain man's address from Being as man's address to Being ('eros'). ... In distinction to this, the taking seriously of the address from Being tends in the direction of making the individual myth, as finite myth, transparent to the entire language of Being."

[20]*GL IV*, 43. In an extended footnote Balthasar explains why he considers the Homeric myths to be superior to other forms of myth. We do not need to recapitulate his reasons here since it is not central to the current discussion. However, it should be noted that here we see once again Balthasar's conviction that the classical Greek heritage forms a privileged locus for theological inquiry into the historical antecedents of Christian revelation. Balthasar states: "Only the West received the grace of birth under the sign of a perfected cosmos, ... the cosmos of Homer's epics." And again: "*Theoria, eidos, nous, nomos, themis, aidos* - all the fundamental modes of the original Greek world-view pass over from the old manner of existence to the new, newly thought-out but surviving the revolution of critical philosophy intact. So it is, once again, in the modern period, where the Homeric world becomes ever more unambiguously evident behind the Vergilian world which is descended from it, that even where for thousands of years faith has no longer been placed in the figures of the gods, the expression of the Homeric world remains self-evidently credible." (45).

humanity.[21] Thus, as Balthasar points out, "We can see two articulations in this structure: first, the irremovable separation of God and man and then man's transcendence into the sphere of God, in which he finds salvation, his greatness and his glory."[22] We see here the two authentic "marks" of myth which, for Balthasar, comprise the essence of its religious insight: 1) the irreducible dualism of the two realms (divine/human); and 2) the undeniable orientation of human existence toward this realm of the divine. The world of humanity is wholly characterized by mortality, by the mark of futility and ultimate death and dissolution, whereas divinity is wholly characterized by that which is immortal, beyond death and transcending futility. Nevertheless, in the Homeric world human self-understanding is always linked with the human relationship to divinity.[23] Homeric myth, therefore, should be characterized as a pre-philosophical, divine-human dialogical dualism that seeks to express through narrative symbolism the primary religious insight that the cosmos is ultimately determined by the category of the "personal".[24] And because the gods are "personal" it follows that our "awe" before existence can be interpreted religiously as an appreciation of the "glory" of the divine *freedom* that lies at the heart of Being. As Balthasar puts it: "The world of myth was fundamentally dialogical: glory streamed forth from the personally divine on to man, who dared to interpret his temporal existence in this light."[25]

Thus, for Balthasar, "dialogue" in the Homeric myths has a clear *theandric* context insofar as the fundamental divine-human dualism is overshadowed by the more primary need to affirm a *real* relationality between the gods and human beings. In other words, of the two fundamental structures of myth mentioned above, "dialogue", rather than "dualism", is the more primary religious reality that myth seeks to preserve. Dualism is simply posited as the absolutely necessary ground of possibility for a real dialogue between the gods and humanity - a dialogue which assumes, since it is a *real* dialogue, that we (and the world) are not

---

[21]*GL IV*, 48. Balthasar states: "We may see a religious decision in the conscious renunciation by Homer of metamorphoses in the other world, ... whereby he equally decisively intensifies man's relationship with an interiority stripped of all magic. ... Now the pure relationship of the hero to his god comes into prominence."

[22]*GL IV*, 45

[23]*GL IV*, 46. Balthasar summarizes this aspect of the mythic dualism as follows: "Men are mortal, wholly marked out by death, whereas gods cannot be killed."

[24]*GL IV*, 55-62.

[25]*GL IV*, 155.

God. Therefore, the two fundamental structures of myth, dualism and dialogue, are intrinsically related to one another and mutually necessary for the other's possibility. The myth, with its naive objectification of the gods as simply other persons (albeit "divine" persons) with whom to dialogue , preserves, nevertheless, the dramatic and moral tension inherent within the dialogical divine-human encounter and thereby also reminds us that Being is expressive of an essential core of freedom - a freedom which bathes all of existence in the mantle of "glory."[26]

But myth has not as yet penetrated beyond a naive dualism into philosophical or transcendental categories and thus the divine freedom which "appears" as the "glory" of Being does so in strictly anthropomorphic categories. Here we run into the limitations of myth as a vehicle for metaphysical and theological insight. The exaggerated anthropomorphisms preclude any serious attempt to overcome the autonomy-heteronomy dialectic at the heart of the mythic dialogical dualism. Ultimately, the divine realm mirrors the conflicts and contradictions of the human realm and its unity can only be maintained by the mystification of the divine will.[27]

But this process of mystification only begs the essential question of the mystery of the "diffusion" of Being into the multiplicity of the world. The world of myth must eventually assert a deeper more unfathomable unity "behind" the multiplicity of localized divine epiphanies. "There is," as Balthasar points out, "no 'fundamental theology' of myth."[28] Hesiod and Pindar had already begun to broaden the Homeric myths by attempting to extend the possibility of the divine epiphany in the hero into every human situation and to inquire into the exact relationship between the transcendent and immutable world of divinity and the individualistic gods of the personalistic epiphanies. Their attempt, although still within the world of myth, is a clear effort at universalizing the basic religious insights of Homer and thus can be seen as precursors to the more serious attempt at universalization found in philosophy.[29] The basic dialogical insight of Homer,

---

[26]*Theo-Drama II*, 42-51.

[27]*GL IV*, 63.

[28]*GL IV*, 155.

[29]*GL IV*, 78. Balthasar states: "The next generation had to ask whether [the Homeric] model was universally valid; whether a knowledge drawn from such an encounter could be broadened to encompass a knowledge of a continuing state; whether every man could find entry to the relationship in which the hero stands; and finally, whether the divinity as such could be understood in accordance with the personal mode of the individual god in his epiphany. The poets

though preserving the sense of the divine freedom (glory) at the heart of Being, could not, for all that, withstand the dialectical scrutiny of the new philosophical reason. In short, Homer's world, precisely because of its status as myth, could not provide an ultimate rational "closure" for the tension between a divine realm of immutable immortality and the human realm of futility and conflict.[30] The real credibility of the "gods" faded into mist and the stage was set for the conflict between the now empty cult of the *polis* and the emerging appeal of the "wise" man whose whole life had a "mimetic" quality which mirrored the perfection of the cosmos. The harmonic union with Being through *mimesis* of the cosmic order now replaces the naive dualistic dialogue of the myth.[31]

B. Philosophy

The world of myth, as we have seen, could not sustain itself. Despite the religious appeal of its dialogical framework, myth did not satisfy the need to universalize the experience of Being beyond the divine epiphanies to a select few.

---

and thinkers from Hesiod to Pindar are occupied in the struggle to give these questions concerning man's lot a responsible answer - that is, an answer that takes account of the entire situation of mankind: and the more universally the question is posed, the more clearly does philosophy emerge from myth."

[30]That is not to imply that Balthasar thinks that the philosophy which follows the Homeric myth is somehow a "superior" mode of metaphysical speculation. Indeed, one of his central points, as we shall see, is that the destruction of myth also brought in its wake the destruction of the "personal" God: humanity is increasingly seen as "alone" in an order of Being which is seen in increasingly impersonal terms. For example, Balthasar states: "As early as the tragedians, the personal characteristics in the divine government are lost and man stands, more and more, alone with his fate. ... One must therefore be very careful when one charges Homer with archaic imperfection as far as his central vision is concerned; one should rather ask whether the later simplifications and removals of ambiguities were not frequently impoverishments." *GL IV*, 63.

[31]I use the word "replace" here only to emphasize that there was, according to Balthasar, a genuine historical evolution at work in this change from myth to philosophy. However, this change should not be exaggerated to the point of exclusion: myth, defined here as the symbolic attempt of the non-philosophical mind to express the dialogical nature of the God-humanity relationship, will always be with us. For example, Balthasar notes: "Is it not a fact that the majority of people continue to entertain an understanding of God that is anthropomorphic and close to mythology, where God is one among many; where God is one place and the world in another; where God is in heaven and man is on earth; where God is one existing thing among other existing things ... ?" *Theo-Drama II*, 192. What Balthasar is recognizing here is, of course, that various forms of mythological piety will always exist among the great mass of the common people. Thus, Balthasar's analysis of the history of the evolution of metaphysical thought is largely an analysis of this change among the educated elite of the ancient Greco-Roman world.

Thus, philosophical reason, through its pursuit of the abstract, universal concept, destroys the world of myth and seeks to apprehend the nature of Being within the purview of reason alone. Balthasar's main objective here is to demonstrate that there is an inherent tension between the mythical world of divine "glory" and its dialogical presuppositions, and the philosophical act which seeks to apprehend the "All" in a single, encompassing, transcendental "movement." Metaphysics now shifts its focus away from the dialogical world of "glory" in the myth toward the "monological" world of rationality. As Balthasar puts it: "The initial juxtaposition of the worlds which we saw in Homer, is no longer acceptable, whatever the consequences for the nature of the *theion*, of the divine."[32] The fundamental nature of human knowledge, its true sources and the extent of its grasp now became the primary focus: could reason alone ascend Mount Olympus in Titanistic fashion and make the "glory" of the gods its own? This desire to know the limits of human reason is at the heart of the new philosophy. Balthasar states: "The undertaking that plots the limits to what reason can achieve in its investigations has borne, since the time of Plato, the name of philosophy."[33] The question which is at the center of this search for rational limits relates back to the world of myth:

> Has the act of transcendence already found the transcendent object? Is it, as act, therefore one with its object or not? Is the light in which we accomplish the act of transcendence identical with the illumination of transcendence? Or, to put the question another way: can the light of reason bring the radiance and the glory of myth within its purview?[34]

But reason seeks a dialectical explanation within its own totality and, therefore, the search for rational "closure" is one of the chief themes of the new philosophy. It is "monological" rather than "dialogical," since reason seeks to grasp the "All" from within its own vital sources. Thus, Balthasar's initial answer to the above question is a qualified "no." It is "qualified" because the monological quality of philosophical reason is not caused by an "anti-dialogical" ideological prejudice but, rather, is caused by a necessary methodological suspension or "bracketing" of the world of "glory" in order to ascertain the limits of reason

---

[32]*GL IV*, 164.
[33]*GL IV*, 155.
[34]*GL IV*, 156.

itself.[35] Thus, philosophy can tend in one of two directions: it can either "bracket" the world of glory while remaining ultimately open to a higher "fulfillment" in a theological metaphysics, or it can close itself off to any "higher" orientation and seek fulfillment within a rational totality that is self-sufficient. If the former path is chosen then "glory" remains a valid philosophical pursuit at the outer limits of reason where theology and philosophy intertwine. If the latter path is chosen then "glory" is effectively eliminated since the possibility of a genuine "address" to humanity from the side of transcendence is ruled out on methodological grounds.

The choice between either a concept of Being which is open to a divine world of "glory" or one which is closed upon itself remains as the fundamental decision which philosophy is always called upon to make. And there should be no mistake as to where Balthasar stands: without the category of "glory" the concept of transcendent Being itself eventually will be lost in the nihilistic, materialistic functionalism of modernity.[36] Or, to put it another way, one cold say that without Christian revelation the concept of Being will be lost to various monistic or idealistic philosophies of "identity" which seek an ultimate metaphysical explanation for the multiplicity of finitude within an overarching "One." And this movement toward "identity" inevitably dissolves the concepts of finitude and individuation within itself (as in pantheism where "Being" is simply equated with "God"), or the "One" is simply formalized into one of the "comprehensive concepts of reason."[37] However, philosophy itself cannot sustain such "identity" without great difficulty and constantly falls back into "mythic" dualistic categories in its attempt to "explain" the outer reaches of human transcendence and the natural instinct of philosophical *eros* to seek an "object".[38] Thus, the history of pre-Christian philosophy is a history of an unresolvable "oscillation" between these two poles - an oscillation which, as we shall see later, can only be resolved in the Christian trinitarian revelation.

---

[35]*GL IV*, 156. Balthasar states: "Reason which inquires about being as a whole is a 'monological' act. At the point where philosophy becomes historically observable the dialogical act of prayer is cut off at a stroke. This break indicates the line of separation. In place of the daring of the heart there is knowledge which keeps itself to itself."

[36]*GL V*, 644-645.

[37]*GL V*, 9-47.

[38]*GL IV*, 196-215.

Before we reach that stage we must first sketch Balthasar's development of this philosophical "oscillation" between monistic identity and mythological "glory" and their "dramatic" correlates: autonomy and heteronomy. To do this we must examine the central role which Platonic philosophy plays in Balthasar's summary of the history of metaphysics. From there we will proceed to an analysis of how Balthasar traces the development of metaphysics from Plato, through the period of "religion," into its final consummation in Christian revelation.

The Ambiguity of Platonic Ascent

Plato, according to Balthasar, was vitally concerned with the question of the limits of human knowledge in the philosophical act. Knowledge of concrete, earthly things was seen as "certain," while knowledge of "heavenly" things was viewed as merely "probable." Thus, the lowliest artisan, insofar as he possessed knowledge of "things," was more of a paradigm for authentic knowledge than any sophist or poet. Thus, for Plato, philosophy should be "an open readiness, service and submission before 'things'."[39] However, philosophical knowledge differs from that of the artisan in its specific object: in every "thing," insofar as it is "real," there is a dimension which can be known only by the philosophical act as such and which Plato refers to as "aspect, appearance, form, content, nature, essential core."[40] This quality of the existent thing is an element in the thing itself and is not an *a priori* projection of human transcendence. The "light" which shines forth from the existent thing comes from neither the perceiver nor, exclusively, from the thing perceived - it is a light which "precedes thought" and is responsible for both our perception and the ability of the thing to be "seen," i.e. its luminosity. In other words, both subject and object participate in a transcendent order of Being which grounds both our inner intellectual light and the intelligibility of the object. Balthasar reaches the conclusion that, for Plato, this light in which the Being of the world participates is itself beyond Being - a kind of "divine extravagance" which is

---

[39]*GL IV*, 177.
[40]*GL IV*, 178.

more than a "mere *a priori* at the heart of reason."[41] But it is precisely here that the ambiguity of Plato's conception of the "divine" enters in. For what is the true nature of the source of this transcendent light? Balthasar states:

> But whence is the light? Is it the return of a mythical revelation from without? Or a mystical experience of union? Or simply an empirical experience of a transcendental structure of knowledge? That an ascent has taken place is clear, as it is that, for Plato, no philosophy can exist without it: it is just in the ascent to the Idea, supremely to the light of the Good which establishes everything, that understanding ... is made possible.[42]

There are two things which Balthasar is at pains to point out here: 1) Plato's conception of "truth" and its establishment is dependent upon an "ascent" into transcendence, into the world of the Idea and the Good, which is more than a mere "ground of possibility" for human transcendence and is truly "beyond" our subjectivity; and 2) that this very notion of transcendence, despite Plato's insistence on a real "ascent", is highly ambiguous and leaves open the question of "divinity" as something which transcends the world-totality or is, in the end, "one" with that totality. This ambiguity, according to Balthasar, can be seen in each of the four ways that Plato attempts to establish our ascent to truth: 1) the doctrine of recollection; 2) the nature of philosophical *eros* ; 3) "authentic" myth; and 4) esotericism.[43] All four of these pathways to ascent, according to Balthasar, share the same ambiguity concerning the nature of the "term" or "goal" of this ascent. Is it a personal encounter with a personal deity beyond Being, or is it simply the "world-soul" which animates the "world-body" in the exact same manner as the human soul animates the human body? If it is the former, how is this to be imagined if not mythologically? And if it is the latter, how do we ultimately distinguish between humanity and divinity?[44]

---

[41]*GL IV*, 180.
[42]*GL IV*, 180-181.
[43]*GL IV*, 180-181.
[44]*GL IV*, 211.

1. Recollection

In Plato's doctrine of the soul all knowledge is a "recollection" of the prenatal existence of the soul in a heavenly realm. Plato uses the soul's "innate" knowledge of geometric principles to prove its preexistence and therefore, by extension, its immortality. However, Plato describes all of this in an elaborate myth whose metaphoric images are later "explained" by a philosophical analysis which sees the soul's ultimate origin and destiny in terms of its simple participation in "divine knowledge," however it was acquired.

But it is precisely the nature of this divine knowledge which is ambiguous. This is illustrated clearly in the divine "hierarchy" Plato establishes. For example, Plato hints at the existence of a "personal" uncreated God who "creates" the "lesser" gods who rule the cosmos. However, it is still unclear how far-reaching this concept of a personal God is for Plato, given its subordination to the Idea of the Good. Does Plato assert its existence simply as a mythic metaphor to be balanced out by the more philosophical Idea of the Good? Add to this the fact that in this hierarchy the human soul, insofar as it is capable of "self-movement" and is therefore "spiritual," is considered by Plato to be equal in its essential nature to the created "gods" who rule the cosmos. These lesser gods, (and by extrapolation the cosmos), are seen as existing in a state of *perfect* harmony and order and are, therefore, perfect reflections of the Idea of the Good and of the Beautiful. Thus, humanity need look no further than the heavens to see the perfection of its own soul. And since the heavenly spheres are themselves a reflection of the Good the ambiguity remains: are humanity and divinity ultimately "one" in their essential nature? Balthasar states:

> Here one suddenly senses the distance between the world of myth - where God and man are in basic opposition - and the world of philosophy, where in principle the "kinship" of both with each other must be pressed to the point of identity.[45]

---

[45]*GL IV,* 182.

2. Philosophical Eros

This same ambiguity overshadows the Platonic doctrine of philosophical *eros* . In the *Symposium* Socrates must confront Agathon and insist that *eros* is neither divinity, nor simply human yearning, but something "in-between," something from the realm of the *daimonic* .[46] *Eros* is an "intermediary" inspiration which lifts the philosopher from his desire for the Good toward the Good. However, from whence does this inspiration come? Divinity? Humanity? Or are these two ultimately the same? On this point Socrates is silent. Instead, the analogy of sexual attraction is pressed into service: in desiring the sexual object we do not simply wish to "behold" but to "possess" in the sense of "entering into" and "begetting within." However, just when Plato seems on the verge of characterizing the ascent of philosophical *eros* toward the Absolute as a relationship of reciprocal love the analysis ends and one is left with a sense of "loose ends."[47] Once again, Plato is ambiguous, according to Balthasar, about the exact nature of the divine. For example, in human terms *eros* always seeks an "object" and therefore cannot be reduced to a formal category of our subjectivity. Nevertheless, we cannot affirm that for Plato the "ascent" of philosophy is anything more than the desire of the "divine" in our soul for harmony and mimetic union with the divine reflected in the cosmos. Plato's use of mythic, personalistic metaphors and analogies to describe the goal of *eros* are not strong enough for us to affirm the presence of a personal God - they may simply be "poetry" at the outer limits of philosophy attempting to express the profound *Mysterium* at the heart of Being.[48]

3. Authentic Myth

This brings us to the third way in which, for Balthasar, Plato seeks to "establish" truth through philosophical ascent: the world of "authentic" myth. Balthasar repeats yet again philosophy's need to posit image and myth as the only adequate tools for expressing the outer limits of reason, while, at the same time, rendering the images ambiguous by reminding us of their purely metaphoric

---

[46]*GL IV,* 189.
[47]*GL IV,* 192.
[48]*GL IV,* 192.

status.[49] What is lacking, according to Balthasar, is the conviction that an address from the divine realm of "glory" is more than a mythic projection of human transcendence, but is instead a true "encounter." Platonic philosophy lacks such a conviction. Therefore, as Balthasar puts it: "the poetical is here the unavoidable substitute for the concretion of a revelation; only together with this form of expression can philosophy express what it must."[50]

Image or myth may be required by philosophy in order to express the inexpressible. However, this need to "go beyond" the limits of pure reason calls into question the philosophical claim to totality. The abstracting mind alone cannot reach the kind of closure it seeks. Unfortunately, Plato's ambiguous development of the "divine," i.e. of what underlies and grounds these poetical expressions, frustrates, once again, all efforts to read into his use of mythic categories the reality of a personal God who is the source of the "glory" of Being. Plato's use of myth as a means for establishing the ascent to truth ends in a profound ambiguity. Balthasar summarizes this as follows:

> This ambiguity affects man's self-consciousness both theoretically and practically right to the end. Personal prayer or pure *theoria* as contemplation? Created being or necessary emanation and participation in the primordially divine? Piety rationally clarified into virtue or virtue finding its perfection in piety?[51]

4. Esotericism

The ambiguity in Plato's development of the idea of "ascent" finally leads him to ground the transcendence of knowledge in a dialectic of being and non-being - a dialectic that ends, according to Balthasar, in a mathematical/mystical esotericism. Plato's attempt to ground truth in philosophical ascent brings him to an affirmation of Parmenides' "closed philosophical system of pure being."[52] However, unlike Parmenides, Plato wished to bring the concept of "non-being" or "becoming" into the system. Thus, Plato is able to bring together dialectically "Idea" and "appearance" in a perfect harmony: no existent thing need any longer be

---

[49]*GL IV*, 195-197.
[50]*GL IV*, 195.
[51]*GL IV*, 196.
[52]*GL IV*, 197.

"ashamed" of its "extension," its "parts," since Being and becoming are now but two poles of a dialectical dance that harmonizes everything within its rhythm. "Symmetry," "measure," and "proportion," become the standards of Platonic perfection and these qualities are most perfectly exemplified in the heavenly spheres.

All of this leads in the direction of a Pythagorean theory of numbers as the final goal of philosophical knowledge: armed with mathematical skill the philosopher can simply "decipher" the code of cosmic perfection based on the symmetry and proportion of the heavenly appearances. Thus, Plato's attempt to ground truth in a philosophical ascent ends in the ambiguity of a "Pythagorean esotericism" which is decidedly unmetaphysical.[53] All that is left is for the distinction between the Idea of the Good and the mathematical perfection of the cosmos to be dropped. God and world collapse into a relationship of identity, and philosophy melts into mathematics.[54] The "glory" of transcendent Being as the term of philosophical ascent is eclipsed and largely forgotten. Balthasar states:

> This rounds off an aesthetic ethic immanent in the world, in which the divine as well as the human appears in a final identity as a harmony of balance; the last glimmer of a revelation from above - some features of which in the middle period were left to the (transcendent) Sun of the Good - fades, or rather passes over into macrocosmic harmony which is accessible to philosophical enquiry. Now is born that philosophical aesthetic of the grand style.[55]

Therefore, according to Balthasar, Platonic philosophy ends with an unresolved tension between a dialectic of intramundane, metaphysical, mathematical "symmetry" and an *eros* whose inspiration moves the philosopher to a *real* ascent. But an ascent into what? Or whom? And with what ultimate ground? There is the ambiguity. Philosophy is, therefore, by the time of Plato, curiously "suspended" between the dialogical world of "glory" and the dialectical world of intramundane "harmony." It is as if, confronted by its own limitations, philosophy is not quite ready to completely relinquish the mythic world of glory. The ecstatic quality of philosophical ascent seems to demand an "objective" (i.e. "other" than the self) goal as the term of its transcendence which is characterized by a dialogical quality and

---

[53]*GL IV*, 200.
[54]*GL IV*, 213-214.
[55]*GL IV*, 213.

can therefore be addressed as "Thou." However, as we have seen, this insight is short-circuited in antiquity by the inability of the classical world's philosophical concept of divinity to encompass "distinction" as a possibility within its concept of immutability.

The person who came the closest to understanding this problem, according to Balthasar, was Plotinus, who was the last great gasp of antiquity; in him the Platonic world of philosophical ascent is clearly mapped out as an ascent born out of a "love" characterized by a deep "longing" (analogous to sexual desire) for the One, for the Absolute.[56] However, not even Plotinus can escape from the ambiguity created by a concept of divinity which is both all-encompassing and "immutable" in a very narrow sense. Plotinus, like Plato, ultimately cannot escape from a philosophy of identity which is unable to completely protect the realm of divinity from the suspicion that it is nothing more than a mere human projection - a "limit concept" which simply objectifies the formal structures of reason itself.[57] Plato and Plotinus remain suspended between these two rival conceptions of divinity: God conceived of as truly "Other" and worthy of true worship, veneration and dialogical encounter, or God conceived of as the self-realization of Spirit in human self-consciousness.

But Plato and Plotinus do, therefore, set the stage for the "decision" which later Western thought must make; the dialogical choice leads us directly into Christian revelation and the path of the Fathers, while the choice for "identity" leads directly to the Kantian and Hegelian revolutions of modernity.[58] But this is getting

---

[56]*GL IV*, 305. Balthasar quotes Plotinus here: "Suppose it happened that the soul was fortunate enough to have the One come to it or, rather, to reveal its presence to the soul once it has turned away from the things around it and made itself ready, as beautiful and as like to it as possible ...: then it may befall that it suddenly sees it appear; and nothing lies between them, they are no longer two but one, there is no more distinction as long as It remains there (the earthly lover and beloved who long to merge into one another are an image of all this)."

[57]*GL IV*, 295. Balthasar states: "But now we can no longer avoid the question of whether Intellect has found what it has been seeking if, in its endless journey through the *noemata* in search of the One, it always returns, in the same moment as it moves outward, to the identity of an encounter with itself." And again: "But if ... self-encounter is what Intellect is, and if Intellect is God and God is Intellect, then it is not evident why the One, which Intellect seeks in its going-forth, can and must be something other than the depths of Intellect (or being) itself, that which is presupposed as the origin of that going-forth and the goal of that return upon itself." (297).

[58]*GL IV*, 291-301. Balthasar is clear about the existential decision which is required when one does philosophy. Since Being is not a neutral or mechanical concept but a reality laden with "value" (hence the transcendentals: One, Good, True, Beautiful) then a choice is demanded in its favor. Balthasar sees the modern decision to abandon a metaphysics of value in favor of the functionalism of a pseudo-scientific concept of Being as a decision fraught with peril; like

ahead of ourselves. Before we can move on to Christian revelation and Balthasar's development of the concept of "form," we must first examine the last great pillar of "metaphysics" and show how it too, according to Balthasar, shares in the ambiguity of a concept of Being which cannot find an adequate grounding for our primal, dialogical experience. This continued need to acknowledge an "address" from the side of Being leads us into the next stage of the history of metaphysics: the realm of "natural religion."

C. Natural Religion

In Plato the question remains open as to the exact nature of philosophical "ascent." Aristotle will add nothing new to the fundamental insights of Plato on this issue.[59] The door is therefore left open for a "natural religion" whose essence is characterized by a syncretistic "bridging" between the world of myth and the world of philosophy. The mythic world, though no longer credible, lives on in the cult of the *polis* and in popular piety. Further, its poetic and metaphoric imagery is posited by philosophy itself in order to express the "far limits" of the rational concept. However, myth also needs philosophy in order to give a rational grounding for the images which undergird the cult, i.e. grant to these "particular" divine "epiphanies" a universal humanistic significance. Thus, neither myth nor philosophy stands alone and the attempt to synthesize their respective roles Balthasar refers to as "natural religion":

> It is in this mutual tendency of philosophy and myth that the uniqueness of religion, formally speaking, is to be found - both in Antiquity and, indeed, perennially. It manifests itself as a bridge

---

Heidegger, Balthasar believes that this "forgetfullness" of Being leads to a "forgetting" of God. Balthasar does not necessarily mean "atheism" as such, but a God robbed of his dialogical qualities and therefore of "Glory." It is important to note here that the world of antiquity, despite setting the stage for this decision, does not yet make such a decision. For example, Plotinus, despite the fact that he cannot ultimately escape from a philosophy of identity, does not fall into a simple monism: there is a hierarchy within all of this "unity" which clearly affirms a differentiation on some level between the Intellect which seeks and the One which is the ground of its seeking. This could be seen as a mere preservation of a mythic concept of duality or, as Balthasar believes, it could be seen as a real insight into the fact that "glory" breaks out and streams forth from the depths of Being: "it is the 'glory' that breaks into the sphere of Intellect and being from what is above being and bestows on it its absolute and transcendental beauty." (301). Thus, Plotinus remains a Greek and not a modern idealist.

[59]*GL IV*, 216.

61

which is being thrown out from two piers on opposite shores and which seems all the time to be approaching the point where both constructions meet, yet always remains intrinsically incapable of being completed. The piers grow towards each other, their behavior is literally "syn-cretistic": the essence of any religion (in so far as it is distinct from true myth and authentic philosophy), not only of religion in the Hellenistic age, is "syncretism".[60]

A great deal could be written about Balthasar's concept of "natural religion" as it is articulated in the above quote. However, for our purposes here we need to focus on Balthasar's assertion that each of the "piers" in this syncretistic synthesis is "incomplete" and never quite bridges the chasm that divides them. Balthasar's ultimate aim here is twofold: 1) to demonstrate that natural religion is just as "ambiguous" about the real nature of divinity as were myth and philosophy; and 2) to outline the exact contours of this ambiguity in order that we might get a better idea of how Christian revelation "completes" the bridge.

The ambiguity of natural religion is the same no matter which "pier" -- philosophy or myth -- one begins on. Religion which arises out of philosophy will inevitably tend toward a universalizing dialectic which undercuts the very mythic images which it needs. Religion which grows out of mythology will tend toward a cultic particularism which violates the rational need for universalization. Balthasar begins his analysis with the kind of religion which has its beginnings on the philosophical "pier."

Philosophical religion cannot escape the two basic "dogmas" of its essential orientation. The first dogma is the idea of the divine as the all-encompassing One. The second dogma is the identification of the divinity of the cosmos as the source and "home" of the "divinity" of the human soul.[61] With regard to the first "dogma," Balthasar notes that religion, like myth, seeks to preserve the world of "glory" which it instinctively believes to be something "Other" than the self - i.e. a transcendence which is not reducible to the formal structures of human self-awareness. However, this dialogical "glory" cannot be maintained in the face of the all-encompassing nature of divinity which philosophical reasoning demands. Therefore, philosophical religion, despite its desire to preserve certain dialogical elements, always tends in the direction of an identity between the human soul and the all-encompassing divinity. Thus, ambiguity arises in a fundamental tension.

---

[60]*GL IV*, 216.
[61]*GL IV*, 216.

Religion, as religion, cannot give up the dialogical mythic experience without simply collapsing into philosophy. However, philosophy itself undercuts the real significance of the mythic metaphors.[62] Plato and Aristotle provide us with perfect examples of this tendency: they could heap scorn on the world of the poets all the while using poetic metaphors to express the inexpressible, e.g. the prenatal state of the soul and its post-mortem destiny. The demands of dialectical reason are constantly undercutting the dialogical quality of myth and force religion, in order to maintain its "religious" quality, into a pantheism which threatens to degenerate at the slightest provocation into a practical atheism. Once the dialogical nature of the divine-human relationship is undercut, there remain few obstacles to a simple equating of "God" with a human projection. Balthasar summarizes this as follows:

> Thus the dialectic of philosophical religion is already thrown into sharp relief: conceived in terms sketched out in a philosophy of identity, the least shift of tone at any moment can tilt godfearing pantheism over into godless atheism, as was to happen later, between Hegel and Marx. What human beings project beyond themselves on to the glory that exists in the supreme God is precisely nothing other than a projection and as such the innate power of the human subject.[63]

Balthasar articulates here his conviction that religious transcendence, just as we saw with philosophical "eros," is profoundly ambiguous. Philosophical religion begins with the assumption that the duality of myth must be transcended in an act whereby all finite limitations in the God-humanity relationship are overcome. Thus, all concepts, all images, all mental "forms" must be negated in our attempt to become "One" with that which is beyond all form, all images, all concepts. However, one can never be certain in this process whether this "naughting" leads to a genuine experience of God or if it is simply the "naught" which undergirds one's own projected transcendence. In short, does this drive toward formlessness lead us toward God or the void?

This kind of philosophical religion pushes inevitably beyond a mere "overcoming of mythic duality" into a nihilism that leaves us with nothing but the void of our own emptiness.[64] Ironically, this kind of religion makes a-theism (the

---

[62]*GL IV*, 217.

[63]*GL IV*, 227-228.

[64]Balthasar, *New Elucidations* (San Francisco: Ignatius Press, 1986) 21-22. Balthasar states: "Non-Christian religions are just such a groping around into what is no longer finite; in

idea that God does not "exist" as other objects in our immediate experience "exist") the practical foundation of all theology. The danger with this approach, according to Balthasar, is that this a-theism is only thinly divided from a simple atheism as such. Walter Kasper, in his analysis of this same dynamic, explicitly concurs with Balthasar: "God is in danger of being swallowed in 'modelessness', of vanishing into nothingness; the (rightly) non-objective understanding of God is in danger of losing its object."[65]

The conclusion to be drawn from this is clear. The philosophical pier of the religious synthesis remains incomplete and ambiguous in so far as the question of a real, personal encounter with a revelation from the realm of glory remains problematical for dialectical reason. However, philosophical religion, in so far as it is "religion," must still posit such a "dialogue" but can only do so in the form of a myth which it must then denude of its specific weight. It therefore ends either in a contradiction or by simply collapsing into a philosophical monism that posits "divinity" as the common possession of the human soul and the heavenly spheres. As Balthasar puts it: "out of the idea of identity, which can emphasize now its pantheistic and now its 'pan-anthropic' tendency, there finally arises a pseudo-dialogue, which allows one pole to be seen as the creator of the other."[66] Thus, philosophical religion cannot preserve the dialogical quality of our religious experience and therefore cannot escape the ambiguity at the heart of human religious transcendence: is the "formlessness" at the edge of our metaphysical perception the formlessness of a God who is beyond form, or is it simply the projection of human transcendence onto the void?

There remains to be considered the type of religion which begins from the pier of myth and attempts a "bridge" to the pier of the universal concept. This kind of "mythic" religion is also characterized, according to Balthasar, by two essential "dogmas." The first is that revelation exists "as an inbreaking of light from above."

---

this attempt the doubt always remains as to whether the ex-perienced 'not' is merely one's own transcendence or one's own creaturely nothingness or really something of God's infinity. Thus non-Christian mysticism always verges on the renunciation of one's own God-given personhood ... or on atheism, insofar as personhood apparently constitutes a limitation to the divine."

[65]Walter Kasper, *The God of Jesus Christ* (New York: Crossroad, 1984) 54. Kasper goes on to state: "Texts expressive of atheism can therefore provide almost as much of a basis for a new God-talk as texts expressive of theism can. Such a mystical understanding of God is in its own way once again very far removed from the personal God of the Old and New Testaments who speaks and acts in history." 54-55.

[66]Balthasar, *GL IV*, 231.

The second is the hierarchical ordering of all Being which this "descent" from "above" implies as its foundation.[67]

The entire tradition of the classical world of myth underscores the dualistic and dialogical character of existence. The divine "epiphanies" of the Homeric myths all converge upon the simple affirmation that God (or the gods) exist and the glory of this divine realm is dialogically communicated to humanity through a descending spiritual hierarchy: God-gods-*daimones* - heroes-kings-common humanity. However, it was the last element in this descending order which presents the problem. The world of myth found itself increasingly unable to universalize the various divine epiphanies by way of application to some common human denominator. The various epiphanies often contradicted one another and the ability of the "god" to "save" an individual through the officially sanctioned cult of the *polis* left open the question of "totality." The local cult was by definition a highly particularized expression of divinity and was therefore unable to make any claim to some sort of humanistic/religious universalism. This was especially true in light of the fact that the god of one's particular cult was often seen to be in conflict with other, hostile divinities who were represented in other cults.[68] Thus, mythic religion inevitably tends in the direction of a philosophical "wisdom" which seeks to ground the particularity of the cultic god in a more overarching philosophical concept of divinity. In its turn this philosophical concept of God, as we have seen, must of its nature push for the ultimate negation of any real significance in the mythic images.[69] What happens in this process, according to Balthasar, is that revelation comes to be seen increasingly as a "cloak" underneath which real philosophical wisdom lies hidden. The mythic image is now viewed as a kind of "disguise" which the "wise man," trained in the proper philosophical "technique," is able to recognize as such. The "mysteries" of divinity lie hidden like some buried treasure which can only be discovered by one who "knows the way." Balthasar

---

[67]*GL IV*, 232.

[68]*GL IV*, 234.

[69]*GL IV*, 234. Balthasar states: "If they are, nevertheless, to be justified at the bar of philosophical reasoning, they must produce something more than a pure appeal to the revelation of a god or a prophetic sectarian leader; they must produce the proof that it is uniquely *these* constructions of phantasy that satisfy the postulates of transcendental reason. Thus, where such systems possess any real self-understanding, they build up towards philosophy from their ground in myth, yet are always unable to reach that goal. For their starting-point is revelation conceived as a particularised *gnosis* and such a perspective is bound always to be transcended by the universal *gnosis* of philosophy."

summarizes this dual tendency of mythic religion toward philosophical wisdom hidden in mythic imagery as follows:

> In the hermetic writings such forms are often no more than makeshift disguises for entirely orthodox philosophical instruction. The god who gives instruction speaks like a professor in the lecture-room and the purely speculative content contradicts the theological form. Not only this kind of literature however, with its reverential genuflections to fashionable half-knowledge, but even serious thinkers as well, build into their schemes of things some sort of knowledge through revelation and attempt to give it a proper justification.[70]

Natural religion, therefore, ends with the same difficulties and ambiguities as did myth and philosophy. The only difference is that religion at least attempts to hold the various tensions in balance. However, bridging the gap between myth and philosophy cannot be accomplished so easily - the natural tendency of religion is to move in one direction or the other while holding the other pole in suspension. A true synthesis wherein the basic tension is overcome in a higher "assimilation" must wait for Christian revelation. Therefore, everything that has been said up to this point is, for Balthasar, simply a "preamble" to christology. All of pre-Christian history is an open and ambiguous question: "open" because all human longing for an Absolute cries out for fulfillment in a real encounter with the "Wholly Other"; "ambiguous" because none of the mythical, philosophical or religious "forms" of antiquity, taken alone or together, are able to completely bear such a fulfillment.

The wisdom of antiquity is a wisdom characterized by a deep frustration - it knows that it is being called to make a decision in favor of the "value" of Being, to embrace reality in the ecstasy that only lovers can comprehend.[71] And yet, it does not know or understand the object of such love and, therefore, frequently obfuscates its quest and confuses the goal with the quest itself, thereby turning the divine glory into a purely humanistic aesthetic and ethic. Not even Plotinus or Vergil, who come the closest to equating Absolute Being with Absolute Love, can overcome the deep, opaque ambiguity of the ancient world's concept of divinity. Clarification comes only after the Christian elaboration of the doctrine of creation

---

[70]*GL IV*, 236.

[71]*GL IV*, pp. 38-39. Balthasar never tires of pointing out the existential decision that is required of the theologian for or against the "value" of Being. This decision is, according to Balthasar, really a decision for or against God.

which established an "ontological difference" between the Being of God and the Being of the world-totality. Only then could the world be seen as pure gratuity and God as sovereign freedom. And, according to Balthasar, there is no better elaboration of this doctrine than that of Thomas Aquinas.

Chapter Three:
Metaphysical Foundations:
The Ontological Distinction and Revelation

A. The Ontological Distinction

As we have just seen, the classical world is characterized by a chronic ambiguity in its concept of the divine and the relationship between divinity and "world." Specifically, the ambiguity resides in the inability of the classical world to formulate a metaphysic which could allow God to be "Other" - and therefore dialogical - while avoiding the mythological anthropomorphisms of an "Objectified" God.[1] Ancient myth and religion certainly preserved profound religious insights which seemed to demand a world of divinity capable of dialogue with the human realm. However, these insights were swallowed up in the dialectic of monistic philosophy causing religion to drift with a certain measure of inevitability into various pantheisms.

What the ancient world lacked, according to Balthasar, was a clear-cut concept of "creation" based upon a sovereign, infinite divine freedom. Without such a doctrine the ancient world could not sustain a clear distinction between God and world without falling back into mythology. In the new Christian framework the old Platonic and Plotinian concept of the "One" which must "emanate" or

---

[1] *Theo-Drama II*, 287. Balthasar states: "In the extra-biblical world, nations can only address their gods as 'thou' on the basis of a mythical assumption, namely, that these gods are limited (by one another or by the world). Where mythical religion passes over into philosophy, either the divinity is no longer addressed as 'thou' at all (Plato) or this manner of address becomes an essentially extrinsic form borrowed from mythical religion, e.g., Cleanthes' hymn to Zeus."

"radiate" its essential nature within an overarching necessity "becomes the absolutely free (and thus personal) God who is under no compulsion, not even from his own nature, and who freely sends forth from himself the world of finite spirits, created to be free."[2] Therefore, imbedded within this Christian doctrine of creation "out of nothing" is the clear affirmation that there is a distinction to be made between the Being of God (Being as such in all its infinite purity) and the Being of creation; the "Being" of the world is real only insofar as it participates analogously in the Being of God.[3] And this distinction between God and the world is grounded in biblical revelation in an antecedent affirmation that there are two "kinds" of freedom at work in reality: God's infinite freedom and human finite freedom. Biblical revelation clearly affirms in a variety of different ways that there is in some sense an "opposition" between God's infinite freedom and human finite freedom. A "covenant" is struck in which the nature of God as sovereign and "One" is maintained even while human freedom is definitely posited as "other" than God.[4] Biblical revelation confronts the mythic-religious-philosophical synthesis of antiquity with two fundamental affirmations. Balthasar formulates the affirmations as follows:

> First, that the "Absolute" is free (which the philosopher can concede in a limited sense); and second, that the "Absolute" has a sovereign ability, out of its own freedom, to create and send forth finite but genuinely free beings ... in such a way that, without vitiating the infinite nature of God's freedom, a genuine opposition of freedoms can come about.[5]

---

[2]*Theo-Drama II*, 191.

[3]*GL V*, 628. Balthasar states: "Biblical revelation rests on the basis of the primal God-world distinction."

[4]*Theo-Drama II*, 190-191. Balthasar states: "It is one of the fundamental assertions of the Bible and of theology that such an opposition exists and that it works itself out dramatically in a variety of forms." 190.

[5]*Theo-Drama II*, 190. We cannot go into detail here and explore all of the theological nuance in Balthasar's development of this concept of opposition in biblical revelation. For our purposes here it is sufficient to establish that Balthasar takes such a God-world opposition as his starting point in developing his Christian "metaphysics". The general scope of the topic we are concerned with - Balthasar's theology of revelation - does not allow us time and space to go into detail analyzing every implication of the *contents* of his theology. It may be that Balthasar exaggerates this theme of "opposition" in biblical revelation at the expense of a more "immanent" biblical strand. However, an examination of that question would require an entire study in its own right. Cf. Balthasar, *The Glory of the Lord VI: Theology: The Old Covenant*, (San Francisco: Ignatius Press, 1991); *Glory of the Lord VII: New Covenant*, (San Francisco: Ignatius Press, 1989).

However, how do such affirmations avoid critical internal contradictions and an inevitable drift back into mythological views of God? Has one preserved the dialogical quality of Being at the expense of philosophical rigor? How can God be "Wholly Other" as Christian theology affirms and still have an ontological relationship with the world that presumes an analogy of Being on some basic level? What becomes of the "reality" of the finite "other" which biblical covenant theology seems to demand? Would it not be easier simply to affirm the basic mythological quality of the biblical narratives and to search for the meta-historical philosophical truths contained therein (which is what the Enlightenment project was all about)?

It is clear that Christian theology, in order to appeal to thinking minds, cannot simply ignore all of the philosophical problems that such a view of God presents.[6] Furthermore, such questions help us to clarify our formulations and avoid pitfalls. For example, Balthasar points out that if we are to affirm that God is "Absolute Unity" then we cannot affirm ourselves as "other" than God in the sense of being "outside" of God or "beside" God or in any way an "addition" to the total "amount" of Being in God. Philosophy helps us to seek the answer (to the God-world opposition) within God in a way that does justice to the affirmations of biblical revelation (opposition) as well as the dictates of philosophical reason (unity). Ultimately these two "tensions" must be bridged within the divine life itself - a synthesis that avoids mythology, monistic philosophies of identity, and pantheism. This means that the Christian solution points us to a conception of God so totally and infinitely "Other" that God can, in virtue of that fact, be the equally immanent "non-other".[7] Therefore, the "task" of Christian theology is to ground the reality of finite freedom within infinite freedom in such a way that the integrity of both is preserved while affirming the absolute priority of the latter. Balthasar states:

> The Christian task, in the face of the Stoic and Plotinian enterprise, is to heighten the formal model into a relationship between freedoms

---

[6]*Theo-Drama II*, 191. This is precisely why, according to Balthasar, we do theology a disservice when we arrogantly snub our noses at the patristic and scholastic attempt to formulate Christian doctrine within the philosophical categories of antiquity. Such "systems" were not simply a distorting "Hellenization" of revelation but, rather, powerful attempts to answer, assimilate and transcend the "common understanding" of ancient humanity within a Christian framework for thinking people. And since such attempts were an answer to the classical world-view they remain as "timely" as the questions raised by such a world-view.

[7]*Theo-Drama II*, 193.

according to which finite freedom can only arise out of, and persist within primal freedom (just as in Plotinus the "other" - over against the "one" - can only be "other" because it itself is a "one" and thus participates in oneness); it is precisely because it has its origin in freedom that it is really free.[8]

Thomas Aquinas gave the doctrine of creation its most consistent systematic grounding with his formulation of the distinction between "essence" and "existence." At the heart of this metaphysical distinction is the theological awareness of a fundamental distinction between God and world. If God is not the world in a relationship of monistic identity, then the "participation" in the Divine act of Being must be mediated to finite creatures in some manner. The old Platonic-Plotinian concept of a direct participation in divinity by way of God's "emanations" is changed by Thomas into a mediated participation, i.e., God's "emanation" of Being must not itself be hypostasized, must not be "divinized." "Thomas," according to Balthasar, "is opposed to the hypostatization of the 'emanations' (being-in-itself, life-in-itself, etc.) and understands them as a single divine cause."[9] If God's emanation of Being to the world was hypostasized, then we would be right back to a metaphysics of identity and this is unacceptable to Christian philosophy.

However, Thomas does speak of God "emanating" Being in a certain sense. The creature is not simply "there" in a kind of raw independence utterly cut-off from any connection with the divine Being. All essences, insofar as they have progressed beyond a merely formal "possibility" as a concept or idea, must be "real" and therefore have "existence" as a constitutive principle.[10] However, this participation in God's Being must not, as we have seen, be conceived of as a direct participation. This mediating level of Being which God "emanates" must be a level of non-subsisting infinite Being which is the Being that each finite essence has as its own proper act of existence. However, if the "Being" of the world-totality is not subsistent Being as such but only its "likeness," then how can we say that it is real? How does it achieve more than a purely formal "actuality"? It does so only in, through, and with its concretization in finite essences. However, it is not reducible to "essences" as such, for then we would have to assert that each finite

---

[8]*Theo-Drama II*, 230.
[9]*GL IV*, 401.
[10]*GL IV*, 401-402.

essence was the sufficient explanation for its own existence. No single essence, or even for that matter all combined finite essences, can ever exhaust the infinite capacity of non-subsistent Being for expression. No finite essence can ever exhaust the infinite possibilities of Being. Therefore, each finite thing possesses what it can never exhaust, participates in what it cannot "grasp" totally as its own. Infinite, non-subsisting Being is, therefore, "that in which all communicate ... It is that which embraces all things (and cannot be exhausted by any number of natures but on the contrary can be participated in more and more in an infinite way.)"[11] Thus, infinite non-subsistent Being transcends the individual finite thing even though such Being, because it is non-subsisting, is "suspended" between the Being of God (upon which it is completely dependent for "act-uality") and the individual finite thing (without which it would never reach subsistence). Thus, there is a real distinction to be made between finite essences and their act of existence, even though the latter only achieves actuality in the finite concretization. Balthasar refers to this Thomistic distinction as the "Ontological difference," and summarizes Thomas as follows:

> Everything is put in a new light by the fact that the doctrine of the transcendentals is interpreted in the perspective of Thomas's major creative achievement - his definition of *esse* and its relation to essences. ... Thomas sees *esse* as the non-subsistent fullness and perfection of all reality and as the supreme "likeness of divine goodness," and so God can no longer in any way be regarded as the being of things, except in the sense that he is their efficient, exemplary and final cause. Thus in a new and much more radical way God is placed over and above all cosmic being, ...: he is indeed "the Wholly Other".[12]

Two related mistakes must be avoided. First, although essence and existence are distinct, existence is not "added to" essence like an extrinsic accident. Existence "inheres" in its essential determination as the most interior act of the finite thing. The second mistake is to picture non-subsisting infinite Being as an "ocean" of potency which is then actualized by being "fragmented" into various "parts" by essences. Indeed, for Thomas, essence is "potency" which awaits actualization in the act of existence. Also, as Balthasar points out, "because *esse* does not subsist,

---

[11]*GL IV*, 402.
[12]*GL IV*, 393-394.

it cannot even be said to release natures from itself as its possibilities; it is only in them that it comes to 'standing' and subsistence."[13] Here one could say that Balthasar sees in Thomas an affirmation of the priority of *Dasein* over *Sein* in the Christian doctrine of creation. The God-world distinction, which initially "de-essentializes" and "de-divinizes" the cosmos, creates a "space" for the existence of finite creatures such that they possess an inner integrity, an individual subsistence vis-`a-vis God that now allows us to affirm that such finite existents are made in the "image and likeness" of God in a much more radical way - they are now "real" and thus reflect something of the divine "realness". Balthasar captures the sentiment of this concept in the following prayer:

> We are not God. ... We step back into distance. Love is found only in distance, unity only in difference. God himself is unity in Spirit only in the distinction of Father and Son. That we stand over against you and are receptive mirrors is in us the seal of your authorship. We are like you in not being you.[14]

It now comes into sharper focus what Balthasar means when he says that God is so totally the "Wholly Other" that he is, in fact, the "non-other." There is now an intimacy between God and creature that is based on an entirely different principle than that of a simple identity. Since the act of "existing" is the Divine act as such, the "real" existence of finite creatures is the greatest gift that Divinity can bestow. And this positing of finite existents is accomplished in a manner which neither diminishes the Divine unicity nor "fragments" Being into various "modalities."[15]

This approach also preserves us from falling into what Balthasar considers the two most common metaphysical errors: the reductive analysis of being from either a rationalistic or an essentialist perspective. Both of these approaches end by destroying the integrity of finitude in one fashion or another. Rationalistic approaches, by turning "Being" into a purely formal concept, a "limit concept" or ground of possibility for the transcendence of knowledge (e.g. the "Frankfurt

---

[13]*GL IV*, 403.

[14]Balthasar, *The Heart of the World*, (San Francisco: Ignatius Press, 1979) 216-217.

[15]*GL IV*, 404. Balthasar states: "[it] is not to be understood as the disintegration or diminution (on the part of the creature) of God's being and unicity ... and the essences of things must not appear as simply the fragmentation of reality, in a negative sense, but must be seen positively as posited and determined by God's omnipotent freedom and therefore are grounded in the unique love of God."

School") ironically end by destroying the essential orientation of finitude toward a real transcendence that is, at the same time, its most intimate possession. This destruction of real transcendence destroys any concept of Being as "beautiful" or "touched" by "glory" and leads inevitably to the positivism of modern science and the destruction of all real metaphysics. The end result is that finitude itself loses its integrity as a participation in transcendent Being and becomes a purely mechanistic reality - just one more faceless "atom" in the great dance of materialistic "chance".

The second approach - the essentialist - has already been dealt with in Balthasar's critique of all metaphysics of identity. Idealistic pantheism destroys the integrity of finitude by reducing all "things" to mere "appearances" or "parts" in a giant cosmic machine. Also, such approaches destroy the truly infinite nature of God by tying him too closely to the cosmos. Thus, as with Plato, "glory" as a dialogical category loses its "salt" and human life degenerates into a mere mimesis of cosmic harmony.[16] And it makes little difference whether such mimesis is conceived along theological, philosophical or artistic/aesthetic lines. The end result is the same: God and world conflate into a single cosmic harmony that destroys the "otherness" of God and reduces the importance of the dialogical quality in the God-world relationship. Thus, only the Christian doctrine of creation preserves the integrity of finitude:

> The de-essentializing of reality, as demanded by Heidegger and as achieved by Thomas, is an extension within philosophy of the illumination by biblical revelation of the idea of God as creative principle. When God, in his knowing and omnipotent love, is seen as freely choosing to create, there can be no question of a restrictive fragmentation of being into finite essences. *Esse* can be suspended without confusion or limitation ... before the free God and only thus become the allusive likeness of the divine goodness. ... Thus and only thus is the creature liberated in the presence of God and in relation to God and can aspire with all its powers towards God and love him without having to comply with the perverse demand that it deny itself in its finite essence. ... The metaphysics of Thomas is thus the philosophical reflection of the free glory of the living God of the Bible and in this way the interior completion of ancient (and thus human) philosophy. It is a celebration of the reality of the real.[17]

---

[16]*GL IV*, 405-406.
[17]*GL IV*, 406-407.

Thus, the Christian awareness of the distinction between God and world and the further distinction between essence and existence opens up two mutually conditioning affirmations. First, the affirmation of the integrity of finite reality. Second, the affirmation of "wonder" at the fact that anything exists at all as our primal experience of Being and, therefore, as the philosophical attitude as such. Our affirmation of the integrity of finitude opens up the category of the "world," as world, for legitimate philosophical and theological inquiry. The fundamental structures of finite being become the primary focus of our attention since non-subsistent Being can only be apprehended through an antecedent awareness of "things." Thus, the fundamental question of existence is not "why am I here?" or even, "who am I?" but, rather, "what kind of place is this?", "where am I?".[18] Therefore, our primal wonder at Being (the philosophical act as such) must be analyzed in our relationship to that world, in our relationship to the realm of the finite.

When we analyze our relationship to the world of finite being we find what Balthasar refers to as a "fourfold distinction" within our primal experience of Being.[19] The goal of this analysis of the fourfold distinction is twofold. First, to show that the source of our "wonder" is not a romanticizing subjectivity but an "enrapturing" created by Being itself, i.e., that Being as such "causes" wonder because it inherently evokes it.[20] Second, to show that the only final explanation for our primal experience of Being as "enrapturing" is that we experience ourselves as being addressed by an infinite subjectivity which must transcend the boundaries of this world.[21] This brings us to the very limits of philosophy and points us toward a theological fulfillment in revelation - a fulfillment which, in its trinitarian dimensions, will finally provide us with a theological grounding within God for the biblical affirmation of the distinction between God and the world. In short, Balthasar now offers us a phenomenology of human self-possession as a further explanation of the ontological difference. This phenomenological analysis deepens

---

[18]*GL V*, 616.

[19]*GL V*, 615.

[20]*GL V*, 614-615. Balthasar states: "It is not only astonishing that an existent being can wonder at Being in its own distinction from Being, but also that Being as such by itself to the very end 'causes wonder', behaving as something to be wondered at, something striking and worthy of wonder."

[21]*Theo-Drama II*, 240.

Thomas's original insight by grounding it in the dynamic relationship between human and divine freedom, which in turn opens the way for a christological and trinitarian fulfillment.

B. The fourfold distinction

The first "distinction" which Balthasar recognizes in our apprehension of Being is the absolutely primal act of "wonder" or astonishment over the fact that "I find myself within the realm of a world and in the boundless community of other existent beings."[22] And nothing in this world of finite existents is a sufficient explanation for my self-awareness of being able to view the world as a totality. Biologically I am the product of a chance "hit," but the world of chance does not seem capable of the intentionality required to bring forth my unique, personal subjectivity. However, despite this awareness of the "non-random" nature of my self-hood, I must nevertheless confront the fact that an infinite number of "others" could just as well have occupied this particular "space" in the universe that I occupy. I do not appear to be an indispensable part of some larger "necessary" web of events and existents. Thus, there is an awareness of "having been allowed in" which begins in infancy; the child's entire subjective world is completely filled with the image of the "other" - the smile of the mother awakens in the child a sense of being welcomed that forms the foundation for all later subjective development of the individual ego.[23] The priority of the "other" in the formation of one's self-consciousness is, therefore, established in the very infancy of life. And this experience of being "admitted" arouses a sense of "play" at the love and grace of it all.

The loving nature of this "admittance" is of primary importance. Do I have a "right" to be here and thus am I a welcome participant, or have I simply been allowed in and therefore stand before the world as a beggar seeking for my sense of self-worth through pleasing that which "allows" me to be here? This "right" to be here must not be viewed along mechanistic lines. It is a metaphysical right. I can lay no claim to it as in a move to grab and to hold on to "power." Being does not empower me in this worldly sense. My sense of belonging here by some kind of

---

[22]*GL V*, 615.
[23]*GL V*, 615-616.

right is not a claim made vis-`a-vis the world. For I am equally aware that the world did not "intend" me, i.e., the world is not what invites me in, but, rather, simply the place in which I find myself. I seem to be invited in by a loving "thou." Thus, my right to participate is analogous to my right to "give" myself in that participation between two people we call "love." The self, therefore, in its relation to the ground of existence, experiences its existence as both grace and necessity. This definition of the self as essentially oriented to an encounter with the "otherness" of the world is central to Balthasar's thinking. The self, according to Balthasar, "is, in so far as it is allowed to take part as an object of love. Existence is both glorious and a matter of course."[24] We are "thrown" into existence and yet find it curiously "non-fatalistic."

The second distinction flows out of the first. The self recognizes that it is simply one existent among others and therefore it understands that all finite existents most likely share the same basic relationship to Being. Balthasar goes on to reach the following conclusion: "It evidently follows from this that, although all existents partake in Being, yet - to whatever extent we were to multiply them - they never exhaust it nor even, as it were, 'broach' it."[25] Thus, all finite existents take on the appearance of being both radically contingent ("I need not have existed") and yet mysteriously willed ("I am a subjective spirit who has been 'invited in'). But "invited" in by whom? The world as a whole is also contingent. Therefore, my primal experience is of participation in a world of radical contingency which seems to have its ontological origin somewhere outside of its own totality. Thus, my primal metaphysical astonishment at Being is not of an "ocean of Being" in which "beings" are swimming. My apprehension of Being is precisely in its indissoluble unity with beings. Therefore, I do not perceive myself as being willed by Being as if I can have some direct experience of Being as such. I can apprehend Being, but only in its indissoluble identity with beings. It thus appears to me as *non-subsisting* in itself. Balthasar states it as follows:

> What this means, once again, is that I cannot appease my primal and overpowering wonder at the fact that "something is" through gazing at Being, in which those things participate and thus exist. Rather, my wonder is directed at both sides of the Ontological Difference,

---

[24]*GL V*, 616.
[25]*GL V*, 618.

... for the fact that an existent can only become actual through participation in the act of Being points to the complementary antithesis that the fullness of Being attains actuality only in the existent; but the fact that (Heideggerian) Being can only be interpreted within existence (Spirit) points to the complementary antithesis that existence (Spirit) grasps the dependence of Being upon beings and thus its non-substantiality.[26]

The third distinction is a simple inference from the second: if the Being of the world is non-subsisting apart from finite entities, then it follows that the essential "forms" which comprise the world cannot be "generated" by non-subsisting Being.[27] In other words, if the distinction between essence and existence ultimately rests on an affirmation of the reality of things precisely in their essential determinations, then they are not emanations of a univocal Being. The Being of the world is not "responsible" for the finite existents. To ascribe such causation to Being is to grant it subsistence - an affirmation which leads directly back to the pantheistic philosophies of identity which Balthasar is seeking to avoid. However, to see Being as non-subsistent also carries with it a certain danger since the world is dedivinized and finite "things" are left to stand on their own subsistence. This "demystification" of worldly Being (and, therefore, of beings) leaves us with two basic existential options. The first option is to be tempted to see the "nothingness" of Being as "nonbeing" and to therefore lose our metaphysical powers of seeing altogether. The nihilism which this spawns can darken entire epochs and lead to a despising of the world and its murkiness.[28] The second option is the one chosen by classical Western metaphysics: "a homage to Being which lets Being in its totality be."[29]

This is as far as classical metaphysics can take us for, as we have seen, the ancients were not able to develop a concept of the "cosmos" which was more than a reduction to an essentializing of univocal Being. The next step was the

---

[26]GL V, 619.

[27]GL V, 619. Balthasar states: "Precisely by virtue of this dependence ... of Being upon its explication in the existent, ... it is impossible to attribute to Being the responsibility for the essential forms of entities in the world."

[28]GL V, 623-624. Balthasar states: "Too much is demanded of the [world] in this case when its own essential light is supposed to suffice for Being as a whole and, since this excessive demand lies clear to view, the forced optimism of the forced worldliness turns perpetually into nihilistic tragedy. The injustice of the world is directly transferred to Being as a whole, which thus itself appears unjust." (624).

[29]GL V, 623.

development of the Christian doctrine of creation which completes and transcends our primal astonishment at Being. This is the "fourth distinction". This final distinction interjects itself into the fissure created by the first three distinctions; the latter all point toward an Absolute freedom which neither the Being of the world can possess (since it is non-subsistent) nor the finite existent entity since "it always finds itself as already constituted in its own essentiality."[30] Thus, the distinction between essence and existence shows us that neither of these mutually dependent "poles" is a sufficient ground for the freedom which undergirds the "glory" of Being and points beyond the ontological difference toward the distinction between God and the world. Furthermore, now we realize that only an Absolute freedom which transcends the world can preserve the integrity of both non-subsistent Being and the finite existent. First, the "glory" of worldly Being is now preserved in a manner which does not attribute to it characteristics which it cannot sustain, e.g., intentionality and subsistence. Second, finite being is preserved from being "swallowed up" in an all-encompassing act of Being which robs finitude of its integrity. Thus, the ontological difference ends by pointing us back toward a grounding unity. Balthasar states:

> If the Ontological Difference must already, as bifurcation, be referred back to a *unicum* ... then it will be secured as the authentic "site of glory in metaphysics" in its deepest affirmation of Being ... and thus of grace within its open-ended sway, in which each "pole" has to seek and find its "salvation" in the other pole: Being arrives at itself as subsistence only within the entity and the entity arrives at its actuality ... only within its participation in Being.[31]

But this Absolute freedom which undergirds the ontological difference must itself be an act of pure "power" characterized by both fullness and poverty. It is fullness because it is, by definition, the complete antithesis of nothingness and pure Being as such. However, it is also "poverty" because, as Balthasar puts it, "it does not need, holding on to itself, to enclose itself in the casing of an entity. ... Rather, fullness as such is pure power ... from whose potency ... all that is potential ... proceeds as rich abundance, which is thus pure freedom, ... pure gift and love."[32] We are now at the metaphysical anteroom to the Christian doctrine of creation and

---

[30]*GL V*, 625.
[31]*GL V*, 625.
[32]*GL V*, 626.

all that it entails. For just as we saw in the first distinction that human subjectivity is constituted in its relation to the "other", to a "world," we now see that Absolute freedom is characterized by a fundamental "ek-stasis" that gives from its "abundance" in an "*excessus*" of Being. The finite subject does not first possess itself in a "grasping" manner and only then reach out to the other; the subject is constituted precisely in this turning toward the other. Likewise, Being does not "underpin" God as an antecedent grounding out of which flows his self-possession and his "ek-stasis" in creation.[33] God's "nature" is characterized by the ecstasy of "excess" born out of an infinite freedom. Thus, an infinite "*excessus*" and an infinite self-possession coincide.

We are now at the outer limits of metaphysical speculation and can go either in one of two directions: we can halt at the ontological difference and declare as "mystery" the exact nature of its ultimate ground (as Heidegger does, leaving worldly Being forever "suspended"), or we can remain open to the possibility that metaphysical speculation on the Absolute freedom that undergirds the ontological difference can be transcended and fulfilled in a revelation.[34] The problem with the first option is that, once chosen, one does not simply "freeze" in a particular stage of metaphysical speculation - the refusal to go beyond the ontological difference into an analysis of Absolute freedom leads in the end to the destruction of metaphysics. The tensions created and the questions left unresolved are decisive and cannot be ignored. One either goes forward, backward, or abandons the project altogether. But once one does posit the reality of such an Absolute freedom then new questions emerge which seek resolution in a heuristic synthesis beyond the scope of metaphysics as such.

We have already touched upon some of these questions. For example, what do we mean when we say that the Absolute freedom is "self-possession" through an "ek-stasis" which overflows into an "excess"? Both Plato and Plotinus touched upon this question in their discussion of the self-diffusion of the "One" or the "Good." And yet, they never reached a clear-cut distinction between God and world that would allow them to develop a consistent concept of the world *as*

---

[33]*Theo-Drama II*, 255.
[34]*GL V*, 625-628.

creation rather than an extension or "effusion" of the divine essence as such.[35] Thus, the question which was raised at the beginning of the chapter must be raised again: How is the God-world distinction grounded without falling into mythological dualism and how is this distinction related to the description of God as "excess"? Balthasar attempts to recapture the "glory" of Being by showing how the metaphysical concept of God developed in the preceding pages is fulfilled and "secured" in the revelation of trinitarian love. Thus, the Christian, through the related doctrines of Trinity and Incarnation, is heir to a metaphysics of love and becomes the real "guardian" of the glory of Being.[36] That is not to say that we can "deduce" the doctrine of the Trinity from all of our foregoing discussions - nothing is more antithetical to Balthasar's theology than the idea that we can "deduce" revelation from historical/philosophical antecedents. However, "grace builds on nature," and the entire history of metaphysical speculation creates a "form" or "type" which the later revelation fulfills as the "antitype." It is the very incompleteness and ambiguity of the metaphysical tradition which throws revelation into sharper relief in its mode as fulfillment.

C. Trinitarian Metaphysics of Love[37]

The ontological difference opened philosophy to the possibility of an Absolute freedom that is underived and utterly sovereign. Furthermore, this

---

[35]*GL V*, 626. Balthasar states: "This mystery of the streaming self-illumination of Being, which was glimpsed by Plato and Plotinus and which alone explains the possibility of a world (that is, the paradoxical existence 'alongside' Infinite Being which fills all things and which stands in need of none), attains its transparency only when, from the sphere of the biblical revelation, absolute freedom (as the spirituality and personality of God) shines in: but not in such a way that the personal God encounters man as one existent marked off from another existent, ... but rather in such a way that the personal and free depths of self-giving absolute Being first bring the mystery of creation ... into the light. God is the Wholly Other only as the ... Not-Other."

[36]*GL V*, 646.

[37]No attempt will be made in what follows to thoroughly analyze Balthasar's trinitarian theology in all of its theological implications. The current discussion is simply concerned with how Balthasar uses his development of the trinity to complete his discussion of metaphysics. Thus, the specific problematic that we will be focusing on is how he uses his doctrine of God to solve the philosophical problem created by the Bible's positing of a distinction between God and world, i.e., how we can call God "thou" without falling into mythological dualism. For a more detailed analysis regarding many of the specific problems with Balthasar's trinitarian theology, e.g., the immutability of God and the dangers of "tri-theism" in such a strongly relational approach, see: Gerard F. O'Hanlon, *The Immutability of God in the Theology of Hans Urs Von Balthasar*, (Cambridge: Cambridge University Press, 1990).

freedom, precisely as sovereign freedom, must also be infinite self-possession. Thus, God's nature can be characterized as the coincidence of infinite Being and infinite self-possession. This fact leads us away from the dual problems of necessity and contingency with regard to God's free act of self-possession and points us in the direction of a proper understanding of the trinitarian relations.[38] First, if God is infinite Being as infinite freedom and self-possession, then it is incorrect to assert that God somehow transforms an antecedent "need to exist" into his self-possession. God's self-possession "belongs" to his nature eternally and as such is in no way the end result of some kind of underlying "need" that the self-possession fulfills. Here we must not confuse the idea that God is a "necessary being" with the idea that God's self-possession is itself the end result of some antecedent "compulsion." Second, since this self-possession is infinite, it is "complete" and "total" and thus excludes that element of capriciousness which nominalistic interpretations of the divine freedom frequently fall into, e.g., the idea that God, as Balthasar puts it, "could primarily affirm something other than himself or could affirm himself otherwise or only partially."[39] This view presupposes an anthropomorphic view of God as a fairly static "nature" with certain attributes such as freedom and intelligence. This view misunderstands God's self-possession as something which comes "after" his essential determination as a subsisting person.

This is, as Balthasar points out, "as far as a philosophy that reflects on the Absolute ... can reach."[40] However, revelation sheds light on the nature of this Absolute freedom as the coincidence of Being and self-possession. God is now seen, through revelation, as so radically sovereign that he can choose to "give himself away" in a "surrender" that is no mere "addition" to his nature but is constitutive of that nature as such. Thus, the possibility opens up for an intra-divine "self-giving" that becomes the foundation for the Father's gift of the Godhead to the Son and for their mutual sharing of the same with the Spirit. God is thereby defined as an infinite self-giving, a limitless self-donation. Balthasar puts it as follows:

> The fact that the absolute freedom of self-possession can understand itself, according to its absolute nature, as limitless self-giving - this

---

[38]*Theo-Drama II*, 255-256.
[39]*Theo-Drama II*, 256.
[40]*Theo-Drama II*, 256.

is not the result of anything external to itself; yet it *is* the result of its own nature, so much so that, apart from this self-giving, it would not be itself.[41]

The Father is not first a "self" that needs to lose itself in the Son in order to regain himself. The Father is from all eternity the act of generating the Son. And the Son is from all eternity the act of "allowing himself to be generated" while the Spirit is "always himself by understanding his 'I' as the 'We' of Father and Son."[42] What opens up in the trinitarian revelation is an image of God's Being which is "One" without being univocal. There is a "differentiation" or a "texture" in the Divine Being that allows us to posit (analogously) a "where" and a "when" between the trinitarian relations.[43] Balthasar means by this that if we are to take God's self-possession as infinite self-donation seriously then we must acknowledge that the relationality that this opens up is a real relationality, i.e., the "freedom" that is involved in the various reciprocal self-donations is real. Therefore, as Balthasar puts it, "something like infinite 'duration' and infinite 'space' must be attributed to the acts of reciprocal love so that the life of the *communio*, of fellowship, can develop."[44] What we have here is the complete coincidence of "Being" and "Having," of "fullness" and "giving away," of "wealth" and "poverty." The trinitarian "hypostases" bear within their reciprocity both an infinite distance and opposition and, precisely because of the distance and opposition, an infinite intimacy and "presence" to one another. They all share the same Divine nature, the same Divine freedom, but not in a "hoarding" manner where they all share it in common with absolutely no differentiation. The "divine nature," states Balthasar, "is defined through and through by the modes of divine being. This nature is always both what is possessed and what is given away."[45] In short, God's subsistence lies precisely in the fundamental trinitarian act of "letting the 'other' be" in an infinite reciprocity between opposition and intimacy.

---

[41] *Theo-Drama II*, 256.

[42] *Theo-Drama II*, 256.

[43] *Theo-Drama II*, 257. Balthasar states: "If there is to be absolute freedom, it follows that, in what takes place between the divine 'hypostases', there must be *areas of infinite freedom* that are *already there* and do not allow everything to be compressed into an airless unity and identity."

[44] *Theo-Drama II*, 257.

[45] *Theo-Drama II*, 258.

What all of this points to is that there can be what we can only refer to as an "exteriorization" within God that coincides with God's infinite self-possession, i.e., God's "interiority." For Balthasar, the concept of God's "interiority" is just as much an analogical predication as is the metaphor "exteriorization." It is, therefore, illegitimate to state that the concept of God's pure self-possession philosophically requires us to posit an image of God's interiority that is similar to human interiority in a univocal manner. Balthasar argues that the concepts "interiority" and "exteriorization" take on an entirely new relationship and meaning when applied to God. Both of these analogical predicates must be seen in their ultimate grounding in the biblical affirmation that "God is love." What this does to our concept of God is to transform it from an image of "absolute power" to one of "absolute love." Thus, the "sovereignty" of God manifests itself in self-abandonment rather than a "holding on" to a static and univocal nature. The world's "oppositional" conception of "poverty" and "wealth" is transcended in a divine interiority that *is* an exteriorization in the "other."[46] This exteriorization within God forms the ontic ground of possibility for the analogous "exteriorization" of a finite world as well as for the Incarnation. Balthasar puts it as follows:

> The exteriorization of God (in the Incarnation) has its ontic condition of possibility in the eternal exteriorization of God - that is, in his tripersonal self-gift. With that departure point, the created person, too, should no longer be described as subsisting in itself, but more profoundly ... as a "returning ... from exteriority to oneself" and an "emergence from oneself as an interiority that gives itself in self-expression". The categories of "poverty" and "wealth" become dialectical.[47]

This concept of personhood, developed primarily to describe the relational hypostases within the Trinity and now applied analogously to spiritual creatures, allows us to overcome the autonomy/heteronomy impasse in our concept of freedom. It is a dialogical "letting be" that fulfills our deepest interiority, our most intimate subjectivity. In the relationship between finite and infinite freedom there is no danger of the creature being "swallowed up" in a divine freedom conceived of as existing "over and against" finite freedom like a master to a slave. If human freedom is made in the image and likeness of God, then it can only come to itself by

---

[46]Balthasar, *Mysterium Paschale*, (Edinburgh: T&T Clark LTD, 1990) 28.

[47]*Mysterium Paschale*, 28.

"going out" of itself and drawing close to the divine freedom in a dialogical relationship of love. "It can only be what it is," states Balthasar, "by getting in tune with the (Trinitarian) 'law' of absolute freedom (of self-surrender): and this law is not foreign to it - for after all it is the 'law' of absolute Being - but most authentically its own."[48] And when this freedom opens itself to the creature, giving it a glimpse of its profound "abysses," pouring itself out in the "unbelievable" paradox of Incarnation, cross, and resurrection, then the "negative incomprehensibility" of God in natural theology and metaphysics turns into the "positive incomprehensibility" of revelation in the "*excessus*" of God's love in Christ. The former is primarily a negation of the ability of all "instrumental" concepts to contain God; the latter is the incomprehensibility which comes from being "flooded" and overwhelmed by a light so bright that it "blinds". The former is dialectical, the latter is dialogical.[49]

And it is within this "blinding light" of revelation that we are able to understand how the world can "be" without "adding to" or existing "along side of" the infinite. It is central to Balthasar's development of the "realness" of the trinitarian relations that we can say that there exists within God something for which our creaturely experience of "spatiality" and "duration" are analogies. The exteriorization of the "interiority" of the trinitarian hypostases demands that we posit the "event-like" quality of these relations without, for all that, diluting the immutability or unicity of God. God does not "become," nor is God "many," even though the "becoming" of creatures in their relations with worldly "others" is an "image and likeness" of the event-like quality of the trinitarian relations.[50] Furthermore, given this assertion we can now posit the "where" and "when" of creation within God. The world finds its "place" and its "time" in the "distance"

---

[48]*Theo-Drama II*, 259.

[49]*Theo-Drama II*, 260. For an excellent treatment of Balthasar's approach to apophatic theology, see: Raymond Gawronski, S.J., *Word and Silence: Hans Urs Von Balthasar and the Spiritual Encounter between East and West*, (Edinburgh: T&T Clark: 1995).

[50]*Theo-Drama II*, 261. The "poetical" and "metaphoric" nature of Balthasar's language here makes it difficult to pin down with any degree of conceptual clarity. What Balthasar is trying to balance here is the seemingly contradictory demands of biblical revelation for God's "involvement" with creation and the philosophical demands for God's immutability. Balthasar rejects both a "process" theology that sees God as "ensnared" in the world process as well as the standard philosophical concepts of God's immutability. He sees both as lacking in theological/philosophical imagination. Once again, for a detailed analysis of all of the ramifications of this debate see: O'Hanlon, *The Immutability of God in Hans Urs Von Balthasar*, 21 ff.

and "duration" within the trinitarian relations. There is an intra-trinitarian spaciousness that "makes room" for the world by incorporating it into the intra-divine relations in a manner which does not simply "divinize" the world in a univocal sense, i.e., the world does not simply "blend into" God and become "moments" within the trinitarian relations. Neither, however, should this incorporating of the world into God be conceived of in terms of a "contracting" of God in order to "create a space" for the finite within God - that would be as anthropomorphic as the former view is overly monistic/philosophic. God does not need to create a "void" within himself in order to "place" creation there: one cannot create a void since, by definition, the void is nothing, sheer non-being.[51] And since the trinitarian relations are characterized in their freedom by an infinite "letting be" of the "other," the "opposition" within the Trinity is an opposition of infinite love and self-donation. Therefore, there is no need for a "retreat" or a "resignation" within God in order to let the others "be". "For that reason," states Balthasar, "God himself does not need to retreat either; he does not need to 'close in on himself', he needs no 'kenosis' when causing the world to exist within himself."[52] The image of a God choosing to become "less" than he is in order to "create" an area of non-being where the world can now "fit" seems to fit in nicely with Balthasar's "kenotic" view of God. However, Balthasar would see this as an overly anthropomorphic development of the divine kenosis that ultimately destroys God's infinity and begs the essential question at the heart of the doctrine of the analogy of Being.[53] Balthasar summarizes this line of thought as follows:

---

[51]*Theo-Drama II*, 262 ff. It should be made clear that Balthasar is not simply replacing theo-ontological categories for personological categories. Infinite Being and infinite self-possession coincide and therefore, Being *as* infinite self-possession is formally primary to a more traditional "substance" ontology. The old Catholic seminary manuals are a good example of the latter where the section on "God" always began with a tract on "*De Deo Uno* " and only then proceeded to a discussion of "*De Deo Trino.* " God as a subsistent unity was thus given a kind of formal priority over the concept of God's Being as infinite "exteriorising" self-possession.

[52]*Theo-Drama II*, 262.

[53]*Mysterium Paschale*, 28-29. Balthasar makes the following point with regard to his own "kenotic" view of trinitarian self-donation: "This [kenosis] does not mean, however, that God's essence becomes itself (univocally) 'kenotic', such that a single concept could include both the divine foundation of the possibility of Kenosis and the Kenosis itself. It is from here that many of the mistakes of the modern kenoticists take their rise. What it does mean ... is that the divine 'power' is so ordered that it can make room for a possible self-exteriorization, like that found in the Incarnation and the Cross, and can maintain this exteriorization even to the utmost point. As between the form of God and the form of a servant there reigns, in the identity of the Person involved, an analogy of natures."

The "not" which characterizes the creature - it is "not" God and cannot exist of itself - is by no means identical with the "not" found within the Godhead. However, the latter constitutes the deepest reason why the creaturely "not" does not cause the analogy of being between creature and God to break down. The infinite distance between the world and God is grounded in the other, prototypical distance between God and God.[54]

We are able to call God "other" precisely because of the "distance" and relationality within God himself. Our "otherness" from God, however, must not be conceived mythologically as a dualistic opposition of two completely distinct "realms" - the human realm of mortality and contingency and the divine realm of immortality and "glory." The "otherness" of creation is grounded within the "spaciousness" of the trinitarian relations in such a way that the integrity of the world as "existing" in its own right is preserved. But it is grounded in such a way that it is "taken up" into the divine life itself and thereby constituted as "within" God (in the sense of participating in the divine life) without simply being reduced (mythologically) to a "part" of God or (philosophically) to a univocal emanation of the divine Being. We are only able to affirm this if we feel ourselves addressed by God as a "thou" in such a way that this address comes from the inner nature of the trinitarian divine life itself. We are thus taken up into God's "oneness" because this oneness of God has "room" for such "otherness" within itself.[55]

D. Christ the Concrete Universal.

The world's "place" within God has its ground of possibility in more than a "generic" concept of "otherness" within God. The world finds its place most appropriately within the Son. Just as the Son is completely "dependent" upon the Father for the communication of his Godhead, so too the world is totally dependent upon the divine freedom for its reality. Thus, both the Son and the world are characterized by an active "passivity," by a "dependence' which is the ground for their most intimate "independence." The Son is divinity in the mode of a passive

---

[54]*Theo-Drama II*, 266.

[55]*Theo-Drama II*, 287. Balthasar states: "God in himself is no one else's 'other': he is the all-embracing One. ... The finite can only dare to call it 'Thou' if, in doing so, it is answering to a 'thou' that comes addressed to itself from the inner nature of the Absolute - from the divine Trinity."

receptivity that allows itself to draw its entire existence, its entire "personhood," from the Father's act of self-donation. Thus, there is a double kenosis at work here. The Father is, from all eternity, "nothing more" than the act of generating the Son in self-donation, while the Son is "nothing more" than the act of letting oneself be generated.[56] Hence, the Son is the ground of possibility for all extra-divine "allowing oneself to be." "Creating" is, therefore, the finite analogue of the intratrinitarian act of "begetting" the Son. Thus, creation does not find its "place" within the trinity in a univocal manner; i.e., there is a theologically legitimate sense in which we can say that creation finds its "place" most fittingly within the Son. However, it must be emphasized that the world, precisely because of its "location" within the Son, is, for that very reason, located within the totality of the Godhead.[57]

The locating of the world within the Son has the further implication, according to Balthasar, that it is through the Son that God creates. The Son, precisely as the infinite, intratrinitarian act of being the Father's perfectly begotten "image," is, therefore, the ground of possibility for more than the abstract concept of "allowing oneself to be." The Son is also the ground of possibility for all possible "images" of the divine and is, therefore, the very paradigm for creation. The Son contains within his act of "being the Father's perfectly begotten image" all possible images of the Father. Creation can be seen, therefore, as the Father's "gift" to the Son. And it is the task of the Son, through the unifying agency of the Spirit, to "take up" the creation and present it back to the Father in that day when God will be "All in All."[58]

---

[56]We are not concerned here with developing the role of the Holy Spirit. The current emphasis is on the 'location" of the world within the Godhead through the Son. That is not to imply that the role of the Spirit can be so easily "bracketed" from that of the Father and the Son. For now, it must simply be shown how Balthasar develops his idea of the Son as the "paradigm" for creation.

[57]*Theo-Drama II*, 261-262. Balthasar states: "Being totally dependent on divine freedom, the world can receive its possibility and reality nowhere else but in the eternal Son, who eternally owes his divine being to the Father's generosity. ... We must add immediately that the world's location in the Son directly implies its location in the totality of the Godhead."

[58]*Theo-Drama II*, 261-262 Balthasar states: "If the Son is the Father's eternal Word, the world in its totality is created by this Word (Jn 1:3), not only instrumentally but in the sense that the Word is the world's pattern and hence its goal. 'Through him' also means 'in him' and 'for him' (Col 1:16). ... The world can be thought of as the gift of the Father (who is both Begetter and Creator) to the Son; ... thus the Son takes this gift - just as he takes the gift of Godhead - as an opportunity to thank and glorify the Father. Having brought the world to its fulfillment, he will lay the entire kingdom at his feet, so that God (the Father) may be all in all; ... as for the Spirit,

The ultimate foundation for such a "taking up" of the world into God without becoming "confused" with God is the hypostatic union of the divine and human natures in Christ. Here we see the true significance of the Chalcedonian insistence upon the "united" but "unconfused" state of the two natures in Christ. Balthasar uses this Chalcedonian formula to develop his own unique approach to the analogy of Being. Through the incarnational union of the divine Son and the created world for which he is the paradigm, Christ becomes and *is* the "concrete analogy of being."[59] Balthasar is attempting here to overcome the confrontation between the "analogy of being" (with a neutral concept of being) and the "analogy of faith" (with its lack of a "natural theology."). The former runs the risk of positing a neutral concept of Being within which both God and the world "share" a "space" (thus "domesticating" God), while the latter creates a dichotomy between God and his creation that can lead to a variety of destructive dualisms. Balthasar puts it as follows:

> We can speak of the "*analogia entis* " here, insofar as, this relationship is distinguished from a pantheism or theopanism which dissolves God. ... On the other side, it must be distinguished from every form of pure dualism, which either isolates God's divinity from the world and closes it in on itself (Deism) or isolates the world's secularity from God (resulting in sin being seen as a fall from the divine realm, secularism and the God-is-dead theology). The possibility of distinguishing between God - who "is all" ... and thus needs nothing - and a world of finite beings who need God remains the fundamental mystery.[60]

However, if Christ is the concrete analogy of being, then two mutually conditioning principles can be held: 1) that creation does participate in some sense in the act of Being and is, therefore, analogous to God's act of existence; and 2) that this analogy is based on a divine initiative where God himself "bridges" the gap between creation and himself through the Son's free obedience in the Incarnation. This latter point is central to Balthasar's entire approach. The initiative in bridging the gap is God's, and therefore any "analogy of being" which does not take into account the world's existence within the "kenoses" of the trinitarian God is doomed to fall back into one of the false polarities. Any approach to the analogy of being

---

he is given the world by both: he is eternally the reciprocal glorification of Father and Son, but now he can implement it in and through the creation."

[59]*Theo-Drama II*, 267.
[60]*Theo-Drama II*, 118-119.

which takes as its methodological point of departure a world which is conceived of as "pure nature" is doomed eventually to see the God-world relationship in either monistic or dualistic terms. The tension created between God and world in such a scenario lends itself to an inevitable reorientation into a philosophy of identity or it will fall back into mythic or secularistic dualisms. A doctrine of creation that emphasizes the creating act of God as a kenotic "descent" (based on the intratrinitarian "kenoses" as it ground of possibility) will be able to affirm that there is an "analogy" between God and the world that has its foundation in the kenosis of the Incarnation. Christ, as the concrete analogy of being, opens up within his person a new, synthesis between the monistic and dualistic options. It is not (contrary to Barth) "idolatry" to see in the analogy of being a "point of contact" between the divine and human realms because it is now clear, in the light of revelation, that the world was made from the beginning for Christ and thus finds its true center in him.[61]

Thus, what is being "elevated" in the analogy of being is not some worldly, "alien" form which obscures God's revelation, but a world which was made from the beginning with this very elevation in view. The analogy of being therefore has a radically christocentric orientation that satisfies the demands of the *analogia fidei* that the world, seen as the *major dissimilitudo,* should never be made to bear a burden which stretches it to the breaking point and beyond. Only God can reveal God. But it must never be forgotten that this creation is radically God's creation and that given its fundamental orientation in its concrete modality toward God, it can reveal something of that inexpressible light. But it does so precisely as that which conceals even as it reveals. Just as God's freedom is a coincidence of fullness and poverty, so too created being reveals something of the divine act of existence precisely in so far as it possesses Being but can never fully "grasp" it in

---

[61]It is, of course, unfair to saddle Barth with a naive and uncritical rejection of the analogy of being since he did undergo a significant evolution in his thinking on this subject. Thus, it is unfair to take his early intolerance for this doctrine as paradigmatic for his entire career. Balthasar, for example, points out that much of Barth's early views on the Catholic concept of the analogy of being took the development of analogy in the work of Eric Przywara as exemplary for all of Catholicism. This is problematical on two fronts according to Balthasar. First, it assumes that there is such a thing as a monolithic Catholic development of the philosophical doctrine of analogy. Second, even assuming that the first assumption is true, it does not necessarily follow that Przywara is exemplary of this tradition. Thus, even Barth came to soften his view on the analogy of being as he grew more aware of the Catholic tradition. For a more detailed analysis of Barth's dvelopment of the analogy of being see: Balthasar. *The Theology of Karl Barth*, (San Francisco: Ignatius Press, 1992).

its totality and thus must "let the other existent be." Therefore, the analogy of being is not predicated upon a static concept of Being but, rather, on one that is open to a fulfillment from above. Here it must be kept in mind that, for Balthasar, the analogy of being is largely an analogy between two freedoms, the one infinite and the other finite. And both freedoms converge in the one figure of the God-man who reveals to us in human form the divine coincidence of self-possession and self-donation. This "trinitarian law" of Being is the ultimate foundation for the analogy of being and it points to Christ as the locus where all human freedom can reach fulfillment. The more finite freedom "lets go" and allows itself to be transformed from within by God, the more it will be itself. Thus, the "theandric" nature of creation and of human freedom finds its foundation in the theandric quality of Christ's existence. Balthasar states:

> The Son's hypostatic distinctness, since it is divine and unique, is what distinguishes each person founded thereon. And the more the person, in response to the Son's call, walks toward his protégé in the Son, the more unique he becomes. Here we can speak of "exemplary identity" (G. Siewerth), which is mediated, living and indestructible, by the analogy of Creator and creature. ... Freedom is communion. Communion is the opening-up of ever-new and unimaginable realms of freedom and dramatic plot; but they are all kept together in the unifying prototype, which is *universalissimum* because it is *concretissimum*.[62]

Christ as the concrete analogy of being reminds us that the inner orientation of finite existence is never, in the concrete, an orientation toward a self-enclosed subsistence: "our hearts are restless until they rest in thee." Just as the *analogia fidei* must acknowledge that creation itself can reflect God's image because it was made from the beginning with the incarnation in view, so too the *analogia entis* must acknowledge that Being cannot be understood apart from this revelation from God. The concept of "pure nature" might be possible in the abstract, but concretely creation has existed from the beginning with Christ in view as its theandric ground of possibility. The world has its own inner "*eidos* ," its own immanent integrity (indeed, Balthasar's entire theology is geared toward preserving the integrity of finitude), but this inner self-possession and immanent teleology are, according to Balthasar, "straining upward" toward an image which is not a part of the world's

---

[62]*Theo-Drama II*, 270-271.

own inner self-possession but is its ultimate fulfillment.[63] The world's *telos* is curiously "suspended" in mid-air between a purely immanent fulfillment and an address from transcendence that seems paradoxically "natural." The Incarnation is the key that unlocks this existential dilemma by revealing "from above" what humanity is most intimately "from below." The true theandric "open-endedness" of the world and of humanity are finally made clear in a revelation which shines with the "glory" of a divine gratuity. And the gratuity of this revelation guarantees that it will never seem "merited" as a "right" of our humanity as such, but will, nevertheless, appear as our most intimate fulfillment.[64] The Word is "sent down" by God to humanity and, according to Balthasar, it is that same Word "that is the force which directs history toward an end at which the same Incarnate Word, who was always its guiding center, awaits it."[65]

Theology, according to Balthasar, is a dialectical encounter with a subjectivity (God's) and is, therefore, a dialectic characterized by a dialogical encounter with the pure actuality of revelation. But "event" and subjectivity presuppose "nature" or integral "substantiality" as a condition of possibility (no matter how hard it is to differentiate "graced" nature from "pure" nature in the *de facto* created order). Therefore, "event" presupposes the analogy of being. However, in Christian theology "nature" may not be viewed statically in isolation from its relationship to the category of "history." In Christian theology "act" and "event" take priority over "substance" in any theology of creation or theological

---

[63]Balthasar, *A Theology of History*, (New York: Sheed and Ward, 1963), 140. Balthasar states: "This struggle of the cosmos for God, and of God for the cosmos ... would never have been so intense if it were not that, in the utmost intensity of immanent strain and tension, a form is struggling to be born which towers in stature above the whole cosmos. History does indeed have its own immanent *eidos*, but in descending into hell and then ascending into heaven and sitting on the right hand of the Father, Christ has taken it aloft with him, and ultimately it is only there that history can seek and recover it."

[64]Balthasar, *A Theological Anthropology*, (New York: Sheed and Ward, 1967), 226. Balthasar states: "This vertical-horizontal axis on which all history turns precludes any progressivism from matter to Spirit in the sense of 'escaping' matter ... and evolving into a new Spirit-form freed from matter. This renders the incarnation superfluous. ... We cannot escape the true 'historical present'. This grounding in the horizontal present is based on our 'vertical' relationship to Spirit. Thus, we go 'forward' horizontally only by remaining grounded vertically. Thus is our form shaped by this vertical-horizontal axis that stretches each to its limit and suspends man (dramatically and dynamically) in the middle. We 'progress' only by living ever more deeply this profoundly mysterious 'suspension' in the middle between the two poles of the axis. Thus is human life marked by a tension overcome only by the Incarnate Logos who bridges this tension on the cross. We progress by moving toward this depth."

[65]*Theological Anthropology*, 227.

anthropology. Nature must be seen, therefore, as a moment within the broader categories of event and actuality. Therefore, just as "substantiality" must be viewed as a presupposition within the more primary categories of subjectivity and actuality, so too is the analogy of being a "moment" within the analogy of faith. Furthermore, the emphasis on history within Christian theology means that "interpretation" of the singularities of salvation history (i.e. revelation) take priority over the abstractions of "theory." Balthasar states:

> History is itself the "system" in Christianity. In Christianity there can be no abstraction, as in Hellenic civilization, but only an interpretation that may not shed itself of the positive fact. And, in contrast to mere "theory," interpretation is only possible from one's own commitment, from being drawn into the event, so that, in Christianity, our solidarity and social bond with the rest of the human race are ineluctably given with the historical. ... But where the absolute is deflected from the direction of the universal concept and from myth and is directed toward the historical, then this changes the very concept of act: God is no longer the pure act of Aristotle in contrast to the potentiality of the world or of its history; God is act as power, deed, love, as what appears in the world and its history as absolute event.[66]

Christian theology, therefore, must be characterized by an ever greater immersion in the "objectivity" and singularity of the Christ-event within the horizon provided by faith.[67] The analogy of being reminds us that the categories of "event" and "Being" cannot be dialectically played off of one other in a theology which emphasizes the finitude of creation as a "contradiction" to God. The nature of revelation as "pure event" or "pure actuality" cannot be used to delegitimate the true inner integrity of the creature's "act," or of the "event" that is creation. This is why Balthasar rejects Christian Platonism. The delicate balance between the pure actuality of grace and the inner integrity of "nature" is destroyed in any system which attempts to eliminate this tension by reducing one of the polarities into the other.[68] Ultimately, the only reality capable of sustaining the unity of the two poles is the divine subjectivity as such. Creation and Incarnation both find their ultimate grounding within a decisive "act" of the divine subjectivity.[69] Along these lines it

---

[66]*The Theology of Karl Barth*, 340.

[67]*The Theology of Karl Barth*, 383-384.

[68]*The Theology of Karl Barth*, 384.

[69]*The Theology of Karl Barth*, 335. Balthasar states: "Our focus will be to try and understand that if the historical *factum* of God's Incarnation in Christ is the meaning and goal not

becomes clear why Balthasar emphasizes an approach to Chalcedonian christology which begins "from above" with the divine "personhood" of the Logos. The Incarnation becomes the central focus of Christian theology because Christ is not simply an abstract "paradigm" for creation but is the very "subjectivity" within whose concrete "act" creation's "act" finds its proper fulfillment. The abstractions of philosophical "theory" and the dualisms of mythic "projection" are transcended within the personalistic categories of the divine subjectivity made historically concrete in the man Jesus. The "singularity" that is Christ, therefore, is the concrete analogy of being precisely because the universal elevation of creation that takes place as a result of the Incarnation is accomplished through the agency of the "person" of the divine Logos acting through, and in union with, the history of a single individual man. And this, according to Balthasar, is what constitutes the "scandal" of Christianity to the human mind. That this concrete singularity could sum up within itself the world's "act" seems inconceivable to human reason. However, it is inconceivable only until one penetrates into the mystery of the divine "act" that *is* the effective cause of the hypostatic union. Balthasar states:

> The natural order, for all its own laws and persisting condition, ultimately rests on the summit of this freest of all events, the Incarnation, and the history that flows from it: that between God and man. ... This history is, in its very center as well as at every other point, the *concretissimum*, concreteness personified. To distance ourselves from this concreteness through abstraction is impossible, indeed sinful. However much there is room for legitimate abstraction and the formation of universal concepts, these remain merely relative to that most concrete reality of all, from which we cannot distance ourselves. ... On the other hand, this *concretissimum* is also the fullest and richest of realities, which is why it is so inexhaustibly rich in interpretative value. ... And within the various interpretations of this event ... we find room for the use of universal concepts, categories, properties and finally of Being itself.[70]

---

only of worldly history but also of nature and creation as a whole, then the necessity of intraworldly history and nature rests on a decision that cannot be reduced to any sort of general norm."

[70]*The Theology of Karl Barth*, 383-384.

E. Conclusion.

The formulation of Balthasar's metaphysics has progressed in a two-fold manner: 1) historically-philosophically, showing the gradual unfolding of a metaphysical dilemma incapable of intramundane resolution; and 2) theologically, showing how the classical concept of Being is transcended and fulfilled in Christ, the "concrete analogy of being." Thus, Balthasar's ultimate aim throughout has been to demonstrate, through a series of historical-intellectual reconstructions, that human subjectivity is a paradox to itself. Our subjectivity seems oriented to a transcendent fulfillment which it can neither "prove" nor "manipulate." It is beyond our power to grasp or to possess and therefore sets before us a curious situation: We can only be fulfilled when we "let go" of ourselves and allow ourselves to be addressed "from above." However, pre-Christian metaphysics, as we have seen, could only approximate an answer to the exact nature of this address. It either posited a mythical dualism or a philosophical monism. Only Christ, according to Balthasar, transforms humanity from within on the basis of a divine initiative and thus presents us with a genuinely theandric solution. This solution allows us to address God as "Thou" without, thereby, falling into mythology.

Theology, therefore, takes on a christocentric form. Since Christ is the divinely appointed means within the economy of salvation for the world and God to be reconciled from within, then Christ forms the material as well as the formal horizon of Christian theology and becomes its most proper object.[71] And since, according to Balthasar, the form of every "science" is determined by the content of its proper object, it follows that theology, seen as the "science" of faith, will have

---

[71] I have deliberately avoided in the foregoing christological discussions any discussion of Balthasar's soteriology. It was not completely necessary for our purposes here to analyse the sophisticated way in which Balthasar develops the theme of the world's reconciliation to God in Christ with specific attention paid to the category of "sin". I have simply sought to establish that Balthasar sees Christ as the concrete analogy of being and thereby to highlight how Balthasar sees revelation as fulfilling and transcending all intramundane metaphysics. The only way in which a discussion of sin would be pertinent to our discussion is in the quality of sin as "anti-God" or, at the very least, as "nonbeing". This raises the thorny question of how Christ can be the concrete analogy of being since the world's sin would seem to pose an obstacle to the total integration of the world within the trinitarian relations. However, it is too far beyond the scope of the current chapter to deal effectively with all of the ramifications of this issue. However, Balthasar's soteriology does grapple with this problem. See: *Mysterium Paschale*, 49-188.

as its proper object the very "substance" of that faith.[72] Theology's proper content is Christ seen as both the proper object of faith and the incarnational ground of its possibility (grace). Therefore, it is incorrect, according to all that we have seen in Balthasar's theology, to set up a false dichotomy between a "theocentric" versus a "christocentric" theology. For the Christian theologian no such dichotomy need exist; it is a violation of the "incarnational principle" deeply imbedded within the revelation of the divine economy to presume that theology can prescind from the concrete form of God made human in the pursuit of some heuristic, abstract synthesis. For the Christian the path to God runs directly through the incarnational form of Christ.[73]

The "Christ form" thus becomes the methodological center of theology. However, this raises certain questions. For example, how does Balthasar's christocentric, contemplative-objective theology fo revelation develop this concept of "form" which we have spoken of so much? What is the source of its self-authenticating credibility? What is the relationship between objective content and subjective perception? Balthasar develops, as we have briefly noted, a "theory of beholding" and a "theory of rapture" (or better, "being enraptured"). How does this theory work itself out? How is the form of revelation mediated to us in the Spirit? What historical form does it take in the Church seen as the mediator? In short, how does Balthasar's theology account for the historicist's objections to the very idea of a "supraessential" divine form within history that is, in some sense, God's "final" word? And how does this divine "superform" get mediated to the believer in the Church's dogmatic, scriptural, liturgical and spiritual structures? The following chapters will build on the current chapter by taking the latter's development of the need for an "objective" divine revelation and developing this "objectivity" into a full-blown theological aesthetic.

---

[72]*The Theology of Karl Barth*, 336. Balthasar states that, "theology [is] a true science of singulars that are nonetheless general and normative."

[73]*The Theology of Karl Barth*, Balthasar quotes Emile Mersch: "Theology is truly theocentric only when it is christocentric." 334.

Chapter Four:
The Form of Revelation.

The preceding chapters dealing with Balthasar's development of a trinitarian "ontology of love" set up the main question which we will pose to Balthasar's theology in the current chapter: If the trinitarian revelation of God in Christ is the fulfillment of all of history and of all of philosophy, then what is the exact theological nature of this revelation and how is it perceived and verified? In short, what is Balthasar's theology of revelation and how is it related to his development of metaphysics? This examination of his theology of revelation will necessitate an analysis of both the "subjective" and "objective" poles of revelation. What this means is that we must examine Balthasar's development of both the objective content of revelation (*fides quae*) as well as the subjective act of faith that perceives and "appropriates" this content (*fides qua*).[1] Furthermore, since Balthasar develops his theology of revelation in conjunction with his elaboration of a theological aesthetics, we must also examine in some detail his analysis of the aesthetic category of "form" or "*Gestalt* " as this applies to God's revelation in Christ.

We will begin with a brief description of why Balthasar emphasizes the need for an "objective" revelation. From there we will examine Balthasar's aesthetic concept of form and how he uses this controlling idea to analyze the relationship between the *fides quae* and the *fides qua* in revelation. We will then conclude with a brief discussion of the "credibility" of the form of revelation.

---

[1] *GL I*, 131.

A. The "Need" For an Objective Form in Revelation.

Since the time of Kant it has become fashionable to emphasize the "subjective" pole of revelation in its appropriation by the human subject. However, Balthasar's theological aesthetic runs directly counter to this trend and seeks to reintegrate the objective and subjective poles of revelation through an analysis of the act of faith, whose inner dynamic is fundamentally characterized by an orientation to the "Light" which streams from the objective form of God's revelation. To that end, Balthasar outlines three basic reasons why an "objective" revelation is both appropriate and necessary.

1. The Foundation of Human Knowledge in Sense Knowledge

Balthasar begins with an argument drawn from the sensible foundation of all human knowledge. Human beings are not pure spirit, and the idea of a divine revelation which is a direct communication between two pure "interiorities" is not true to our experience.[2] Just as all other human knowledge comes to us through our experience of the "outside" world (i.e., the world of "not me"), so too must divine revelation make use of the material of our sensible world in order to communicate. This is a constant theme which Balthasar never tires of repeating. The God of the Old and New Testaments is the sovereign and absolutely free Creator - a Creator who does not shy away from the messy limitations of finite materiality. Here we must remember Balthasar's development of a trinitarian metaphysics of relational love that overcomes the false dualism of myth and the facile identities of monistic philosophy. The God of the Bible is no Pythagorean harmony of oppositional dualities within an architectonic cosmology of the "spheres."[3] This creation is radically God's creation and there is not a hint in the

---

[2]*GL I*, 430. Balthasar states: "In the concrete, we have always already made some contact with God as we approach him through the worldly and material creation, knowing nothing of a pure communication between two interiorities."

[3]For an interesting intellectual history of the interrelatedness between Greek music, mathematics, philosophy and religion see: Jamie James, *The Music of the Spheres: Music, Science, and the Order of the Universe*, (New York: Grove Press, 1993).

Biblical narratives of any "strain" on the infinity or transcendence of God when God has dealings with finite creation. Therefore, it is entirely fitting that the God of the Bible should make use of creation in the divine self-communication. Furthermore, we must avoid at all costs seeing such material "forms" and "images" as obstacles to our knowledge of God that must somehow be "gotten beyond." In other words, our knowledge of God does not "increase" in direct proportion to the distance we can muster between ourselves and the material, sensual world:

> It is a matter of faith that we should not simply give ourselves over to God mystically, as to an Absolute that transcends all worldly forms and relativizes them, not only as to a primal Ground that destroys all of these forms, but that we should at the same time entrust ourselves with the confidence of faith to the *Creator Spiritus*, to the Spirit who from the beginning is a Creator and who, in the end, aims not at a Hindu dissolution of the world through mystical dance, but at creative form, regardless of how much in the form of man and of the world remains to be burnt away as dross.[4]

2. The Objective "Glory" of God in Creation and Covenant

Balthasar's second argument for the appropriateness of an "objective" revelation flows logically from the first. If God has revealed himself as the Creator, and if "this creation is necessarily ... a manifestation of God, it follows that this manifestation takes its form from the form of the world itself."[5] What Balthasar is attempting to say here is that God is present in creation not as another "object" alongside of or behind the material form but is revealed precisely in the very "Being of things." God's omnipotent and eternal Being is symbolically and analogously revealed in the very Being of finite creation. Creation is not an "allegory" of God's Being, nor is it simply, taken as a whole, a "metaphor" for God which can be dispensed with once we have penetrated beyond materiality and

---

[4]*GL I*, 35-36. See also, Balthasar, *In The Fullness of Faith: On the Centrality of the Distinctively Catholic*, (San Francisco: Ignatius, 1988). Balthasar states: "God ... is Spirit ... and he chooses the descending path into matter, not only in order to meet man intimately and in his totality, but also in order to show him the full meaning of salvation that resides in man's relation to matter, namely, that souls are (defenselessly) open to one another in the medium of the senses; the fact that man is fettered to vulnerable, corruptible bodiliness is something crucifying and humiliating, but it also has something glorious in store, which will shine forth at the 'resurrection of the flesh'" (115). Elsewhere Balthasar makes mention of God "getting his hands dirty" with "Adam's clay" (111).

[5]*GL I*, 430.

gleaned the "kernel" of divine "truth" lurking "behind" the material image.[6]
Balthasar turns to St. Paul for support on this point. The famous Pauline
statements concerning the knowability of God through creation are taken by
Balthasar to mean that the light of God's Being shines through created Being in
such a way that it is no mere "aspect" or "part" of God which is made visible.[7] The
culpable nature of our ignorance of God (according to Paul) in the face of this
revelation points to its "completeness" on some basic level. It is the divine Being
which radiates in its integrity through the medium of the Being of the world. This
radiating of the divine Being is referred to by Paul as the "glory" of God, and is
immediately differentiated from the created world as such. Being a pious Jew, Paul
would never confuse the divine glory with the Being of the world. Nevertheless,
Paul affirms the knowability of the divine Being in the structures of the finite
world. Balthasar states:

> The text [Rom. 1:23] does not specify the precise nature of the
> analogy between man or beast and their form, on the one hand, and
> that between cosmos and creating Godhead, on the other. But the
> answer is there implicitly: everything which is said of God - his
> divinity, his eternal might and glory, his power as Creator -
> consistently underscores the ever-greater difference between him
> and creatures. However, this does not preclude God's doxa from
> radiating and "being seen" (kaqoratai) in and through the form of the
> world.[8]

The created world, imbued with the divine glory which "overshadows" it, is
similar to the presence of God in Jewish history. Just as the *Shekinah Yahweh*
went before the Israelites and manifested itself during their wanderings (Ex. 14:19),
and then later came to rest in the "glory" of the holy city as a "light to the nations"
(Is. 60:2), so too does God's glory manifest itself within the created world as a
whole. Stories such as that of Jonah in the prophetic literature were constant
reminders to the Jews that the particularity of their covenant was meant as a "sign"
of God's fidelity to, and presence within, the rest of "the nations."[9] And just as the
presence of the divine glory in Jewish history prefigures and anticipates the

---

[6]*GL I*, 430.

[7]GL I, 430-431. Balthasar quotes the following texts: Rom. 1:19f., Rom. 2:4, Rom.
9:22, 1 Cor. 1:25.

[8]*GL I*, 431.

[9]*GL VI*, 207-209.

presence of God in the Incarnation, so too does the divine presence in creation prefigure Christ.

However, as Balthasar frequently makes clear, we must be careful not to draw this pattern of "promise-fulfillment," "type-antitype" in an overly neat fashion. It may be true that Christ is "simply" a making visible of a divine presence which pervades all of creation. However, it would be wrong to see in this fact a license to develop an evolutionary view of the progressive nature of revelation such that the Old Testament,[10] seen as the paradigmatic intensification of all creaturely "longing," easily flows into the New.[11] Much of the "prefiguring" of Christ in creation is in the form of a radical ambiguity which leads to paradoxical answers to vexing existential questions. We saw this with regard to ancient metaphysics, with its internal vacillation between myth and philosophy. Thus, one can "see" the fulfillment which Christ brings only to the extent that one antecedently carries within oneself the felt need to find an answer to all of the aforementioned ambiguities.[12] And the same is true of the Old Testament. There is no "magic thread" which runs through the entire Old Testament tying it directly to the New. We will see in chapter five how the various "types" within the Old Testament jostle

---

[10]The designation "Old Testament" is retained here for definitive theological reasons. Although Christian exegetes must be accutely sensitive to the sad history of anti-semitism that Christian triumphalism has often led to, nevertheless, Balthasar retains the use of this designation because he does exegesis self-consciously as a Christian exegete. As we will see in chapter five, Balthasar's approach to exegesis is controlled by his christological theology of revelation. Thus, the "Tanak" is, for him, both the "Hebrew Scriptures" and the "Old Testament."

[11]*GL I*, 431-432. Balthasar states: "The revelation of the triune God in Christ is not simply, to be sure, the prolongation or the intensification of the revelation in the creation; but, in their essence, they are so far from contradicting one another that, considered from the standpoint of God's ultimate plan, the revelation in the creation is seen to have occurred for the sake of the revelation in Christ, serving as the preparation that made it possible. ... In this way the form of the world itself ... in the Holy Spirit ... becomes a temple which, like the tabernacle and Solomon's edifice, harbours within and above itself the *kabod* of God."

[12]Balthasar, *Truth is Symphonic: Aspects of Christian Pluralism*, 47-57. Balthasar states: "Revelation can come to terms with every form of the genuine philosophy that seeks to plumb the difference between the world's ground and existence, whether such philosophy comes from the Mediterranean world, the Far East or Africa. But the dialogue will begin by eliciting the question that is fundamental to philosophy and is contained in and behind the various answers that are apt to conceal the question." 52. Therefore, revelation has a certain iconoclastic quality to it insofar as it seeks to "get behind" the various philosophical constructions to find the deeply imbedded existential question about Being. Balthasar states: "So revelation has no choice but to remove this roof superstructure and dismantle the philosophies until it uncovers the genuine search common to them all ... the 'restless heart'." 54. However, revelation has nothing to say to the unphilosophical and utterly pragmatic "disciplines" which dominate the academic world of today: "In this ... context, revelation has nothing to say, since no question arises to which it alone can give an answer." 56.

one another in an uneasy alliance. There is no single "form" to the Old Testament, only a series of textured pluralities spanning several centuries tied together within the faith consciousness of the Hebrew people - - a consciousness which is convinced that somehow these often paradoxical images find a common origin in their God. And since this faith consciousness seeks this common origin in a God who acts in history, then it necessarily looks to its own future as a people for the fulfillment of all of its ambiguous and paradoxical expectations. However, there is no predetermined manner in which such fulfillment must take place. Hence, the many-faceted and vague nature of the messianic expectation and its often confused relationship with the national political identity, is a natural by-product of the open-ended nature of the Old Testament narrative itself.

What all of this points to is that God's revelation in Christ, although it flows from the antecedent revelation in creation and in the Old Covenant, is of a wholly unexpected and unpredictable nature. Only the revelation of the triune God in the earthly form of Christ could fulfill all of our paradoxical expectations by first shattering the illusory quality of our answers and then laying bare the heart of the question. Everything is transformed from within by the radiating light of revelation and elevated to a new plateau. Thus, although the historical form of Christ is the product of its historical antecedents, the true significance of this form can only be seen through the eyes of faith, which sees these same historical antecedents "taken up" into the hypostatic union. The true significance of Christ can only be discerned through an affirmation of the truly theandric quality of everything that he accomplishes. What you see in Christ is the wholly unique union between the archetype (God) and the image (humanity). The image is of no interest apart from its union with the archetype. The form of Christ's humanity becomes the perfect image of the "form" of the triune God. The world of the "divine" is not an amorphous "ocean" of Being which then "delimits" itself in order to make itself visible in the "foreign" world of form and finitude. The triune nature of the divine means, among other things, that God possesses, and is, a "superform." Balthasar states:

> Now, what makes its appearance in Christ in no way represents itself as a *phainomenon* of the One as opposed to the Many, but as the becoming visible and experienceable of the God who in himself is triune. The form of revelation, therefore, is not appearance as the limitation ... of an infinite non-form ..., but the appearance of an

infinitely determined super-form. And, what is more important: the form of revelation does not present itself as an independent image of God, standing over against what is imaged, but as a unique, hypostatic union between archetype and image. In the form of revelation, what is image is of no interest in isolation and for itself (the man Jesus), but only in so far as in this image (Christ!) God portrays himself - indeed, in so far as this man is himself God.[13]

3. The Objective "Form" of Revelation, The "Form" of God, and the "Incomprehensibility" of God in Negative Theology

Here we see the third and most important reason Balthasar gives for the appropriateness of an "objective" form in revelation. Since God is not infinite "formlessness," but rather, is infinitely determined within the divine self by a triune "superform," then we can begin to see why Balthasar places such great emphasis on the aesthetic objectivity of revelation and its power to "enrapture" the beholder. The concrete historicity of the divine self-revelation should not be viewed, according to Balthasar, as a "concession" to the pitiful material beings that God has created. Nor is the material creation as such a place which exists in opposition to God (antagonistically) and which must be "overcome" and "gotten beyond" in order to attain salvation in the heavenly realm of pure, formless Spirit. The entire world of "things" reflects something of the infinite self-determination of God and as such comprises no "obstacle" to our knowledge of God. Just as we saw in chapter three that Balthasar posits something analogous to "space" and "duration" in God, so too here: The multiplicity of the world's forms does not constitute a contrary cosmic principle opposed to God's Oneness and formlessness. God made "things." God is the author of specificity and form. Thus, it is not unreasonable to say that there is something analogous to "form" in God. Balthasar refers to this within his trinitarian theology as an infinitely self-determined "superform."

However, at this juncture a caution must be registered. Since we are talking about an analogical predication, the concept of "form" cannot be affirmed in an overly positivistic manner when applied to God. A cautionary warning arises within "negative" theology concerning the always "greater dissimilarity" that exists between God and the world in any analogy. Negative theology reminds us that any

---

[13]*GL I*, 432.

theology that reflects upon revelation must be sophisticated enough in its approach to the analogical nature of human language when applied to God, that it does not fall prey to the rationalistic temptation to reach some kind of systematic "closure" in its doctrine of God. The term "closure" is used here to denote any theological attempt to reduce the mystery of God's nature as such into a monistic identity with revelation. This in no way is meant to call into question the validity of what God has revealed, nor its consistency with God's inner ontological Being. Therefore, Rahner's famous dictum that the "economic Trinity is the immanent Trinity, and vice versa," is not called into question. All that is meant by Rahner's definition is that we need not fear that there is some kind of bifurcation between who God really is in God's inner self, and the God who is revealed in salvation history. Furthermore, it also implies that we can extrapolate from the economy of salvation and make certain statements about God's inner life without being accused of engaging in Gnostic musings about what is essentially unknowable. The Church, therefore, is granted a certain amount of latitude in its doctrinal statements concerning God's inner life that go beyond a mere repetition of biblical language.[14]

However, God's inner mysteriousness (the only true "Mystery" in the strict theological sense) must not be collapsed into a relation of strict identity with revelation.[15]   To do so destroys God's transcendence, and shows a misunderstanding of revelation as a set of propositions out of which we "deduce," rationalistically, who God is. The question, therefore, arises, as to how Balthasar reconciles his stress on the objectivity of revelation with the traditional cautions of apophatic theology against an exaggerated literalism in our approach to the "positive" aspects of revelation.

Balthasar acknowledges that every analogical affirmation contains within itself an inherent tension that cannot be avoided. But an awareness of this tension is nothing new. The Christian tradition has grappled with this issue ever since the need for a philosophical defense of the faith arose in the early patristic era. Christianity has had to come to terms with two seemingly contradictory elements in its doctrine of God: the affirmation of God's absolute transcendence and sovereignty, *and* of God's "communio" with the world through the hypostatic

---

[14]Karl Rahner, *Encyclopedia of Theology: The Concise Sacramentum Mundi*, Karl Rahner (ed.), "Divine Trinity," (New York: Crossroad, 1975),1755-1764.

[15]Karl Rahner, *Sacramentum Mundi*, "Mystery." 1000-1004.

union. The New Testament affirms that God dwells in "unapproachable light, whom no person has ever seen or can see" (1 Tim. 6:16) while at the same time stating that in Jesus dwells the "fullness of the Godhead" (Col. 1:19), and "He who sees me sees the Father" (John 14:9). So Christians have learned to live with a certain tension in their God-talk as they walk a thin line between the legitimate demands of negative theology and the "visibility" (i.e., historicity) of revelation.[16]

This same tension has threatened to reduce Christian theology and spirituality to one pole or the other down through the centuries. Platonic elements have always tempted the mystical tradition toward a false matter-spirit dualism (as well as a constant temptation to flirt with various forms of Quietism), while revelational positivism helped to create the false theological rationalism of much of the post-Tridentine manual theology.[17] There is no escape, according to Balthasar, from this ongoing tension:

> Christians today must be capable of withstanding the tension which is contained within these statements. On the one hand they must abandon every attempt to penetrate into the hidden and free being of God with unbaptized reason, and on the other they may reject no path which God himself offers men into the mystery of his eternal love. They may neither on the one hand push God away into a realm of inaccessible transcendence which then ultimately becomes a matter of indifference for men, nor on the other hand so draw him into the historicity of the world that he forfeits his freedom over the world and falls victim to human *gnosis*.[18]

It is tempting to leave the issue here, suspended in "tension." However, Balthasar attempts to shed further light on the exact nature of this tension by raising it from the level of a philosophical impasse concerning the limits of language, to a truly theological tension created by the inner dynamic of revelation itself. He does so by distinguishing between two different kinds of "incomprehensibility." First, there is a purely negative incomprehensibility characterized by the philosophical impulse to ground all statements about the Infinite in the ultimate mystery and unknowability of Absolute Being. This is the path of classical apophatic theology.

---

[16]*Elucidations*, 24.

[17]*GL V*, 48-140. Balthasar develops the history of the mystical tradition in a section titled "The Metaphysics of the Saints." He traces in great detail this constant temptation for Christian spirituality to reduce itself to one pole of the analogical tension.

[18]*Elucidations*, 25.

Balthasar sees merit in this approach as a necessary "balance" against any tendency toward revelational positivism and as a guard against all forms of idolatry. The iconoclastic quality inherent in this approach is an absolutely fundamental component of the biblical revelation, with its constant warning against creating "images" of the divine.[19] Iconoclasm (in its milder forms) has acted as a corrective throughout the entirety of the Church's history and, in point of fact, helps to preserve the genuine aesthetic "form" of revelation from adulteration. The sober quality of this more negative kind of incomprehensibility protects the image of Christ from being "extended without any critical distance whatever into other images which, regardless of all their religious relevance, nonetheless belong to the sphere of aesthetics."[20]

However, Balthasar cautions against an exclusive reliance on such a model for the incomprehensibility of the Absolute. First, the iconoclastic tendency, valuable though it may be, must never be taken to its radical extreme, i.e., the denial of all images whatsoever. That would be anti-Incarnational. The iconoclastic tradition cannot go beyond the level of a "practical call to the constant vigilance required to keep the transcendental beauty of revelation from slipping back into equality with an inner-worldly natural beauty."[21] Second, the impression can be all too easily given that the finite world of images is somehow "foreign" to God in the sense of an oppositional principle of some kind. Thus, the tendency can creep in whereby the individual is tempted to seek a non-mediated "direct" contact with the divine and to disparage the world of finite "things" as an annoying nuisance on one's purely spiritual journey to God.[22]

Balthasar's approach to the incomprehensibility of the Absolute begins with an assumption drawn from the idea of revelation itself: God wills to be known and, no matter what difficulties may be involved, Christian theology must start from the premise that God has in fact engaged in a self-revelation and has become known in

---

[19]*GL I*, 40-41.

[20]*GL I*, 41.

[21]*GL I*, 41.

[22]*GL I*, 217. Balthasar states: "Where, for ... unenlightened eyes, there seem to stand intermediary figures as obstacles, there precisely it is that faith perceives its own light within the form of revelation."

Jesus Christ.[23] It would be unworthy of the Christian concept of God if we were to assert that God can be self-revealing but only in a manner which is utterly impenetrable to reason.[24]

Balthasar also asserts with equal force the dictum: *si comprehendis, non est Deus*. The difference from the more negative concept of incomprehensibility is that in revelation it is precisely the incomprehensibility of God's eternal triune love that is revealed. Even in the beatific vision God will remain incomprehensible to us since we will then see "face to face" the infinite depths of God and that God is the "always and forever greater." Thus, in revelation it could be no different. If what is revealed is nothing less than the very nature of God, then "a necessary part of this manifestation is his eternal incomprehensibility."[25] However, here "incomprehensibility" is not a purely negative determination denoting the dark and shadowy hinterlands of ambiguity, i.e., of what one does not know. The incomprehensibility of God given in revelation is, according to Balthasar, "a positive and almost 'seen' and understood property of him whom one knows."[26]

---

[23]*GL I*, 186. Balthasar states: "We must begin by replying that the first and pre-eminent intention of the self-revealing God is, precisely, really to reveal himself, really to become comprehensible to the world as far as possible."

[24]*GL I*, 186. Balthasar states: "If his first intention were to make those who believe in him assent to a number of impenetrable truths, this would surely be unworthy of God and it would contradict the very concept of revelation."

[25]*GL I*, 186.

[26]This approach to the incomprehensibility of God in Christian theology finds an echo in Aquinas, who notes that the "negative" moment in all theology, although of fundamental importance, must not be seen as a complete negation of our ability to speak about God's attributes. Negative theology, according to Aquinas, must be viewed as a necessary moment within our attempt to know God through analogy. The alternative would be to view analogous language about God as a futile moment within a relentless negative approach that ultimately annihilates the possibility of God-talk altogether. See: *Summa Theologica*, I, q. 13. ("The Names of God"). Aquinas views our engraced "knowledge" of God in this life as a "union" with that which remains, in itself, unknowable. The "union" spoken of here implies a certain kind of "real" knowledge" of God appropriate to our human condition. It falls short of a direct vision of God and, therefore, does not "know" its proper object in the same way as an empirical object of natural reason. However, with regard to faith Aquinas states: "Although by the revelation of grace in this life we cannot know of God *what He is* , and thus are united to Him as to one unknown; still we may know Him more fully according as many and more excellent of His effects are demonstrated to us, and according as we attribute to Him some things known by divine revelation." *ST., q. 12, a. 13, ad. 1*. Therefore, the incomprehensibility of God must be viewed in Aquinas as precisely that which is revealed to the believer in God's revelatory self-donation. But it is something truly *revealed* . The paradoxical quality of such an assertion means, therefore, that caution must be used when dealing with God's incomprehensibility; the integrity of God's transcendent mystery must be preserved, but not in such a way that the integrity of the finite world as "creation" is dismissed. The incarnational principle within Christianity, as well as the biblical

The more a great work of art is known and grasped, the more concretely are we dazzled by its 'ungraspable' genius."[27]

Here we see once again Balthasar's aesthetic emphasis on the "objectivity" of revelation. Even God's very incomprehensibility is somehow "seen" and made visible in a finite form. The triune love of God poured forth in Jesus Christ is beyond our ability to "encapsulate" in a rational concept. Our human faculties are overwhelmed by the blinding light of God's *excessus* of love in Jesus Christ. Thus, our "blindness" is created by an excess of light rather than its lack. The negative philosophical incomprehensibility of God is transformed and lifted up into the positive theological incomprehensibility of God's triune love revealed in Jesus. This is the triumph of God's *kenotic agape* over all forms of human *gnosis* which seek to "tame" God's love in either sterile rationalisms which trap God in human systems of thought, or a pious transcendentalism which pushes God into a comfortable Deistic distance. Jesus has revealed in his very person and existence that God wishes to be addressed as "Thou," and has established the theological conditions for its possibility. The infinite divine profundity that makes such a bridge possible is the truly incomprehensible mystery at the center of all Christian theology. Thus, far from destroying negative theology, Christian revelation shows us the true contours of the divine incomprehensibility for the first time. Balthasar states:

> It is true that in Jesus Christ the mystery of the ground of the world burns out more brightly than anywhere. But, on the other hand, it is precisely in this light that for the first time and definitively we grasp the true incomprehensibility of God. It is here that God breaks *for ever* all the "wisdom" of the world by the "folly" of his love ... . This incomprehensible love of the God who acts in the event of Christ raises him far above all the incomprehensibilities of philosophical notions of God which consist simply in the fact of negating all statements about God, which may be ventured on the grounds of our knowledge of the world, out of regard for his total otherness.[28]

---

concept of creation, demands that the "tension" between the divine realm and the finite realm be reconciled, not "gotten beyond" by simply reducing one pole of the tension into the other.

[27]*GL I*, 186.

[28]*Elucidations*, 22-23. Walter Kasper, as noted before, correctly pinpoints the visible "incomprehensiblity" of God's love in the Incarnation as one of the central motifs of Balthasar's theology of revelation. Kasper. *The God of Jesus Christ*, 54-55.

Thus, revelation has an objective form which does not "objectivize" God, precisely because it is the revelation of a love which breaks all barriers and categories and remains forever beyond all systemization. What lover would dare to submit his/her beloved to the cold analysis of rational categories in order to ascertain the hidden "secret" which is the very core of the beloved's personhood and "lovability"? To do so would be the destruction of real love. And yet, love is something truly "known" and experienced in the very depths of our being. Love, therefore, seen as the deepest communion and self-donation between persons, has an iconoclastic element to it even as it enlightens. All expectations and preconceptions are shattered as the reality of the beloved exceeds all of the normal categories for understanding our day-to-day reality. Furthermore, only love, viewed as the deepest expression of our innermost freedom, has the power to reveal the depths of personhood. As Balthasar puts it: "Only that which is given by the unsearchable freedom of love has power to reveal. And so analogously ... the free-self-disclosure of the divine heart sheds over all our existence ... an incomparable light; and yet it comes from God 'who dwells in unapproachable light.'"[29]

The central idea which runs through all of Balthasar's observations concerning the objectivity of revelation is that we cannot artificially separate the act of revelation from the content. The Word, in the Incarnation, does not exist somehow behind or "in" the flesh of the historical Jesus, but, rather, *is* the flesh of the historical Jesus. Jesus does not represent the Word but *is* the Word in the form of human flesh.[30] Therefore, the visibility of revelation must not be overlooked simply because it involves the knotty problem of particularity. It is an illegitimate and ill-conceived Christian theology that sees in the historical particularity of revelation a stumbling block to universality. Furthermore, Balthasar emphasizes that the "visibility" of God in revelation, although it flows from historical and worldly antecedents is, nevertheless, a theandric event with divine authorship. We must take the divine element with the utmost seriousness and recognize that in

---

[29]*Elucidations*, 24.

[30]*GL I*, 182. Balthasar states: "We should never tire of reminding ourselves that, from a Christian standpoint, there is no possibility of distinguishing between's God's act of revelation and the content of this revelation, for this revelation is inseparably both the interior life of God and the form of Jesus Christ. For the Word of God is *both* the divinity which expresses and reveals itself in the Trinity's eternity and in the economy of time *and* the man Jesus Christ, who is the Incarnation of that divinity. He is Word as 'flesh', a 'flesh' which in its human totality and in the life-figure in which it exists is the concrete presentation of this Word."

revelation we do not have "merely" a projection of the mythopoetic imagination, but that we also have an image placed before us by God.[31] This "image," states Balthasar, "offers itself as something that could not have been invented by man - an image that can be read and understood and, therefore, believed only as an invention of God's love."[32] Therefore, the first task of fundamental theology should be to ask the question of how God's revelation comes to us in history and how this revelation is perceived by human beings. It is, therefore, "the question of perceiving form - an aesthetic problem."[33]

B. Beauty, Form, and Revelation
1. Beauty

The concept of "form" has frequently arisen in the course of analyzing Balthasar's theology, but only now are we in a position to deal with this issue on a substantive level.[34] In order to avoid a theological aesthetics which is nothing more than an "aestheticizing theology" that deals in the sentimental world of mere "appearance," the concept of form must be situated within the broader context of the category of "beauty" seen as one of the transcendentals of Being.[35] Thus, the first stage of our analysis of "form" will be a discussion of how Balthasar develops the interrelationship between Being and beauty. From there the concept of form will itself be more specifically defined, and an analysis offered of how Balthasar applies this concept to the category of revelation.

The first thing to be pointed out is that Balthasar never engages in a detailed, systematic development of a highly academic "theory of beauty."[36] Instead,

---

[31]*GL I*, 172. Balthasar states: "What is involved [in revelation] is not at all a projection of the mythopoetic religious imagination, but rather the masterpiece of the divine fantasy, which puts all human fantasy to naught."

[32]*GL I*, 173.

[33]*GL I*, 173.

[34]The word "form" is a translation of the German "*Gestalt.*" This translation of Balthasar's use of *Gestalt* has become the standard English translation with few exceptions. Therefore, it will be retained throughout the current discussion.

[35]*GL I*, 79-117.

[36]It is important to note at this point that Balthasar, surprisingly, never develops a sustained, systematic presentation of his "theory of beauty." This is for two main reasons. First, as we shall see, Balthasar's approach to the subject takes place largely within patristic-medieval metaphysical categories. And, as in so many other places in his prodigious writings, Balthasar has a tendency to assume that the reader shares his enormous erudition and, therefore, is as familiar with the sources being dealt with as he is. Louis Dupre refers to Balthasar's frequent tendency not

Balthasar begins his analysis with a metaphysical discussion of the relationship between beauty and the other attributes of Being. Here we immediately get a clue as to where Balthasar wishes to situate his discussion of beauty -- squarely within the domain of Being as such. It is also clear that Balthasar's development of beauty as a "transcendental" places much of his discussion within the context of the history of patristic-medieval thinking on this issue.[37] Balthasar never engages in a lengthy systematic debate about whether or not "beauty" is a transcendental in the same way that the *unum* ,*bonum* and *verum* are. Indeed, Balthasar makes the categorical statement that the Church Fathers, as well as the medieval scholastics, "unhesitatingly" granted to beauty the status of a transcendental.[38] He asserts this, despite the fact that there is still debate about what Aquinas had to say on the issue, or even if all of the patristic and medieval discussion about beauty ever reached any real clarity.[39] However, Balthasar makes such a claim based more on what is implicit and latent in the great patristic and medieval theologies than on what they

---

to lay bare the full theoretical apparatus behind an idea as an "intellectual *desinvolture* if an argument fails to warrant the author's patient attention." "The Glory of the Lord," *Hans Urs Von Balthasar: His Life and Work,* David Schindler (ed.) (San Francisco: Ignatius Press, 1991), 206. The second major reason for his lack of a systematic theory of beauty is more intentional. Balthasar himself refers to his approach to beauty as that of a "layman." This is necessary, according to Balthasar, at least in the initial stages of inquiry, in order to avoid prejudicing our contemplation of what God puts before us in revelation. An overly developed "theory of beauty" might "read into" revelation its own ideological orientation. Thus, Balthasar's initial theoretical apparatus with regard to beauty remains fairly simple on the conceptual level. See, *GL I*, 117. This self-analysis on the part of Balthasar finds further support from Frank Brown who concludes: "Von Balthasar himself, it should be observed, employs a quite minimal theoretical apparatus, albeit one applied with great theological insight." Frank Durch Brown, *Religious Aesthetics: A Theological Study of Making and Meaning,* (Princeton: Princeton University Press, 1989), 18.

[37]Some might object to "situating" Balthasar's approach within the confines of "classical" Catholic metaphysics. The implication might be that Balthasar's theology is, therefore, out of date. However, to state that someone's metaphysical categories are largely shaped by a particular school in no way implies a slavish adherence to every aspect of that school. Furthermore, it is far from a closed question as to whether or not such "ancient" approaches are, in fact, out of date in terms of their primary, foundational insights. For example, Aristotelianism is far from dead even though Aristotle's cosmology is antiquated and false. Balthasar's theology may represent a more "classical" approach but that fact alone does not imply that it is antiquated.

[38]*GL I*, 38.

[39]For an excellent. although somewhat idiosyncratic, treatment of this issue see, Umberto Eco, *The Aesthetics of Thomas Aquinas,* (Cambridge: Harvard University Press, 1988), pp. 20-48.. It is Eco's conclusion that Aquinas did view beauty as a transcendental. However, beauty is closely related to the good since they are both transcendentals of Being under the aspect of "form." What seems to differentiate them in Aquinas is a purely logical distinction between the *bonum* as a final cause which "draws" the appetite toward the desirable form, and *pulchrum* as a purely formal cause. This seems also to be the conclusion of Gilson in his interpretation of Aquinas. See: Etienne Gilson. *The Elements of Christian Philosophy,* (New York: Doubleday, 1960), pp. 174-178.

say explicitly about beauty as such.[40] The fundamental point which is important here is simply Balthasar's assertion that beauty is, in fact, one of the attributes of Being and has been implicitly and explicitly affirmed as such in the tradition. It is not, therefore, necessary to analyze this tradition in detail in order to situate Balthasar's aesthetic.

There are two important features of Balthasar's concept of beauty which stand out as a result of his designating *pulchrum* as a transcendental: 1) Beauty is an attribute of Being and can therefore only be understood in its ultimate foundations from a metaphysical perspective; and 2) Beauty cannot be divorced from its fundamental grounding in all of the other transcendentals.[41] There are several consequences which flow from these two observations. First, theology has difficulty engaging in dialogue any system of thought which is indifferent to metaphysics, since Christianity is, at its root, an answer to metaphysical ambiguity. Similarly, theology will have difficulty engaging in dialogue with any worldview which has stripped beauty of all metaphysical significance. Secondly, the consequences of ignoring beauty's deep spiritual significance are disastrous. For once beauty has been banished, the other transcendentals are not far behind and the death of metaphysics will follow in due course.[42] The "primal wonder" which is the heart of the philosophical act will not long survive the death of beauty as an attribute of Being. The ancient world understood this deep inner connection between truth, goodness and beauty and the danger of losing the significance of

---

[40]See, *GL II*, and *GL III*. These two volumes comprise a series of extended monographs on individual Christian theologians, philosophers and poets with the intended purpose of drawing out the latent theological aesthetic inherent in them all. In no way does Balthasar claim that any or all of these thinkers were explicitly aware of developing "beauty" as an attribute of Being and developing a theological aesthetic therefrom. What they all shared in common was a belief in the "glory" of a creation which was "good" and, therefore, "beautiful." Furthermore, they believed in the redemption of creation which points to an eschatological fulfillment where all earthly forms and values will be lifted up into a divine "form." Thus, for example, Aquinas may make contradictory statements about the nature of beauty as such, but his theology of creation and redemption contain an implicit theological aesthetic which Balthasar draws out. Balthasar states explicitly: "It makes no difference whether or not they are expressly speaking of the beautiful, or even whether or not they are conscious of the aesthetic moment as they ... order and elucidate their material." *GL I*, 78.

[41]*GL I*, 118.

[42]*GL I*, 19. Balthasar states: "Thomas described Being (*das Sein*) as a 'sure light' for that which exists (*das Seiende*). Will this light not necessarily die out where the very language of light has been forgotten and the mystery of Being is no longer allowed to express itself? What remains is then a mere lump of existence which, even if it claims for itself the freedom proper to spirits, nevertheless remains totally dark and incomprehensible even to itself. The witness borne by Being becomes untrustworthy for the person who can no longer read the language of beauty."

truth and goodness if beauty were banished to the margins of respectability. Balthasar states:

> Beauty is the last thing which the thinking intellect dares to approach, since only it dances as an uncontained splendor around the double constellation of the true and the good and their inseparable relation to one another. Beauty is the disinterested one, without which the ancient world refused to understand itself, a word which both imperceptibly and yet unmistakably has bid farewell to our new world, a world of interests, leaving it to its own avarice and sadness. ... Our situation today shows that beauty demands for itself at least as much courage and decision as do truth and goodness, and she will not allow herself to be separated and banned from her two sisters without taking them along with herself in an act of mysterious vengeance.[43]

From this foundation one of the primary tasks of a theological aesthetic becomes readily apparent: to "guard" the integrity of Being. We have already seen how necessary metaphysical "awe" is to the theological task, according to Balthasar. We can now further specify that within this close relationship between metaphysics and theology the category of the "beautiful" takes on special importance as the "guardian" of this wonder. "Man," states Balthasar, "philosophises in a transport of awe, illumined by the light of eternal Being as it shines forth in the world."[44] To lose the power of this "light," a light which is the splendor and beauty of Being, is to lose the ability to philosophize at all. Theologically this translates into a specific concern for the "Glory" (*Herrlichkeit*) of God as it manifests itself in the "form" of historical revelation. For just as metaphysics suffers when "beauty" is banished or ignored, so too does Christian theology "lose its salt" when it capitulates to the modern spirit of functionalism and no longer attends to the "Glory" of God as its central motivation. "Theology," states Balthasar, "is the only science which can have transcendental beauty as an object."[45] This transcendental beauty fulfills the splendor of creaturely Being from within. When theology and philosophy become artificially divorced, the aesthetic dimension in philosophy is reduced to a mere "appearance," while theology, therefore, banishes beauty as a theological category to the realm of pure spirit.[46]

---

[43]*GL I,* 18.

[44]*GL I,* 71.

[45]*GL I,* 70.

[46]*GL I,* 45-78. We cannot go into great detail concerning the historical evolution of the split between philosophy and theology and what this has meant to aesthetics as a specifically

The "middle realm" of the *daimon*, that natural *eros* of the cosmos, becomes either the truly demonic (a mistake made by many Christian thinkers) or it becomes a simple projection of human subjectivity (a mistake made by many moderns).[47] The true nature of beauty as an attribute of Being as such -- and, therefore, analogous to the "Glory" of God -- is lost. The world, therefore, suffers a dual loss. It suffers the loss of its own most inner integrity and subsistence, as well as its ability to act as a vehicle for the splendor of God. In short, it loses its status as *creation* . Theologies which lose sight of the connection between the "splendor" of Being and the "Glory" of God in revelation and creation (*Gratia perficit naturam*) end in a "joyless" rationalism which is no longer convincing. Balthasar puts it as follows:

> Nothing expresses more unequivocally the profound failure of these theologies than their deeply anguished, joyless and cheerless tone: torn between knowing and believing, they are no longer able to *see* anything, nor can they, therefore, be convincing in any visible way.[48]

2. Form

The ultimate foundation of Balthasar's concept of beauty resides in its ontological status as an attribute of Being. But as we have noted on several occasions, for Balthasar, "Being" does not connote a "formless ocean" compared to which "specificity" and finite form become insignificant drops of water which will eventually "merge" with Being and lose all individual identity. Rather, beauty,

---

theological category. It is enough here to note that it is Balthasar's contention that aesthetics has been eliminated from theology and marginalized in philosophy due to the tragic consequences of artificially "sealing off" philosophy from theology. Balthasar deals with this from a historical perspective in two sections entitled, "The Elimination of Aesthetics from Theology."

[47]*GL I*, 62-63. In analyzing the thought of Gerhard Nebel, Balthasar quotes him with approval concerning this realm of the worldly *daimon* : "What exactly is the *daimon* ? Reality cannot be exhausted either mythically or Biblically merely with the double affirmation of man's interior space and of the exteriority of the creating and redeeming God. The phenomena compel us to establish the existence of an intermediate realm proper to the *daimon* of the beautiful, a realm which for centuries now has been progressively restricted, suppressed, and finally even denied. The history of the modern world lies just as much in the ruination and abolition of this daimonic *intermundium* as it does the de-Christianization of public life and culture." Balthasar goes on to conclude: "Nebel recognizes that the beauty both of nature and of art makes a claim to wholeness and thereby discloses the wholeness of Being - yes, the *wholeness* of it, but only as the goodness of God's most excellent work." (Here we see once again the close connection which Balthasar draws between *pulchrum* and *bonum* .)

[48]*GL I*, 174.

although it has an ontological status, still finds its specific "character" in the inner "luminosity" and "splendor" that radiates from the depth of "form." Balthasar states:

> Those words which attempt to convey the beautiful gravitate, first of all, toward the mystery of form (*Gestalt*) or of figure (*Gebilde*). *Formosus* ("beautiful") comes from *forma* ("shape") and *speciosus* ("comely") from *species* ("likeness"). But this is to raise the question of the "great radiance from within" which transforms *species* into *speciosa* : the question of *splendor*. We are confronted simultaneously with both the figure and that which shines forth from the figure, making it into a worthy, a love-worthy thing.[49]

This "inner radiance" is the result of an interiority that seeks to express itself through the outward manifestation of form. The form is expressive of interiority precisely because it represents the achievement of an inner freedom that is able to gather together into the service of expression that "which had been indifferently scattered."[50] Here we come face to face with the great mystery of the interaction between interiority and its communication, soul and body. However, no dualism whatsoever is implied here. This interaction results in an integral expressive form that "radiates" an inner luminosity. This expressive luminosity, which is the product of the intersecting of inner splendor and outward form, is the *locus classicus* of all metaphysical thinking about beauty and is referred to by Balthasar as the "primal phenomenon."[51]

It is easy to make two fundamental mistakes regarding this primal phenomenon. The first mistake was made by Plato and by all subsequent spirit/matter dualisms: the attempt to "get behind" the outward form in order to get at the real truth of a thing which resides in a kind of pure spiritual interiority. "Reality" is reduced to spirit or interiority and it exists in a kind of "*Urzeit* " all its own. It then seeks a "field of expression" which it "uses" during its sojourn in time and abandons when it is "finished" with it. This approach makes the world of matter and form into a secondary moment in the history of spirit. The world thus loses its true inner integrity and is reduced from the level of the truly symbolic to

---

[49]*GL I*, 19-20.
[50]*GL I*, 20.
[51]*GL I*, 10.

the level of a mere "allegory" for spirit.[52] The other mistake is to see the material world in the modern, materialistic sense as a "spiritless" body which is somehow thrown together through the interplay of blind material forces. Here, too, the finite world of form, including mind itself, loses all ontological luminosity and simply becomes an epiphenomenon of matter.

In the ancient world only Aristotle seems to have taken the integral simultaneity of interiority and its outward form seriously. Unfortunately, Aristotle had no clear vision of what happens to this integral wholeness after death, and thus failed to satisfy the deep longing of the human being for some kind of transcendent hope beyond the grave. The Greek tragedies were the tortured cries of the Greek psyche as it struggled with such despair. The only alternative appeared to be a return to an even more intense Platonism that had long-lasting effects well into the Christian era. Only the concept of the resurrection of the flesh could eventually overcome Platonic dualisms and give an ontological/theological foundation for the integrity of interiority and form:

> Only God's gift from the New Earth and the Flesh that rises to eternal life can quench this question and prevent the reversion to an intensified Platonism which has had such grievous consequences even for Christian theology. ... The freedom of the spirit that is at home in itself, therefore, is simultaneous with the "keyboard", which it has appropriated and which allows the spirit self-expression. Such simultaneity is possible because it is the spirit's native condition always to have gone outside itself in order to be with another.[53]

The Christian concept of the resurrection of the flesh and the ultimate holistic integrity between the New Earth and the Old gives Balthasar one of his basic principles regarding form: "Our first principle must always be the indissolubility of form, and our second the fact that such form is determined by many antecedent conditions."[54] Form is "indissoluble" because it is always more than a simple "sum of its parts." For example, one does not appreciate a great work

---

[52]It was understandable for Plato to make such a mistake since he lacked any clear concept of the "resurrection of the flesh." Thus, in order to prove human immortality after death there was a need to disengage the human personality (soul) from the world that eventually "disintegrates." However, this does not alter the fact that this position is essentially dualistic and treats the world and the body as a mere "shell" for the soul.

[53]GL I, 21.

[54]GL I, 26.

of art by first breaking it down into its "parts" and then attempting to understand it by examining all of its antecedent causes in an atomistic fashion. Aesthetic appreciation demands an ability to accept the form as a totality, as a heuristic synthesis of otherwise disconnected fragments. That is not to say that a form's antecedent causes should be ignored. Nothing could be further from the truth. Part of the enjoyment of aesthetic perception is precisely understanding each of the antecedent causes in its own individual *telos* and to see the genius involved in weaving together disparate antecedent "components" into a new whole -- a whole which forces no "part" to violate its own inner integrity while it is being "taken up" and "used" in a higher synthesis. The "indissolubility" of form can, therefore, be synonymously expressed as its nonreducibility.[55]

So what exactly then does Balthasar mean by his concept of form? We have already seen that he refers to it in conjunction with the "radiance" or the "inner light" that emanates from the very depths of Being. Granted, it also comprises the typical aesthetic categories of proportion and harmony and can therefore be expressed through certain kinds of numerical relationships. As such, "form" is a purely intramundane and measurable phenomenon.[56] However, form is most properly seen as the mysterious "knowability" of Being which is the result of the deeply expressive nature of Being in its very depths. As Gilson puts it in his treatment of Thomas on the same subject: "The beautiful is a variety of the good. It is the particular kind of good to be experienced, by a knowing power, in the very act of knowing an object eminently fit to be known."[57] Thus, the splendor of form arises from the depths of Being in its mode as knowable, as expressive, as "grace."

Furthermore, it must never be forgotten that this more metaphysical view of "form" means that it must be viewed within a comprehensive approach to Being -- an approach that must include the good and the true. As Balthasar puts it: "When beauty becomes a form which is no longer understood as being identical with Being, spirit, and freedom, we have again entered an age of aestheticism, and

---

[55]*GL I*, 31: "For we can be sure of one thing: we can never again recapture the living totality of form once it has been dissected and sawed into pieces, no matter how informative the conclusions which this anatomy may bring to light. Anatomy can be practiced only on a dead body, since it is opposed to the movement of life and seeks to pass from the whole to its parts and elements."

[56]*GL I*, 118.

[57]Gilson, *The Elements of Christian Philosophy*, 176.

realists will then be right in objecting to this kind of beauty."[58] Therefore, out of an aesthetic concern for the form of Being there arises an ethical concern and a concern for truth. But these dimensions of Being do not transcend and leave behind the aesthetic. Rather, they reveal themselves as "beauty's inner coordinate axis, which enables beauty to unfold to its full dimensions as a transcendental attribute of Being."[59] Therefore, it is the totality of Being that is manifested in each and every individual finite form within the context of each form's integration of its various parts and elements. Finite form, therefore, requires both a "surrounding world" and the totality of Being as such. "In this need," states Balthasar, "it [form] is ... a 'contracted' representation of the 'absolute,' in so far as it transcends its parts as members and controls them in its own confined territory."[60]

In this sense it could be said that everything is "beautiful" insofar as everything that exists is possessed of some kind of form which is expressive of Being. Things become more or less beautiful depending on how perfectly they have integrated their form. As one ascends the hierarchy of complexity from inorganic molecules up to highly complex organisms possessed of a deep spiritual interiority, beauty becomes much more richly textured due to the vast array of potential interrelationships in the various components of the form. Balthasar's concepts of beauty and form are not, therefore, univocally predicated of all existents equally. There are "analogical gradations" between the various hierarchical manifestations of worldly form that make some forms more suitable expressions of the depths of Being than others.[61] Here we can truly see the deep connection between interiority and outward, expressive form. As Balthasar puts it: "As we proceed from plant to animal to man, we witness a deepening of the interiority, and, at the same time, along with the continuing organic bonds to a body, a deepening in the freedom of the expressive play of forms."[62] And the "light" which shines forth

---

[58]*GL I*, 22.

[59]*GL I*, 22-23.

[60]*GL IV*, 29.

[61]*GL I*, 119: "Protestant theology ... has been wholly right consistently to reject the application to Biblical revelation of the schema inherited from pre-Christian, and especially Greek, philosophy, a schema that distinguished between a 'ground of Being'; and an 'appearance of Being.' But ... this schema exhibits different analogical gradations even in the worldly realm, since the expressions of a free spirit (namely, as word and creative deed) are structured differently from those of organic and subspiritual nature, and yet they are not excluded from the schema."

[62]*GL I*, 21.

from the depth of a form is, at one and the same time, both the light of the form itself and the light of Being in which the form is immersed. Thus, as Balthasar puts it, "the transcendence increases along with the immanence."[63] Therefore, Being, on this higher spiritual level, becomes most uniquely itself precisely when it seeks to communicate itself to the "other" in its outward expressive form, i.e., communicability is a function of the form's very immanence as form. Ultimately, form is an indissoluble union of two things:

> It is the real presence of the depths, of the whole of reality, *and* it is a real pointing beyond itself to these depths. ... Both aspects are inseparable from one another, and together they constitute the fundamental configuration of Being. We "behold" the form; but, if we really behold it, it is not as a detached form, rather in its unity with the depths that make their appearance in it. We see form as the splendor, as the Glory of Being. We are "enraptured" by our contemplation of these depths and are "transported" to them. But, so long as we are dealing with the beautiful, this never happens in such a way that we leave the (horizontal) form behind us in order to plunge (vertically) into the naked depths.[64]

3. Form and Revelation.

We have seen how Balthasar develops a metaphysical view of form as the expressiveness and communicability of Being. But how does Balthasar relate this metaphysical definition of form to revelation? We cannot go into the actual theological unfolding of the Christian form in salvation history, in Scripture and in the ongoing tradition.[65] The question before us now is more theoretical. What is the relationship between form as an attribute of Being and form as a concept within a theological aesthetic applied to revelation? If, as we have already seen, *gratia*

---

[63]*GL IV*, 31.

[64]*GL I*, 118-119.

[65]Balthasar spends several volumes dealing with the dimensions of the Christian form. See, *The Glory of the Lord VI: Theology, The Old Covenant,* and *The Glory of the Lord VII: Theology, The New Covenant.* Also, the second and third parts of his theological trilogy, as we have noted before, deal with both the dramatic (*bonum*) and the logical (*verum*) dimensions of the Christian narrative. Thus, as we have seen in his approach to beauty as a transcendental within a comprehensive view of Being, so too here we cannot divorce his theological aesthetic from his theological dramatics or his theo-logic. All three of these perspectives are required in order to "flesh out" the dimensions of the form of revelation. Therefore, we must not make the mistake of isolating Balthasar's concept of form wholly within aesthetic categories as such.

perficit naturam, non supplet, then how does the metaphysical concept of form get "taken up" analogously into the theological concept of form?

"God's Incarnation," states Balthasar, "perfects the whole ontology and aesthetics of created Being. The Incarnation uses created Being at a new depth as a language and a means of expression for the divine Being and essence."[66] This is possible because form, especially in its higher spiritual levels, "always expresses more ... than what goes into the thing formed itself (namely, the infinity of glory), [and this] makes the beautiful as such available as a form of revelation."[67] What then are the specific elements within the metaphysical concept of form that Balthasar uses, analogically, in building his theological aesthetics? Fundamentally, there are two. First is the idea (discussed above) concerning the form of Being as the outward "expressiveness" of a deep spiritual interiority. Form as "expressive image" of the inner depths becomes Balthasar's most fundamental theological building block. The second element is implied by the first. "Expressiveness" implies "freedom," which is why form as an attribute of Being is most itself when worldly Being reaches the level of spiritual subjectivity. The patristic idea of humanity as the "mouthpiece" and pinnacle of creation finds an echo here in Balthasar's development of the freedom in the depths of Being that finds expression through human subjectivity. But this freedom to express outwardly implies an *eros* , an "enthusiasm" which loses itself in the other. Therefore, Balthasar's metaphysical concept of form contains the enthusiasm of *eros* as a basic category, which he uses as his second main building block in the theological aesthetic.[68]

With regard to the first "building block," the expressive image, Balthasar insists that we must avoid any attempt at an easy transposition from worldly form to the form of revelation. Protestant theology has been correct to reject the idea that

---

[66]*GL I*, 29.

[67]*GL IV*, 34.

[68]Cf. Peter Casarella, "Experience as a theological category: Hans Urs von Balthasar on the Christian encounter with God's Image," *Communio XX* (Spring, 1993), 118-128. I am indebted to Casarella's analysis for developing these two elements of Balthasar's concept of form as the primary building blocks in his theological aesthetic. However, I disagree somewhat with Casarella's description of the second element of form. Casarella describes kenotic love as the primary characteristic of the "enthusiasm" engendered by the form. And although Balthasar frequently describes the hiddenness of God in the form of revelation and, therefore, the *kenosis* that is involved in such a "hidden" descent into human flesh, nevertheless, I think it is better, for reasons that will become clear later, to designate the enthusiasm generated by form as "*eros* " rather than agapaic *kenosis*.

any worldly aesthetic schema could be simply transposed to theology. However, Balthasar argues that the concept of expressive form can be applied to revelation in a super-eminent manner. Balthasar states:

> To use the analogy in a supereminent sense, what is the creation, reconciliation, and redemption effected by the triune God if not his revelation in and to the world and man? Not a deed that would leave its doer in the background unknown and untouched, but a genuine self-representation on his part, a genuine unfolding of himself in the worldly stuff of nature, man and history - an event which in a supereminent sense may be called an "appearance" or "epiphany."[69]

Our worldly experience of the expressiveness of Being in the outwardness of form is analogous to the experience which is created by faith when the light of grace gives us "new spiritual eyes" for "seeing" the expressiveness of God. The experience of seeing with spiritual eyes does not descend from above and force itself upon us as something foreign. It builds on our creaturely ability to see the expressiveness of Being in worldly forms. Therefore, even though we cannot simply apply worldly form and aesthetics directly to revelation, we can still say that were it not for our ability to see worldly form we would be unable to perceive the form of the divine epiphany in Christ. Revelation cannot escape from the fundamental metaphysical law that immanence and transcendence, as we have noted, increase together. This is the foundation for the analogy between the expressiveness of Being in finite form and the form of revelation:

> To put this in the language of aesthetics: the higher and purer a form, the more will light shine forth from its depths and the more will it point to the mystery of the light of being as a whole. To put this in religious language: the more spiritual and independent a being is, the more it is aware in itself of God and the more clearly does it point to God. It is not possible that the biblical revelation should escape from this fundamental law of metaphysics. ... And so the absolute being makes use of the form of the world with its duality of language (inalienable finitude of the individual form *and* unconditional, transcending reference to this individual form to being as a whole) in order to make itself known in its unfathomable personal depths.[70]

Balthasar states that despite the legitimate concerns of apophatic theology to avoid all false revelational positivisms, there still remains the bedrock fact of all

---

[69]*GL I*, 119.
[70]*GL IV*, 31-32.

Christian revelation that there is, in fact, something to be seen and grasped. God does not approach us in total darkness and then ask of us a completely blind faith in something that remains totally hidden. "Something," states Balthasar, "is offered to man by God, indeed offered in such a way that man can see it, understand it, make it his own, and live from it in keeping with his human nature."[71] Furthermore, the analogy posited between the expressiveness of Being in the metaphysical paradigm of transcendence/immanence and the form of revelation, is not negated by apophatic theology but, rather, affirmed. For the more a form becomes most perfectly itself, the more does it radiate the depths of a deep mysteriousness that is revealed, precisely, as that which is "ever greater" and which can never be grasped in worldly concepts.

This truth can be seen in the relationship between the human soul and the human body, the way the spirit manifests itself as "concealed" in history, and the way God is present as "hidden" and "latent" in creation and the order of redemption. In none of these examples can the inner reality of "the depths" be "read off" of the phenomenal surface like some mathematical formula or easily measured proportion. Indeed, form would lose its own most proper radiance were it not for the presence of the unfathomable, mysterious depths of Being. As Balthasar states: "form would not be beautiful unless it were fundamentally a sign and appearing of a depth and a fullness that, in themselves and in an abstract sense, remain beyond both our reach and our vision."[72]

With this in mind, Balthasar is fond of quoting the liturgical prayer found in the Christmas Preface: "Because through the mystery of the incarnate Word the new light of your brightness has shown unto the eyes of our mind; that knowing God visibly, we might be snatched up by this into the love of invisible things."[73]

---

[71] *GL I*, 121.

[72] *GL I*, 118. This idea of the hiddenness of the depths finds a humerous yet serious expression in Walker Percy in a manner which echoes Balthasar's statements about the ultimate mystery of the human being to himself/herself. Percy points out that of all the things in the universe that are most mysterious to humanity, none remains more of an enigma than the one thing we ought to know better than anything: the human animal itself. He sees in this fact a confirmation of the deeply spiritual nature of the human psyche and the delegitimation of all attempts to understand the human from within our modern functionalist, technocratic, reductionistic worldview. See, Walker Percy, *Lost in the Cosmos: The Last Self-Help Book*, (New York: Washington Square Press, 1983), esp. pp. 10-17.

[73] *GL I*, 119-120. The Latin text reads: "*Quia per incarnati Verbi mysterium nova mentis nostrae oculis lux tuae claritatis infulsit: ut dum visibiliter Deum cognoscimus, per hunc in invisibilium amorem rapiamur.*"

There are two fundamental elements in this prayer which coincide with the two analogical elements of form outlined above: the expressiveness of God in an outward form, and the "love" (*eros*) which is engendered in humanity for God precisely by the "light" which emanates from the form. Here it must be pointed out how Balthasar sees in this prayer confirmation of his emphasis on our "knowledge" (*cognoscimus*) through the mediation of a visible sacramental form of an "object" which is actually God. This very real knowledge is caused by the new light of grace (*lux*) which shines on the "eye of our mind." The prayer emphasizes the "newness" of the divine light which cannot, therefore, be equated with the light of worldly forms. However, even the divine light must shine into the eye of our mind. Furthermore, it must make use of visible forms in order to do so:

> The "new light" will ... make seeing the form possible and be itself seen along with the form. The *splendor* of the mystery which offers itself in such a way cannot, for this reason, be equated with the other kinds of aesthetic radiance which we encounter in the world. This does not mean, however, that that mysterious *splendor* and this aesthetic radiance are beyond any and every comparison. That we are able to speak here of "seeing" ... shows that, in spite of all concealment, there *is* nonetheless something to be seen and grasped (*cognoscimus*).[74]

Before we move on there is one last aspect of form as "expressive image" that must be mentioned. Just as we saw that it is precisely the incomprehensibility of God which is revealed in the positivity of revelation, so too here it is precisely the "expressiveness" of God which is revealed in the expressive form of revelation. For Balthasar, Christ is the perfect expressive image of the Father. Being is expressive into outward form precisely because God, within the inner divine life of the trinitarian relations, is expressive.[75] What is therefore expressed in revelation is the donability of God - a donability which, in a supereminent manner, is analogous to the donability of Being. Thus, one of the primary aspects of the content of revelation is its formal structure as such. Christ, the *Logos* in human flesh, takes on the form of an "obedience" which is the obedience of the image to its archetype. In this case, the obedience is so complete that it forms a unity within distinction which the tradition refers to as the hypostatic union. Furthermore, since he is both God and a human being, the significance of who he is and what he accomplishes is

---

[74]*GL I*, 120-121.
[75]*GL I*, 69.

universal.[76] Christ is the archetypal image for all created forms. His "form" is the form into which all created forms are to be incorporated. True to his aesthetic concerns, Balthasar emphasizes that earthly form, though it will one day die and pass away, does not pass into formless oblivion. Rather, all earthly forms will undergo a death and a resurrection and make the transition from the Old Earth to the New Earth. Seen in this light, Christianity becomes the aesthetic religion *par excellence*.[77] Created forms do not lose their own inner integrity by conforming to the archetypal image. Rather, all created forms become closer to what they are in themselves by conforming to the image. Here Balthasar is fond of quoting a passage from Bonaventure: "The likeness which is the truth itself in its expressive power ... better expresses a thing than the thing expresses itself, for the thing itself receives the power of expression from it (i.e., from the likeness)."[78] Here, on the level of our incorporation into Christ, we find once again the general metaphysical law that immanence and transcendence increase together as a function of one another. In this instance, it is the very engraced expressiveness of the human form as such which "con-forms" to its archetype's expressiveness as an image of the Father.

The question remains, however, as to the precise manner in which our form becomes incorporated into the Christ form. Balthasar answers this question by referring to the subjective stance of Jesus *vis-a-vis* the Father. Balthasar departs from the tradition here somewhat insofar as he ascribes real faith to Jesus. The traditional (largely Thomistic) approach emphasizes that since Jesus possessed the

---

[76]It is important to note again that Balthasar's development of the universality of Christ's significance relies on an anthropology that sees humanity as the "pinnacle" and "mouthpiece" of creation. Thus, Christ can be the archetype for all created forms precisely because he is the very perfection of humanity itself. Christ can, therefore, act as a mediator between creation and God, nature and grace, precisely because of his perfected humanity. However, a caution is important here as well. Balthasar would see no significance to such a "perfected humanity" were it not for the fact of its union with divinity. Indeed, such a perfected humanity would be impossible without it.

[77]*GL I*, 216: "And although, being finite and worldly, this form must die just as every other beautiful thing on earth must die, nevertheless it does not go down into the realm of formlessness, leaving behind an infinite tragic longing, but, rather, it rises up to God *as form*, as the form which now, in God himself, has definitively become one with the divine Word and Light which God has intended for and bestowed upon the world. The form itself must participate in the process of death and resurrection, and thus it becomes co-extensive with God's Light-Word. This makes the Christian principle the superabundant ... principle of every aesthetics; Christianity becomes *the* aesthetic religion *par excellence*."

[78]*GL II*, 293.

beatific vision he could not possess faith since, by definition, faith is a hope for things not seen.[79] Faith, in the Thomistic sense, is a theological virtue that infuses into the soul an inchoate knowledge of, and an anticipatory participation in, eternity. However, the "perfected" vision of God in heaven known as the "beatific vision" renders faith superfluous.[80] And even on the level of purely "human" faith (a "natural" virtue), one has no need for such faith when the object of that faith becomes empirically known. Balthasar broadens this traditional concept of theological faith into the total existential response of the individual to what God has revealed. As we saw regarding the incomprehensibility of God, the more that is revealed of the divine nature, the more God's incomprehensibility comes to the forefront. Even in the next life, where we will all possess the beatific vision, we will never comprehend God, and our "knowledge" of God will not, therefore, be opposed to our vision of God. The more we "know" God, the more we know that God is the "ever greater." Thus, faith, far from being done away with by the "vision" and "knowledge" of the beatific vision, is only increased and made more itself through the vision of God's self-revelation. In other words, true to his development of our vision of form, Balthasar states that the more we are enraptured by God's trinitarian "super-form," the more we are drawn into the genuine mysteriousness and incomprehensibility of God.

Balthasar uses this broadened concept of faith and applies it to the subjectivity of Jesus. The theandric subjectivity of Jesus becomes the archetype of all Christian subjectivity and faith. The goal of Christian faith is to grow into an image of the archetype through an ever closer "grafting" into the "mother plant" who is Christ.[81] Christ is the archetypal form, not in some idealistic Platonic sense nor in a dualistic mythic sense, but, rather, precisely as a singular subjectivity that incorporates into itself as archetype all human faith, indeed, all human subjectivity. Thus, the form of earthly existence is most characterized by the category of the personal. At the end of all earthly longing there exists, not some impersonal cosmic

---

[79]Thomas Aquinas, *Summa Theologica: IIIa, q. 10* .

[80]*Summa Theologica: IIa, IIae, q.5, a.1* : "Now the principle object of faith is the First Truth, the sight of which gives the happiness of heaven and takes the place of faith. Consequently, as the angels before their confirmation in grace, and man before sin, did not possess the happiness whereby God is seen in His Essence, it is evident that the knowledge they possessed was not such as to exclude faith."

[81]*GL I*, 224.

principle of "union," but a countenance.[82] The hypostatic union is not created by two independent and isolated natures which somehow "come together" and "create" Christ.[83] The union of the divine and human natures is accomplished within the category of the personal. It is the Word who "descends" and effects the union within its (the Word's) deepest interiority. Therefore, Christ is the "concrete analogy of Being" precisely within a subjectivity that unites the divine and human realms within the singularity of personhood.[84] The expressiveness of Being in outward form finds its ultimate ground of possibility in the expressiveness of a divinity that is able to "exteriorize" itself in a concrete human being:

> The Son's infinite hypostatic distinctness, since it is divine and unique, is what distinguishes each person founded thereon. And the more the person, in response to the Son's call, walks toward his prototype in the Son, the more unique he becomes. Here we can speak of "exemplary identity." ... It follows, therefore, as we have already said, that the person's opening-up to the prototype must coincide with the abolition of all limitation vis-a-vis everything that shares in being: freedom is communion. ... But they are all kept together in the unifying prototype, which is only *universalissimum* because it is *concretissimum*.[85]

The category of the personal leads us into the second element of "worldly" form that is analogous to the form of revelation: the expressiveness of Being seen as an *eros* for communicating with the "other." Being is expressive in form

---

[82]Cf. Joseph Ratzinger, *Introduction to Christianity* (New York: Herder and Herder, 1970), 247. Ratzinger echoes Balthasar's concern for the category of the personal. He beautifully summarizes the point as follows: "This confirms ... the precedence of the individual over the universal. ... The world is in motion towards unity in the person. The whole draws its meaning from the individual, not the other way about. Perception of this also justifies once again Christology's apparent positivism, the conviction ... that makes one individual the centre of history and of the whole. The intrinsic necessity of this 'positivism' here becomes apparent afresh: if it is true that at the end stands the triumph of spirit, that is, the triumph of truth, freedom and love, then it is not just some force or other that finally ends up victorious; what stands at the end is a countenance."

[83]*Theo-Drama III*, 223: "The synthesis [in the hypostatic union] is a free act of the divine Person; it is not a quality impressed on the divine Person by the two natures."

[84]Balthasar's emphasis on the subjectivity of the incarnate Word as the archetype for all Christian subjectivity bears the clear mark of Kierkegaard's influence. Kiekegaard sought to maintain the possibility of actually hearing a word of God without falling prey to either Kantian subjectivism or Christian scholasticism. He sought the answer in Christ's subjectivity which he equated with truth itself. Thus, the believer must seek to conform to this subjectivity. The credibility of Christ becomes visible in the apostle who has totally identified himself with the subjectivity of the Christ. But this subjectivity presents the world with an intolerable paradox which impels the apostle toward a cruciform subjectivity. Cf. Balthasar, *Love Alone*, 39-41.

[85]*Theo-Drama II*, 270-271.

because it is possessed of a deep inner interiority that points to an ultimate freedom that undergirds all of finite existence. The form of worldly Being, therefore, points to the communicability of Being, to its orientation to a "world," or a field of expressive discourse. This orientation of Being toward a field of communicability finds its culmination in human personhood, which is essentially constituted by its own fundamental dynamic toward the "other," by its "going out" into a "world." Balthasar refers to this dynamic as a form of *eros*.. We spoke earlier of the "middle area" occupied by *eros* , by the *daimon*, which is threatened by the iconoclastic tendencies of many Christians, and by the reductionistic subjectivism of many moderns. Balthasar refers to it as a "middle area" because it occupies the ground between human subjectivity and the realm of divinity. Consequently, a naive dualism, either of the old mythic type or of a more modern positivist/subjectivist type, constantly threatens to rob this middle area of its own integrity as finite form in an effort to make a "direct link" between the two interiorities.[86] And when this mediating world of finite forms is robbed of any ontological value or meaning precisely as form, then aesthetics degenerates into a superficial aestheticism which deals with the transitory, subjective/sensual impressions created by mere "appearances." One of the consequences of this reduction of a metaphysical grounding of form to a superficial psychologistic aestheticism is that *eros* is robbed of its true inner significance as the movement of the soul toward that which is inherently desirable because it is "valuable." The process of genuine aesthetic perception is set on its head: instead of the "enthusiasm" of the enraptured soul which goes out of itself in a natural movement of desire toward the object of its rapture -- an object which is seen as valuable ("good") in itself -- we have the egoistic "grasping" of a subjectivity which sees all worldly form as a mere "amusement park" of appearances for one's personal enjoyment.[87] The other

---

[86]*GL V.* 643. Both of these tendendencies are linked by a single common denominator: their desire to bypass the middle realm of *eros* in a mistaken desire for an aprioristic immediacy between finite spirit and the divine spirit. Balthasar states : "Being is left out of the picture in a pseudo-Augustinian aprioristic immediacy of relation between God and Spirit, and the metaphysical act is bound up with a somehow mystical love of God."

[87]It is important to point out here the close connection between Balthasar's theological aesthetic and his theological dramatics. The "desirability" of finite form is closely connected with the "good." Here, the "good" is viewed as a transcendental property of all beings insofar as they participate in Being as such. All finite existents are "good" insofar as they are "real." "An existent being," states Balthasar, "is good for me because it complements my particularity; but since it is real, I cannot absorb it into me: I must allow it to maintain its own independent

129

extreme is that of the iconoclastic Christian who, fearing aesthetic rapture as the idolatry of the finite form, seeks to place all worldly form, and therefore all finite *eros*, within the category of that which is "passing away" and of little importance.[88]

These various truncated forms of *eros* are especially tragic when their consequences threaten to destroy the inner integrity of human love and relationality. And human beings who have lost the genuine capacity for worldly *eros* and the rapture of love will no longer be able to recognize the revelation of God's love in history. When metaphysical *eros* is lost, and the mystery at the heart of Being is forgotten, then the loss of the human realm is not far behind. If everything in the "world" has no ultimate ontological value, and is, in the final analysis, of only provisional and functional value, then it follows that such is also the case for myself and for humanity as a whole. Balthasar states: "If I am no more than a means, then so too is the Thou whom I love."[89] Furthermore, when the entire world of finite form is stripped of its ontological value as the manifestation of the depths of Being, then it is also stripped of its genuine ontological desirability. The "desire" of the subject for its object now becomes a self-serving act of manipulating phenomenal

---

reality, for only then can it be regarded as good." *Theo-Drama II*, 240. Balthasar includes this discussion in his theological dramatics within his wider analysis of the nature of human freedom and its role in the subjective self-possession of the human being: "Now the soul is 'for itself,' and in the immediacy that this implies lies its freedom, which cannot be lost; however, it only possesses it in virtue of the luminous quality [*Gelichtetsein*] of the totality of being. Therefore it is an integral part of this imperishable freedom ... that the soul, precisely because it possesses itself in freedom, necessarily respects all other beings on account of their freedom (they are true and real) and *lets them be* ; only on this basis does it seek to embrace them." *Theo-Drama II*, 240. Therefore, the "value" that the "good" represents to me is precisely in its independence from me. The world of "things" and persons does not exist for my utilitarian comfort. And the more that I empty myself of all "claims" upon reality, the more "valuable" does that reality become for me.

[88]Balthasar acknowledges the legitimacy of the Christian fear of the idolatry of the finite object on account of its seductive beauty. But here it must be remembered that beauty, especially in its higher spiritual levels, is the expression of a deep interior freedom. Thus, the realm of the "*daimon* " can be either the expression of the truly demonic or it can be an expression of the good, of the divine. Thus, the difficult job of the "discernment of spirits" can never be dispensed with. Indeed, in so far as the Christian vocation is to "leaven" all of the structures of the world with the "yeast" of God's revelation, it could be said that this process of transforming worldly *eros* from within, i.e, the constant process of the discernment of spirits," is *the* Christian task *par excellence*. Therefore, a metaphysical history of aesthetics, as Balthasar states, "must be a place of continuous, very fruitful theological decisions: for being as a whole, in its transcendence which cannot be fixed, points through to God or to nothing, according to the illumination man gives it." *GL IV*, 38.

[89]*GL V*, 644. Balthasar goes on to state: "This means that there is no gleam of glory surrounding personal love anymore, or at most the deceptive illusion of one, which lovers are always supposed to see through in a melancholy or cynical way - for the glory of love can flourish only within the context of an at least intuited glory of Being."

appearances for one's subjective aims rather than the "disinterested" pursuit of the "good" for its own sake. Real *eros* is debased and vulgarized where beauty is turned into a mere appearance and the subject grows incapable of discerning real beauty or of sustaining real love. Is it any wonder, according to Balthasar, that in such a world the beauty of revelation should fall upon eyes that have lost their capacity for form, for people who have lost the real dimensions of genuine *eros* ? Balthasar borrows a term from Goethe and refers to such people as *Geistlos* : devoid of spiritual senses and unable to appreciate the inner dignity of all worldly *eros* for the goodness of the good.[90]

In contrast to all of these negative tendencies, Christian revelation establishes the aesthetic principle on a firm metaphysical foundation. But that foundation is not some impersonal cosmic principle but the revelation of the divine *eros* for creation - an *eros* that also posits, in an act which is simultaneous and coextensive with the act of revelation as such, the human response. Revelation is, therefore, characterized by a dual *eros* : the *eros* of God for his creation and the *eros* of the engraced human desire for God. The human response is not to be conceived of psychologistically as a subjective response to a vision of inner worldly beauty. Human *eros* for God can only be founded on "the divine light of grace in the mystery of Christ."[91] Furthermore, it is important to note here that Balthasar's application of the term *eros* rather than *agape* is intentional. From the perspective of the human ascent to God, what is most central is the aspect of the objective form of revelation which draws the human being out of himself/herself toward that "which has been shown."[92] The term *eros* preserves the specifically aesthetic element in this spiritual *ekstasis* better than *agape* , since the ascent of the soul to God is best characterized as an "enthusiasm" for the beauty of revelation. Likewise, the divine *kenosis* in creation must not be viewed mechanistically or impersonally in the sense that God is somehow simply "obeying" some intra-divine

---

[90]*GL I*, 23: "The beholder's spirit, enjoying a mysterious empathy with the spirit of what he beholds, [is not] without influence upon the efficacious reality of the beautiful - whether as the spirit of an individual or as the spirit (*Geist*) and demon (*Ungeist*) of an epoch. Works of art can die as a result of being looked at by too many dull (*geistlos*) eyes, and even the radiance of holiness can, in a way, become blunted when it encounters nothing but hollow indifference."

[91]*GL I*, 121. Balthasar goes on to state: "The whole truth of this mystery is that the movement which God (who is the object that is seen in Christ and who enraptures man) effects in man ... is co-effected willingly by man through his Christian *eros* and, indeed, on account of the fact that the divine Spirit enthuses and inspires man to collaboration."

[92]*GL I*, 121.

"law" which dictates God's descent into creation. God is not an "explication" of an antecedent "need to exist," -- i.e., God is not dependent upon Being but is an act of pure existence as such. God is most deeply characterized by an inner sovereignty and freedom. The divine *kenosis*, therefore, is not the blind emanation of an impersonal force, but the expression of a deepest freedom. And if God was under no constraint in creation, then creation is seen, fundamentally, as an act of the deepest gratuity motivated by nothing more than the divine *eros* for the work of God's hands. Here we see why it is important to emphasize the divine *eros* before we plunge into an unreflected discussion of the divine *kenosis* . Theology can grow so accustomed to "explaining" the "why" of God's act of creation and of God's "descent" in the Incarnation by appealing to *kenosis* that the biblical motif of the jealous "nuptial" God filled with the "enthusiasm" of *eros* for creation can be easily forgotten:

> Here the theological aesthetic of the commentaries on the Song of Songs should - with an indissoluble union of *agape* and *eros*, of the glory of God and the beauty of the soul - afford an almost inexhaustibly variable treasury of themes: from Origen and Methodius, from Gregory of Nyssa, Ambrose and Bede, there stretches the unbroken procession of these commentaries through the monasteries and universities of the Middle Ages to Luther and into the Baroque period. The biblical *eros* -motif, expounded in relation to Christ and his Bride ... , leads both to the heart of the distinctively Christian mysteries. ... Or to put it another way ... all revelation ... takes place for the sake of the marriage feast of the Lamb.[93]

"*Kenosis* " becomes impersonal when it denotes an "emptying out" that is seen as part of a "process" of "going-forth" and "returning" that lacks real narrative tension -- the tension which can only be created by real drama with real characters. Here we see part of Balthasar's aversion to Rahner's evolutionary christology, with its neat ascent "from below" with hardly a bump along the way. Balthasar's constant criticism that Rahner's theology lacks a real theology of the cross finds its place here. Rahner, according to Balthasar, lacks a well defined theology of the cross precisely because his theology lacks the element of real drama.[94] And real theo-drama can only be created by the presence of a divine *eros* which jealously enters the world stage in a search for the pure human response. Here too we find

---

[93]*GL IV*, 322.
[94]*Theo-Drama III*, 253; *Gl VII*, 218; *The Moment of Christian Witness*, 64-65.

the chief difference between the enthusiasm of Christian *eros* and that of paganism. The Christian ascent to God rejects all of the false systemizations and idealizations of Being found in the Platonizing tendencies of antiquity. It also rejects the pseuedo-utopian ideologies of all secular eschatologies. In contrast to these tendencies, Christian *eros* is an enthusiasm that is characterized by the sobriety of the real, of the concrete.[95] As Barth observes, only Christian revelation shatters all of our previous aestheticizing concepts of beauty because it alone provides us with the drama of the God who is able to transform from within the disfiguring ugliness of the consequences of sin: death, decay and the God-forsakenness of the tomb.[96] Balthasar quotes Barth: "If we seek Christ's beauty in a glory which is not that of the Crucified, we are doomed to seek in vain. In this self-revelation, God's beauty embraces death as well as life, fear as well as joy, what we call 'ugly' as well as what we call 'beautiful'."[97] The world's anomic horrors are transfigured from within and transcended in a Christian realism that begins with the cross and ends with the resurrection of the flesh.[98] In the paschal mystery we see the revelation of a divine *eros* that is so enthusiastic it descends to the very depths of ugliness and reclaims it within the furnace of the heart of Christ.[99] This "descent" of the divine

---

[95]*GL I*, 123: "We can never approach Christian *eros* and Christian beauty from a merely Platonic tradition and expect to interpret them adequately. The enthusiasm which is inherent to the Christian faith is not merely idealistic; it is, rather, an enthusiasm which derives from and is appropriate to actual, realistic Being. This is why God's Word constantly brings the false kind of enthusiasm which hovers about suspended on aestheticist and idealistic proleptical illusions back down to the level of sobriety and truth."

[96]*GL I*, 124: "As Karl Barth has rightly seen, this law extends to the inclusion in Christian beauty of even the Cross and everything else which a worldly aesthetics (even of a realistic kind) discards as no longer bearable. This inclusiveness is not only of the type proposed by a Platonic theory of beauty, which knows how to employ the shadows and the contradictions as stylistic elements of art; it embraces the most abysmal ugliness of sin and hell by virtue of the condescension of divine love, which has brought even sin and hell into that divine art for which there is no human analogue."

[97]*GL I*, 55-56.

[98]Cf. Peter Berger, *The Sacred Canopy: Elements of a Sociological Theory of Religion*, (Garden City, New York: Doubleday & Co., 1969), 23. The use of the term "anomic" is borrowed from Berger's analysis of the religious response to the problem of evil. According to Berger, one of the chief problems created by our experience of "evil" is that it threatens the "nomos" which has been created by one's religious worldview. For the human being, therefore, one of the most negative consequences of such "anomic" experiences is that they threaten not only physical and/or mental anguish, but also they threaten to destroy the very philosophical/religious framework that can give such horrors any meaning at all. Balthasar's development of the descent of God into the horrors of human evil goes so far as to emphasize Christ's salvific engagement with the ultimate anomic horror of all: the meaninglessness of death and hell.

eros into the ugliness of sin is not merely Luther's positing of revelation in that which is *sub contrario*, but, rather, the very "transvaluation" of sin from within."[100]

In this context we find that one of the secondary connotations of "*kenosis* " in the Greek takes on more importance. The "descent" or "emptying" which it denotes carries with it the implication of a certain futile vanity, a recklessness in the face of an almost certain fruitlessness. For what could better characterize the "foolishness" of the divine wisdom than the *ek-stasis* of an *eros* that spends itself to the point of inner exhaustion for the sake of creation? Here is where Balthasar parts company with Kierkegaard. Whereas Kierkegaard, despite his distaste for Schleiermacher's subjectivism, continued to place the bulk of his emphasis on human subjectivity in its conforming to the cruciform paradox of Christ's subjectivity, Balthasar emphasizes the transforming light of God's glory in the objective form of revelation.[101] The divine *ekstasis* is not a wild dance into the oblivion of formlessness and irrationality, but the revelation of an *excessus* that pours itself out into the specificity of creation. Balthasar puts it thus:

> This objectivism ... is the result of taking seriously the *ekstasis* of love, its going out of itself: only in this way can man achieve an act of serious love which corresponds to God's own act of taking love seriously - the act of the divine Eros which goes out of itself in order to become man and die on the Cross for the world. ... The only enthusiasm to be taken seriously is filled with that God who is no other than he who loved the world so much that he preferred it to his only Son. The power of an enthusiasm that shatters all fetters

---

[99]We do not have time here to discuss Balthasar's unique development of the theology of "Holy Saturday" and the relation this bears to his conviction that Christians should not abandon their obligation to hope for the eventual salvation of everyone. Balthasar develops the traditional doctrine of Christ's descent into hell in conjunction with his reflections on Holy Saturday. Christ's "descent" is a solidarity with the dead, with all of those who are "cut off from the land of the living" and languish in the God-forsaken silence of death. And precisely because Balthasar takes the controversial (and paradoxical) stand that Christ himself entered into a real God-forsaken state while remaining in union with the Father in the Spirit, he can assert that Christ has tasted "hell" and has redeemed, not just those who "choose" to leave hell (this is mythological), but hell itself. For Balthasar, it is no accident that the Old Testament lacked a clear concept of either heaven or hell. The true eschatological dimensions of human destiny only become clear after the paschal mystery. Heaven and hell open up as real existential possibilities in the heart of the Lamb who "became sin for our sakes" and was slain. See, *Mysterium Paschale*, 148-188.

[100]*GL I*, 126.

[101]*GL I*, 153: "Whatever else we might say about God's hiddenness, his 'guising' (Luther), his 'incognito' (Kierkegaard) in Christ ... the fundamental thing is that here we have before us a genuine, 'legible' form, and not merely a sign or an assemblage of signs."

reaches its end and proper goal, not when it tears all forms to shreds in Dionysian fashion or dances them away in the manner of the Hindus - thus finding in death itself its final shackle - when it can transvaluate death itself into life and shattering force.[102]

The dual aspects of form we have been discussing, expressive image and the *ekstasis* of *eros*, have some far-reaching methodological consequences for theology, according to Balthasar. The first consequence has to do with the proper theological outline for a theological aesthetic. The first principle of a theological aesthetic must be that theological speculation never loses its foundation in the economy of salvation. Metaphysical speculation about the harmonious beauty of the divine attributes is certainly a legitimate enterprise. Furthermore, dogmatic theology is certainly justified in stretching theological reason to the limits of speculation concerning such things as the Trinity and so forth. However, the Christian theologian must always come "home" to the bedrock of the form of God's historical revelation in order to remain true to the aesthetic specificity of God's concrete activity.[103] Therefore, all theological aesthetics will be developed, according to Balthasar, in two "phases." The first phase revolves around a "theory of vision." This would be a fundamental theology that would explore "aesthetics" in the Kantian sense as "a theory about the perception of the form of God's self-revelation."[104] The second phase revolves around what Balthasar refers to as a "theory of rapture." This is dogmatic theology, and it deals with aesthetics as a "theory about the Incarnation of God's glory and the consequent elevation of man to participate in that glory."[105]

We have already discussed Balthasar's development of the "rapture" or *ekstasis* of *eros* as one of the primary building blocks in his theory of form. Here it becomes the central determining feature of dogmatics as such: "This double and reciprocal *ekstasis* -- God's 'venturing forth' to man and man's to God -- constitutes the very content of dogmatics, which may thus rightly be presented as a theory of rapture: the *admirabile commercium et conubium* between God and man."[106] The theory of vision (fundamental theology) can in no way be detached

---

[102]*GL I*, 216-217.
[103]*GL I*, 125.
[104]*GL I*, 125.
[105]*GL I*, 125.
[106]*GL I*, 126.

from the theory of rapture (dogmatic theology). In Rahnerian terms this would be stated as the impossibility of dividing the subjective pole of revelation (the inner movement of grace elevating human subjectivity) from the objective (the historical revelation as such). This subjective/objective paradigm is also adopted by Balthasar. However, Balthasar develops this paradigm aesthetically to such an extent that the subjective and objective poles seem to coalesce in a single dynamic characterized by the reciprocal "give and take" between that which "raptures" and that which is "enraptured." According to Balthasar, this is especially true of theology: "In theology, there are no bare facts, which, in the name of an alleged objectivity of detachment, disinterestedness and impartiality, one could establish like any other worldly facts, without oneself being ... gripped so as to participate in the divine nature."[107] The theologian's "object" is the human participation in God seen as the unitary interplay between the dual movements of *eros* : the divine *eros* expressed in revelation and the human *eros* expressed in faith.[108]

C. The Form of Revelation and the Act of Faith.

All of this brings us to the question of the act of faith as such and how it is related to the form of revelation. The first thing to be noted is that, for Balthasar, given the close link he establishes between subjective faith and the objective pole of revelation, one must be careful about drawing too neat a distinction between the *fides qua* and the *fides quae* in the act of faith. It must be remembered that Balthasar sees Christian faith as an incorporation into the "faith" of Christ himself. Thus, as Balthasar states: "The *fides quae* of the Christian is the *fides qua* of Christ as he faces the Father, and even the Christian's *fides qua* lives from the radiance of this light of Christ."[109] The light of revelation meets and enraptures a human subjectivity whose eyes have been "trained" in the school of worldly form to recognize form and its qualities. Grace builds on this worldly knowledge in a supereminent manner and orients the mind's eye to a perception of God's revelation in Christ.

---

[107]*GL I*, 125.
[108]*GL I*, 126-127.
[109]*GL I*, 218.

A caution must be raised here. Balthasar insists that specifically Christian knowledge does not lie "hidden" in some antecedent manner only to suddenly come out into the light when it "recognizes" its teleological fulfillment in Christ. Balthasar does not see the human subject as being that transparent to itself even when engraced. The religious *a priori* remains a question mark for humanity and, at best, points to the tension and ambiguity inherent in its own frustrated *telos* . Therefore, Balthasar emphasizes the wholly unexpected quality of Christ's revelation and of the "shock" and scandal that it creates even in those people who have developed their spiritual senses in the light of grace.

Two errors are to be avoided here. The first error is to see revelation as a "pure paradox" having no connection with our antecedent worldly knowledge. The second error is to see in the analogy of being a too- smooth transition from worldly knowledge to the "knowledge" imparted by divine revelation. A better paradigm is to be drawn from the world of aesthetics, where a great work of art does not lose its unexpected freshness and uniqueness just because it flows from easily recognizable historical antecedents. The "divine art" in revelation both builds on nature and transcends it in a wholly unexpected manner.[110] It transcends worldly form, not by negating it and leaving it behind, but by transforming it from within and integrating it into a new spiritual plane. "Form," aesthetically conceived, becomes an indispensable theological category for upholding the analogy of being within the analogy of faith and for preserving the universality of reason without robbing revelation of its specificity. The specifically Christian "knowledge" which faith brings cannot be separated from the objective form of revelation in Christ. The religious *a priori* needs the theological *a priori* in order for *pistis* to be lifted into Christian *gnosis* .[111]

The two errors mentioned above, the "knowledge" of faith as pure paradox and the "knowledge" of faith which is a smooth transition from worldly expectations, translate into two different "kinds" of theology which also must be

---

[110]*GL I*, 164: "This state of things is best explained by analogy with aesthetic judgment, which registers with admiration the aesthetic necessity in the free creations of art: that they must be just so and not otherwise. Could not Bach have equally chosen a different third theme for a triple fugue, and have interwoven it with the other two in just as necessary a manner? We may answer yes in order to pay greater tribute to Bach's genius. But, aesthetically speaking, that would mean nothing. The study of aesthetic necessity starts with the strict givenness of the completed work."

[111]*GL I*, 167-168.

avoided. The first of these approaches views revelation in an overly positivistic sense as a set of "facts" or "data" which God has planted in history and invested with a certain credibility and evidentiary force. The purpose of these signs is to establish the credibility of revelation as coming from God, and, therefore, its utter reliability. It makes little difference for our analysis here as to how rationalistic such a schema becomes. It makes little difference whether the recognition of the credibility of the signs is a purely rational process, or a process that is, in itself, already a part of the movement of grace and, therefore, part of the act of faith as such. What Balthasar wants to point out is that these "signs," in and of themselves, are not seen in such a theology as a self-revealing of God himself, but "pointers" to a deeper, eternal truth which God wants to impart. Balthasar states:

> Thus understood, the rationality of faith rests totally on the persuasive character of the revelatory signs, their power to convince man's reason: the credibility of the witnesses is verifiable, as is the imperative to believe a credible witness. But in this way the divine witness becomes one (exceptional) case among others; the divine quality does not leap into prominence, neither on the side of insight or vision nor on the side of faith. This is an anthropological theory of faith which dispenses with the philosophical dimension, the faith-theory of positive theology as developed primarily by the Baroque scholasticism and Neo-Scholasticism of the Jesuits.[112]

The second approach which is to be avoided (in its extremes) has much deeper roots in the tradition and a higher degree of theological legitimacy. This approach can be roughly characterized as an analysis of the act of faith as the engraced "completion" of the natural inner dynamism of human cognition. Here we encounter Augustinian illuminism with its equating of Being with "Light" (the "Word" of Being) and the participation of human rationality in this Light-Word. All human longing, all of the disquietude of the human heart, is part of the general human dynamism toward God who is seen as ultimate transcendence. For Thomas as well as for Augustine, theology rests on the same two foundations: 1) the inner dynamism of human cognition with its determination to press on to the vision of God; and 2), God's revelation seen as the "bestowal of the innermost light of Being."[113] The modern heirs to this tradition are many (Blondel, Marechal, Rousselot) and they argue from an analysis of the dynamics of human subjectivity

---

[112]*GL I*, 148.
[113]*GL I*, 149.

to the "appropriateness and reasonableness of the transcendent faith-act."[114] But this analysis is short-circuited in its extreme manifestation in the subjectivism of modern thought.[115] In this approach the objective form of revelation loses its own proper "light" and is swallowed up within the inner dynamic of the human spirit as it seeks to "exteriorize" its own inner, formal categories. Revelation runs the risk in this schema of being reduced to a mere mythopoetic projection which may exhibit a powerful appeal, but is, in the final analysis, simply a projection of the formal structures of human subjectivity:

> The question remains whether on such a view the objective foundation of the specifically Christian fact is as successful as the subjective foundation, and whether this whole orientation is not constantly threatened by a secret and, occasionally, even by an open bondage to philosophy which makes the internal standard of the striving spirit, even where it is conceived only as "emptiness" or "void", as *cor inquietum, potentia oboedientialis*, and so on, nevertheless to be somehow the measure of revelation itself. ... All the historical positive aspects of revelation from the outset tend to dissolve (spiritually and allegorically) into the elements of an enlightened Christian supernatural "philosophy".[116]

What both the subjectivist and positivist theologies share is a view of the objective form of revelation as a mere sign or pointer to the eternal truth or goodness which lies "behind" or "beyond" the sign. The sign itself is of only provisional and transitory value, and can be dispensed with once a "direct" mystical contact with the divine has been made and faith is replaced by "vision" - a narrow

---

[114]*GL I*, 149.

[115]*GL I*, 177. That Balthasar is only criticizing here the exaggerations of this aspect of the tradition is clear from numerous citations, of which the following is representative: "The modernistic tendency ... represents an exaggeration of the subjective-existential light of faith, as described by Thomas."

[116]*GL I*, 149-150. This is the basic reason for Balthasar's much publicized criticism of Rahner's transcendental theology. However, this aspect of the rift between Balthasar and Rahner has been greatly exaggerated. Balthasar himself frequently engages in a transcendental analysis of human subjectivity. Furthermore, Balthasar has made it clear that his primary objection to the transcendental analysis of human subjectivity is its proclivity to be used in the extreme subjectivist manner described above. However, it hardly seems fair to judge Rahner's theology by its extremes. It goes without saying that Balthasar would not want to be judged based on the "objectivist" and authoritarian extremes to which his theology has been taken by many "conservatives." The real, substantive differences between Balthasar and Rahner revolve around what Balthasar perceives to be a lack of aesthetic and dramatic qualities in Rahner's Christology and Trinitarian theology. For a good discussion of the differences between Rahner and Balthasar see: "Balthasar and Rahner on the Theology of Nature and Grace" *Communio* (Thematic issue, Summer,1991).

definition of faith which Balthasar rejects. In the positivist approach the "signs" do not stand under the light of divine Being, but merely point to it. In the subjectivist approach the "signs," according to Balthasar, "become so transparent to this light that in the sign only the signified is of interest, and in the historical only that which is valid for eternity."[117]

The positivist approach is animated by a concern for the truth of revelation and its ultimate credibility founded upon God's authoritative truthfulness. The subjectivist approach is concerned with God as the "goal" of human transcendence and the final resolution of all inner inquietude. Thus, God is seen under the aspect of the good as the infinite fulfillment of all human dynamisms and desires. What both lack is the element of the beautiful, which alone can save their approaches from the "parallelism of ostensive sign and signified interior light."[118] Beauty, as we have noted, is the radiance which shines forth from within form itself. Beauty is not an external light which shines upon form rendering it beautiful, but a quality which breaks forth from the "comeliness" and splendor of the form itself. When "truth" is considered without the quality of beauty, then it degenerates into a formalistic pragmatism that captivates no one. As Balthasar puts it, "the very conclusions are no longer conclusive."[119] And our relationship to the good becomes utilitarian and hedonistic whenever the good is robbed of *voluptas*. Only when revelation is perceived in its integrity as a "form," which is the unity of outward expression and inner splendor, do we see a way out of the positivist/subjectivist dialectic. Balthasar states:

> Only the apprehension of an expressive form in the thing can give it that depth- dimension between its ground and its manifestation which, as the real *locus* of beauty, now also opens up the ontological *locus* of the truth of being, and frees the striver, allowing him to achieve the spiritual distance that makes a beauty rich in form desirable in its being-in-itself ... and only thus worth striving after.[120]

All of this leads us directly back to where Balthasar wants us to be: the center of Christian revelation in God's visible, historical, revelation. In Christ

---

[117]*GL I*, 150.
[118]*GL I*, 151.
[119]*GL I*, 19.
[120]*GL I*, 152.

content and form are inseparable. The theological *a priori* cannot be detached from its ultimate foundation in this objective content. The *lumen fidei*, that inner divine light which bathes the mind's eye, must constantly turn to the concrete object of revelation in order to find its realization. And once it does reach its final realization in its object, the *lumen fidei* brings with it a change in our ability to perceive the divine form. We are given the spiritual eyes necessary to recognize the light which shines forth from the form of revelation. However, here we must be careful not to conceive of this relationship in an overly temporal manner. One does not "first" receive an "inner light" which "implicitly contains within itself the whole substance of faith," and only "subsequently" have this already complete "knowledge" brought to the surface of consciousness through an encounter with the object of revelation. Revelation, in such an approach, is reduced to the level of a mere "catalyst."[121] "It is much truer," states Balthasar, "to say that the readiness of the interior light is wholly oriented toward the objective form of revelation .. so as to arrive at its content."[122] The "inner light" is, in some sense, "incomplete" without its objective fulfillment. And this holds true even for the non-Christian. In some mysterious sense, states Balthasar, "every person outside Christianity who receives a share in this interior light of faith receives it only by the objective mediation of Christ's atoning life, death and Resurrection."[123] Furthermore, the "infused" quality of the

---

[121]*GL I*, 177.

[122]*GL I*, 177.

[123]*GL I*, 180; Se also, 167-171. Even here Balthasar emphasizes that we are not talking about non-Christians reaching salvific faith through some sort of unmediated, direct illumination from God. Balthasar is quite clear that the theological *a priori* must be granted to all, since all are called to the vision of God. But this "inner light" is mediated to the non-Christian through the forms and constructions of the various myths, philosophies, religions and "mystical" disciplines. This creates a certain tension in Balthasar's theology since he is now caught between the need to emphasize the uniqueness of God's revelation in Christ as well as the integrating power of this revelation through the universal offer of grace. Does not the analogy of Being and the breaking down of the old scholastic two-tiered hierarchy of nature and supernature imply a more positive evaluation of non-Christian religions than what Balthasar is willing to grant? Has Balthasar taken seriously his own theology of grace or does he occasionally continue to fall back into the comfort of the old distinctions? Here Balthasar makes a clear distinction between the "forms" of the various "religions" and the form of Christian revelation. The former are a purely human projection and creation while the latter is from God. Balthasar insists that this distinction is necessary in order for the incarnation to "stand out from the crowd," as it were. Therefore, immediately after Balthasar states that non-Christian religions can mediate the "light" of revelation, he adds that this only happens because these "forms" are "reflecting back" on to the believer his or her own projected "inner light." But this inner light, bereft of the truth of the singular Incarnation, falls prey to a host of possible blunders which Balthasar lists. Thus, there is no substitute for the singular Incarnation of God in Christ.

lumen fidei must be maintained against all those who would treat faith within the boundaries of a purely human possibility. As Balthasar puts it: "As long as he [the Christian] continues to treat 'his' faith as his own possibility, he still does not believe at all."[124]

The emphasis Balthasar places on the role of the objective pole of revelation can be further illustrated by comparing the specific nature of the light of reason with the light of faith. In Thomistic epistemology the agent intellect, in order to attain the true realization of the known object, must always resort to the *conversio ad phantasma* . Balthasar appeals here to Thomas's development of the sensible foundation of all knowledge and the constant need of even the abstracting intellect to return to the concrete image.[125] Likewise, the infused, inner light of faith which grace brings must always seek its ground and orientation in the objective content of God's revelation -- i.e., it too must return to the level of the concrete in order to reach its own deepest realization. Neither the light of faith nor the light of the agent intellect will ever become objectified as such, but can only be known formally in the act of knowing the object. However, here the similarities between the light of faith and the light of reason breaks down:

> In the act of knowledge what shines forth at the *conversio ad phantasma* is the light of being, an "aptitude" possessed by the *intellectus agens* as such. But in man's turning to Christ what shines forth is not man's own aptitude for faith, but rather Christ's aptitude to give to the inept a share in his own light and power.[126]

In an act of knowledge from within the light of reason both subject and object are "carried" in the same light of Being. It is Being that forms an "identity" between knower and known. However, the light of faith stems entirely from within the object of revelation and draws the subject out of his/her isolation and into the field created by revelation. What takes place is a progressive incorporation of the believer into the "world" of the objective pole of revelation rather than the other

---

[124]*GL I*, 180.

[125]*GL I*, 170: "On the plane of revelation the light of faith and the form of revelation may together constitute that synthesis which according to Aquinas corresponds, on the plane of natural perception, to the encounter of the senses and the light of the intellect. If the ontological light of the active intellect can become objectified only by turning to the phantasm, God's supreme light can become objectified only when it falls, not on any random worldly phenomenon ..., but on *the* phenomenon which God's light has fashioned for itself in order truly to make its appearance *there* and not elsewhere."

[126]*GL I*, 181.

way around.[127] "We must," states Balthasar, "beware of vitalistic comparisons, which suggest that, in the act of faith, subject and object 'float' together in a common medium of 'divine life'."[128] We must not, according to Balthasar, lose sight of the "permanent onesidedness" inherent within the process of Christian revelation. The initiative is God's. It is God who grants to us a share and a participation in God's very Being through God's "act" in Jesus Christ. Christ is the "Primal Image," the Archetype from which the *lumen fidei* receives its power. What unites the believer with God is not Being -- that would make Being antecedent to both God and world -- but the very Spirit of God.[129]

This leads us to our final point in Balthasar's discussion of form and revelation. Since it is the Spirit of God which binds the believer to God by drawing the believer into the "field" of the objective form of revelation, then it follows that the "credibility" of this form does not reside in any worldly scheme or thought. Granted, the objective form of revelation has its worldly analogue, as we have seen, in Being as expressive image and Being as an *eros* toward the other. Nevertheless, revelation does not depend on these worldly analogues for its inner warrant and credibility. David Tracy is, therefore, somewhat correct in his assessment that, for Balthasar, all worldly analogues for revelation bear only an *ad hoc* apologetical or "correlational" value.[130] Such analogues are important, according to Balthasar, for two basic reasons. The first reason is somewhat pragmatic. The mere fact that one has recourse to analogy acts as a "limit concept" that helps to preserve us from falling into an extrinsicist view of the nature-grace

---

[127]*GL I*, 215-216: "The light of faith cannot for a moment be thought of or even experienced as a merely immanent reality in our soul, but solely as the radiance resulting from the presence in us of a *lumen increatum*, a *gratia increata*, without our ever being able to abstract from God's Incarnation when considering this light and this grace. Now, if this light and this grace possess the form of Christ, then what is luminous about them is also determined by the objective form, and there is no possibility, for reasons of religious interiority, of dismantling this synthesis instituted by God. ... It is impossible to dissect the objective Christ into a form, whose sole property it is to 'appear' externally, and a formless light which is what remains for the religious interiority."

[128]*GL I*, 181.

[129]*GL I*, 196: "This identity of God's Spirit, uniting subject and object (whether it is understood more as the work of the person of the Spirit or of the whole trinitarian spiritual God), is the very foundational possibility which cannot be absent from any conscious and psychological act of faith and which cannot be excluded from the consciousness of the act of faith as being unimportant or irrelevant. 'In your light we see light.'"

[130]David Tracy, "The Uneasy Alliance Reconceived: Catholic Theological Method, Modernity, and Postmodernity," *Theological Studies*, (1989), 565.

relationship. Second, and more importantly, they point to the deep onto-aesthetic integrity of the world in its status as *God's* creation. However, to "tie down" the credibility of revelation to these analogues (with their inner probative force and existential power), is to establish something extrinsic to revelation as its antecedent principle, and, therefore, its "judge." Christ, the Primal Image and Archetype, is finally credible only as the manifestation "in the flesh" of God's triune love. The worldly analogues of "expressive image" and "*eros* " do not render the Christ form "credible," but, rather, "recognizable." And it is this distinction that differentiates Balthasar's approach to the relationship between revelation and its analogues from that of most critical correlationalists, like David Tracy. Balthasar, it seems to me, would argue for the fact that the worldly analogues for revelation, as well as revelation's historical antecedents, create the conditions for revelation's intelligibility but not its credibility. The credibility of the form only comes when one has been granted the "eyes of the Spirit," when one has been infused with the "sensuality" of the Spirit and the ability to recognize the specifically divine element radiating from the historical Christ form. Here we must go back to Balthasar's repeated insistence that it is only the category of the beautiful that compels us to respect the "truthfulness" of truth, and to desire and love the "goodness" of the good. Without beauty, truth and goodness "lose their salt" and are reduced to a merely functional status, bereft of joy. Likewise, in revelation, the worldly analogues and the historical antecedents help us to "recognize" its basic intelligibility and to "acknowledge" its lofty moral message - perhaps even to recognize its divine origin - but only the inner radiance of the form itself can "compel" us to faith through its divine credibility. As long as faith remains within the realm of worldly "proofs" and apologetical warrants for faith, it remains a fundamentally anthropological affair with merely "psychologistic" roots. Specifically Christian faith, with its inner kerygmatic "force" and "certainty," is a divine gift and a thoroughly theandric act. It is the revelation of God's love that shocks us with its beauty and moves us toward its light. It is a beauty that gives credibility and force to the truth and goodness of revelation and causes us to yearn for and to love the divinity of the divine. As Balthasar puts it: *Glaubhaft ist nur Liebe* ("only love is credible"). This is why fundamental and dogmatic theology can never be artificially separated. Apologetics is, at its root, simply a well explicated dogmatics.

We have seen how Balthasar's development of his theological aesthetic and his theory of form tries to stake out a "middle path" between a rationalistic theological extrinsicism on the one hand, and a subjectivistic, reductionistic "transcendentalism" on the other. Balthasar develops a concept of form that emphasizes the inner credibility of the object of revelation - an object with worldly analogues and historical antecedents but which, ultimately, brings its own warrant for faith. The topic of Balthasar's relationship with "correlational" theology was also briefly discussed. All of this leaves us with two fundamental questions which need to be answered in the next two chapters. The first question is how the form of revelation is mediated to us in its scriptural attestation. The second question deals with how the Church can mediate revelation and, therefore, form the proper context for all Christian theology.

Chapter Five:
The Scriptural Mediation of the Form of Revelation

In the preceding chapter Balthasar's development of the concept of "form" was examined in its relationship to revelation. However, this analysis would not be complete if we did not examine Balthasar's analysis of how the "form" of revelation is mediated to the believer down through the centuries. The two primary ways, according to Balthasar, that the form of revelation is mediated is through Scripture and Church. It will be shown that these two mediating agencies are intrinsically related to one another, as well as to the form that they seek to mediate.

The primary concern of this chapter will be an analysis of Balthasar's approach to biblical exegesis with an eye to how his overall theology of revelation guides his exegesis as it confronts the issues raised by modern, historical-critical approaches. The relationship between Balthasar's development of the concept of form and his approach to the Scriptures as a mediation of this form, will become clear in the course of the analysis. Our concern here is not to engage in an in-depth analysis of all of the major trends in modern biblical exegesis. That would demand a major study in its own right. Our only concern is with how the form of revelation is made "contemporaneous" to the believer through the historical medium of the Scriptures. The bulk of the chapter will concentrate on Balthasar's critique of the Enlightenment presuppositions that undergird the historical-critical approach to exegesis. Balthasar's own "aesthetic" approach to exegesis will be developed in the midst of this critique.

A. Enlightenment presuppositions of modern exegesis.[1]

The first thing to be noticed is that for Balthasar exegesis is a *theological* activity carried out from within the faith of the living Church.[2] And it is a theological activity precisely because the Scriptures themselves are self-consciously theological creations and demand to be dealt with on that level. Therefore, contrary to what many might think, exegesis is not a branch of the philological or historical sciences. Biblical exegesis might use these resources, but it is at root a theological activity born out of the substance of faith.[3] For Balthasar, "exegesis is the progressive returning of everything history has formed back to the original Light and the interpretation of it by reference to this origin."[4] This "origin" is Christ and we must accept him within the totality of the image the Scriptures present us with just as we accept a great work of art on its own terms. The exegete is, therefore, analogous to the art critic: "The point of access to the artist's genuine inspiration must be an inspiration akin to the artist's. Scholarly enquiry must become contemplation."[5]

But such theological/contemplative exegesis requires that one place oneself, as much as is humanly possible, within the world of the text as it stands and to allow oneself to be assimilated and transformed into its milieu. This requires an affirmation of the integrity of the text's theological/canonical unity as the ground of

---

[1]Cf. Balthasar, *Theo-Drama II*, (San Francisco: Ignatius Press, 1990) 420. Balthasar never provides us with a succinct definition of what he means by the term "Enlightenment." He uses it almost always in a narrow and pejorative sense as an intellectual movement characterized by a reductionistic, naturalistic and rationalistic attack upon the idea of supernatural revelation as a basis for religion. Thus, he seems to define "The Enlightenment" in the Kantian sense of humanity "coming of age" from the state of prescientific and precritical infancy - a state characterized by a tendency to spurn one's own reason and to depend on an alleged revelation from God. For Balthasar, therefore, the Enlightenment is characterized by a kind of Promethean Titanism that replaces the integrity of the Christian revelation and the unified world-view it spawned, with a host of chaotic and secondary human ideologies. It is in this sense that this term will be used.

[2]*GL VII*, 103. Balthasar sees no substantive difference in form between the theology of the Bible and the later theology of the Church: "It has already become clear that theology in the Bible can have no fundamentally different form from later theology in the Church: each is an interpretative act of standing and circling around a midpoint that can indeed be interpreted, but is always in need of interpretation and has never been exhaustively interpreted."

[3]*GL I*, 536-538.
[4]*GL I*, 101-102.
[5]*GL I*, 102.

possibility for Christian exegesis. And for Balthasar, much of modern critical exegesis continues to ignore both the reality and the importance of establishing this overall unity of biblical revelation because it has changed little in its fundamental assumptions since its beginnings in the Enlightenment.[6] Therefore, Balthasar's critique of the Enlightenment is the key to understanding his critique of modern, historical-critical exegesis. This critique revolves around three main points: (1) the "naive realism" of the Enlightenment heritage and its subsequent polarization of "objective fact" and "subjective faith"; (2) its inability to appreciate the significance of the historical particularity of revelation; and (3) its chronic inability to preserve the theological unity of the canon within a heuristic, intratextual framework. Each of these topics will be dealt with in order.

1. Naive Realism. Jesus of History-Christ of Faith.

The cornerstone of Balthasar's critique of the Enlightenment's approach to exegesis is his criticism of the latter's attempt to divorce the process of exegesis from the living faith of the Church in some vain hope of producing a more "scientific" view of the historical Jesus.[7] This latter approach is predicated upon a pseudo-scientific distinction between "objective" historical fact (naturalistically and materialistically conceived) and "subjective" faith (mythologically conceived). And as we shall see, Balthasar rejects such an approach to scriptural exegesis since it is based upon a kind of "naive realism" that does not take into account the fact that human reason, even when it is reflecting upon "empirical facts," is itself grounded in culture.[8]

This naive, "dualistic" polarization of "empirical fact" and " subjective faith," as it applies to the process of biblical exegesis, carries with it some far-

---

[6]GL I, 533-535.

[7]GL I, 31-32: "One should first ask whether such attempts to work back 'scientifically' to real or alleged sources are not most useful when they once again demonstrate the indivisibility of the definitively expressed Word. ... And [this] would further suggest that the main fruits to be gathered from the very unfruitfulness and failure of the scientific experiment would be the ever clearer exigency of returning to the one thing necessary."

[8]Convergences, 51: "The theory which was favored at the beginning of our century - in which objective scientific method and subjective commitment were regarded as separable - even should it be applicable elsewhere, cannot be used here."

ranging consequences. For Balthasar, one of its most negative features is that it creates an immediate "tension" between the Jesus of history and the Christ of faith; in true "Humean" fashion everything that is not empirically reducible to naturalistic explanations must run counter to our "uniform" human experience and is therefore inherently questionable and suspect. Thus, "religious" interpretations of historical events, born out of the "bias" of faith and the "immaturity" of the precritical, mythopoetic mind, are not reliable. Accurate information about what "really" happened must be "retrieved" by systematically peeling back the layers of the scriptural onion until we reach some sort of historical nucleus which is transparent in its meaning to all rational minds. Balthasar has the following to say about such an approach:

> This [method] is usually the result of opposing a Jesus of history, who is perceived with anything but overwhelming clarity, to a Christ ... of faith. ... Such an either/or misses precisely the point which is here at stake and which alone can provide the bridge between the "historical-critical method" of an obstinate historical scientism (to which apparently only the theologians cling any more and which understandably can never attain to vision since it is already methodologically blind) and the way of faith which, because of the definition of faith it presupposes, is in no better position to attain to real vision. The "historical-critical" destruction of the form put forward by the Evangelists, for instance, only makes sense as an exercise if one supposes that faith ... as such can only be subjective and cannot correspond to any objective evidence.[9]

This "obstinate historical scientism," which Balthasar sees as the central methodological assumption of much of modern exegesis, sets within the heart of the theological act a moment of "methodic doubt" which can only cause theology to begin theologizing by questioning and doubting its own most essential sources. This leads us to a very straightforward question that is at the heart of Balthasar's critique: are we to pursue a hermeneutic of radical discontinuity between the Jesus of history and the Christ of faith in order to retrieve the former from the ecclesial distortions it is trapped in, or do we approach the scriptural and ecclesial witness as a unified "*Gestalt*" which is entirely credible in its own right and on its own terms as an explanation of who Jesus of Nazareth was?[10] Along these same lines one could pose a related question: is theology faced with a choice, in the area of biblical

---

[9]*GL I*, 466.
[10]*GL I*, 466; 536.

exegesis, between a "hermeneutic of suspicion" or a "hermeneutic of trust?"[11] This latter posing of the question is probably a more apt one since the position one adopts is usually a function of one's antecedent attitude toward the classical theological forms of the received tradition.[12] For Balthasar the choice is clear: methodologically speaking, "suspicion is an unprofitable attitude and the reverse of inclusive."[13] What is at stake in this debate, according to Balthasar, is nothing less than the fundamental trustworthiness of the Church's *kerygma* as well as faith in the abiding presence of the Holy Spirit in the Church's classical formulations of that same *kerygma* . Balthasar does not mince words here:

> Will we take seriously this reference which faith itself makes to the historical event? It seems we must, if, that is, we scrutinize critically the sources accessible to us and are willing to hear the *kerygma* of the primitive Church for what it claims to be: a testimony about the man Jesus Christ, who died and rose for us. But taking this testimony seriously will necessarily lead to the automatic dissolution of the dualistic Protestant position which

---

[11]The term "hermeneutic of suspicion" or "hermeneutic of trust," is used here in the sense outlined by Juan Luis Segundo, S.J. in, *The Liberation of Theology*, (Maryknoll, New York: Orbis, 1988), 9: "There must ... be four decisive factors in our [hermeneutic] circle. *Firstly* there is our way of experiencing reality, which leads us to ideological suspicion. *Secondly* there is the application of our ideological suspicion to the whole ideological superstructure in general and to theology in particular. *Thirdly* there comes a new way of experiencing theological reality that leads us to exegetical suspicion, that is, to the suspicion that the prevailing interpretation of the Bible has not taken important pieces of data into account. *Fourthly* we have our new hermeneutic, that is, our new way of interpreting the fountainhead of our faith." There are many elements of this analysis with which Balthasar would not disagree. Balthasar believes very strongly in the counter-cultural nature of the gospel and the need to confront the "powers" of this world with the "iconoclastic" message of Jesus Christ. Nor would Balthasar disagree with the idea that we must read the Scriptures with an eye toward their present day application. However, Segundo (as well as others) take this "suspicion" and apply it to the "ideological" forces that were already at work in the writing and formation of the Scriptures. Thus, it is possible in such an approach to assert that, in many ways, the "Christ of faith" that we find in the New Testament already represents the ideological distortions of the early Church. The task of historical criticism, therefore, is to "peel away" these "distorting" ecclesial ideologies and to lay bare the "real" historical Jesus. Once we retrieve the "historical Jesus" we are then free to bring our own concerns to the message and work of Jesus without the distorting mediation of ecclesial interpretation -- be that ecclesial interpretation intra-biblical or post-biblical. Cf. Segundo, *The Historical Jesus and the Synoptics*, (Maryknoll, New York: Orbis 1985), 28; 30-31. Also see: Hans Kung, *On Being a Christian* (New York: Doubleday, 1976), 119-126; 145-166. It is this use of "suspicion" to which Balthasar objects.

[12]Cf. Hans Urs von Balthasar, *Explorations in Theology I* , "The Place of Theology," 159-160.

[13]*Explorations in Theology I*, 159: "The theology of today must have such a certainty and fullness - derived from the eternal fullness of revelation, of the Spirit given at this time, and of the fullness of the tradition received - as to embrace the riches of past theology as a living thing, and to endow it with fresh vitality."

considers faith and reason to be irreconcilable and does not want to see that, in the theological domain, it is faith alone that can guarantee the full objective ("rational") knowledge of things as they really are.[14]

Thus, for Balthasar, it seems inconceivable that we can affirm, at one and the same time, the authoritative trustworthiness of the *kerygma* and a material distinction between that same *kerygma* and the historical events it purports to interpret with normative force. Either we will gradually come to see that there is no radical discontinuity between the "objective facts" of Jesus' life and the "subjective interpretation" of this life in the ecclesial witness, or we will gradually be made aware of the fundamentally untrustworthy character of the *kerygma* and simply abandon any notion of biblical normativity and ecclesial authority. But, according to Balthasar, the two poles of this contradictory situation cannot be maintained forever, as the history of exegesis in this century attests. Balthasar puts it as follows:

> A danger, it is true, is never far off when the existential dimension is played off against the "historical-critical" dimension (which occurs when the modern scientific concept of truth is accepted for theology) and the result is a "Christ of faith" versus an "historical Jesus." ... The figure which confronts us in Holy Scripture is more and more dissected in "historical-critical" fashion until all that is left of what was once a living organism is a dead heap of flesh, blood and bones.[15]

For Balthasar, it is not surprising that the so-called "quest for the historical Jesus" came to ruin insofar as it was a quest for transparent historical "facts" that would enable exegesis to become truly "scientific" and put an end to inter-confessional squabbling. The "facts" turned out to be not so transparent and the figure of Jesus became a curiously "plastic" thing which more or less corresponded with the prevailing *Zeitgeist* .[16] Balthasar summarizes this nicely:

> Protestant theology's sense of shock at the "non-existence" of a credible historical Jesus before and apart from faith resembles the shock experienced by the naive realist at the non-existence of the

---

[14]*GL I*, 536.

[15]*GL I*, 174.

[16]*GL I*, 533: "The 'historical Jesus' thus exposed presented the most varied faces, all of which more or less corresponded to modern expectations or ideals."

world in which he had "believed." The same un-philosophical shock then impels this theology to see "faith" as purely subjective.[17]

What is at issue here is not so much the *historical* "method" of modern exegesis (which is absolutely necessary), but the theological presuppositions which direct its use: "From Reimarus to Wrede ... the ruling presupposition was that only the historical-critical outlook, unprejudiced by faith, was in any position to see the truth of what happened at that time in Palestine."[18] The key phrase here is "unprejudiced by faith," since there is nothing inherent within the historical-critical method as such which makes it incompatible with the "contemplative" exegesis promoted by Balthasar.[19] However, it is Balthasar's contention that modern exegesis since the time of the Enlightenment has treated the faith-witness to Christ found in Scripture as a predominantly distorting force rather than an authentic and normative interpretative voice.

This predilection to see faith as "distorting" rather than enlightening is an assumption which has its roots in the naive realism of the Enlightenment's "empiricist" universe.[20] As we have seen, Balthasar sees in modern exegesis the full-flowering of the "naive realism" of the Enlightenment with its crude opposition between an empirical fact (the truly real) and its subjective interpretation (the questionably real).[21] In most forms of "naive realism" interpretations are not seen as necessarily wrong, they are simply not as reliable as the easily demonstrable fact. Unfortunately, the "easily demonstrable fact" is rare and is usually lacking in significance or interest for the deeper questions of human life. Most of the great problems which exercise our minds in the hurly-burly of the everyday world are complex, divergent problems and require extremely synthetic interpretations and responses. Furthermore, when one is dealing with facts of an "interpersonal" nature, i.e. all of the major human interactions that make life worth living, then interpretation is not only desirable, it is required by the nature of the "fact" itself.

---

[17]*GL I*, 535.

[18]*GL I*, 535.

[19]*GL I*, 542. We will return later in this chapter to the positive evaluation which Balthasar makes of the historical-critical method.

[20]*GL I*, 533-535.

[21]*GL I*, 533: "Historical biblical research was predominantly a child of the non-believing Enlightenment (Reimarus, Lessing), which directed its theses polemically against an uncritical belief in the Bible. They undertook to remove the layers that faith had painted over so as to expose beneath them the authentic historical figure of Jesus."

For Balthasar, brute facticity and cold logic remain uncompelling for the human being when they are divorced from questions of meaning, beauty and teleology. Indeed, when science, employing a methodology of reductionistic materialism, assumes a condescending "superior" attitude *vis-a-vis* more "subjective" pursuits (e.g. poetry, theology, philosophy), then it is science itself which is eventually destroyed by its own inherent nihilism.[22]

Theologically, this translates into an awareness of the limitations of a reductionistic kind of empiricism as an interpretive model for exegesis. For if the Scriptures are a kind of "spiritual" writing then they demand a kind of "spiritual exegesis" similar to, but not identical with, artistic interpretation.[23] Thus, the Scriptures, by their very nature, require an entering into their "subjectivity" in order to understand them on an "objective" level.[24] Contemplation of the unified christological form presented to us and for us by the biblical authors is essential if exegesis is to avoid treating the "data" concerning Christ in an overly "clinical" fashion, using the popular model of the "hard" physical sciences as a paradigm.

The "hard" scientific approaches (e.g. physics, chemistry etc.), which rely upon empirical observation and inductive logic, are well suited to the task of universalizing into general "laws" the uniformity of physical reactions and relations between discrete material phenomena. Furthermore, within these disciplines the goal of neutral objectivity, although ultimately impossible on a perfect scale, is nevertheless the desired ideal: phenomena are best analyzed when the observer's subjectivity filters information with the least amount of distortion. The paradigm for this kind of "scientific subjectivity," inherited from the Enlightenment and with us still, is that of the "detached observer" who does not allow such "subjective" heuristic categories as "*telos*," "significance," "meaning," and the like to intrude upon the observation of physical events. And even though there are very few logical positivists or "naive empiricists" still remaining within the modern scientific

---

[22]*GL I*, 19.

[23]Cf. Avery Dulles, S.J. *The Craft of Theology: From Symbol to System*, (New York: Crossroad, 1992). 73-74. Dulles, in a chapter entitled "The Uses of Scripture in Theology," includes Balthasar, along with Henri de Lubac, Louis Bouyer and Yves Congar, under the heading of "spiritual exegesis." I think he is essentially correct in this designation as well as in his clear implication that such "spiritual exegesis" is a central component of the theological tradition developed by *ressourcement* theologians.

[24]*GL I*, 85: "For exegesis historical expertise is, of course, needed: but to a far greater extent there is required the divining power of imaginative reconstruction ... - that youth of the heart which is able to feel at one with the historical and eternal youth of mankind."

community as such, nevertheless, there remains still a kind of unspoken bias in favor of Archimedean objectivity as the goal of science within the mass consciousness of western "pop" culture.[25] For Balthasar, it is this conception of science within popular consciousness, as we have inherited it from the naive realism of the Enlightenment, that has infected theological exegesis and has, in effect, "vulgarized" it. The Archimedean search for the "brute facticity" of the life of Jesus, purged of the "subjective distortions" of apostolic and post-apostolic theologizing, is, for Balthasar, every bit as "pedestrian" and "vulgar" as the naive quest of the crude, scientific empiricist for a materialistic, reductionistic explanation for all phenomena. It is a self-contradictory quest destined for futility. Balthasar states:

> Once this is grasped, the full futility becomes apparent of the efforts of those exegetes - whether they are believers or not - who strive to achieve something like a "neutral" photograph and tape-recording of the historical Jesus. Taking photographs is a physical event, and the equipment can by its nature capture nothing other than what is offered to it physically, even if this is the features of a human face. The writing of history, on the other hand, asks questions about meaning, and essentially it cannot obtain any more meaning than it itself is ready to deposit and invest in anticipation.[26]

For Balthasar, in spiritual and artistic matters there is no such thing as a "bald fact" which can be empirically observed and universalized into general laws without reference to the dialogical relationship between the "subjectivity" of the artistic object and the subjectivity of the observer. Thus, to speak once again in the categories of art, in order to truly "see" a piece of art one must, on some level, come to an approximation of what the artist sees. If you do not, then you have not even understood the piece on a purely "objective" level. The artistic object presents itself on an objective level precisely as that which is *given* for subjective

---

[25]Cf. Stanley L. Jaki, *The Purpose Of It All*, (Edinburgh: Scottish Academic Press, 1990) 29-31; 107-109. Jaki notes that the debate within the scientific community over the relationship between the oberver and the observed is still ongoing. There are strong voices in favor of the "anthropic principle," who champion the idea that the universe only comes to a certain reality when it is in fact "observed" by intelligent beings like ourselves, i.e. the "observer" in no way stands "outside of" the observed phenomenon nor should he. There are, however, voluble proponents of a more traditional observational realism who posit a fundamental distinction between observer and observed as the only way to preserve the exact sciences from utter solipsism. All of this post-Enlightenment debate on the philosophy of science is a healthy indication that science may yet rid itself of its crass, materialistic, "physicalism." Nevertheless, Jaki notes that popular culture still retains the old prejudices.

[26]*GL I*, 543.

appropriation. Nor is this a purely solipsistic appeal to "romantic" sentimentalism: "vision" in art and theology requires a certain rapture or ecstasy precisely because one has first been "enraptured" by the inherent, transforming power of the object itself.[27] Balthasar puts it as follows:

> A consideration of the presuppositions, now generally accepted, that govern a science dealing with spiritual and artistic works would have necessarily convinced the theologians of the naiveté of such a methodological conception [the empiricist assumption]. ... A work of art can be grasped objectively only within a certain subjectivity which corresponds to the work, and an analysis of its objective structure presupposes that such a realization of its content has at least occurred at some time even if such a moment has passed.[28]

2. The Significance of Historical Particularity for Biblical Exegesis.

This connection between theological and aesthetic sensibility, which forms the cornerstone of Balthasar's theology of revelation and which he uses to criticize the naive realism of the Enlightenment, also leads us into the second major area of Balthasar's critique of the Enlightenment's approach to exegesis: the dark cloud of suspicion which Enlightenment thinkers cast over historical particularity as a suitable vehicle for supernatural revelation of the kind found in the Bible. For Balthasar, art and theology are connected by their dual concern for "*das Ganze im Fragment*," i.e. the search for the universal and necessary "truth" within a particular, unique, and wholly gratuitous "form." Indeed, to go a step further, Balthasar would say that the "whole" is not simply *in* the "fragment" (this is a dualistic and latently "docetic" way of thinking), but rather, the "whole" *is* the "fragment" and is expressed precisely *as* "fragment." Balthasar states:

> In order to know how God heals that which is not whole, one must learn from him himself that man is his creaturely word which has its existence in his eternal Word, and that God, so that his covenant and his dialogue with man should not be broken off, would rather let the heart of his eternal Word break on the cross. Thus, the whole *in* the fragment only because the whole *as* the fragment.[29]

---

[27]*GL I*, 125-126.

[28]*GL I*, 535.

[29]Balthasar, *A Theological Anthropology*, (New York: Sheed and Ward, 1967), 233.

As in a work of art where the "universal meaning" is not to be found behind, underneath or "in" the work but precisely through and with the work, so too in theology we see the "content" of the divine revelation precisely within the particularity of the historical events that express it. In the case of revelation, "particularity" is not the opposite of "universality," nor is "matter" the opposite of "spirit." God is indeed the "Wholly Other" but precisely for this reason he is the "Not-Other" (*Non- Aliud*).[30] Therefore, there exists a deep and abiding analogy between God and creation such that God is able to "speak" clearly and simply to his creatures.[31] Here we see the deep connection between Balthasar's analogical, aesthetic, theology and his approach to biblical exegesis:

> My "method," in contrast to that of the Protestants, is neither dialectic, as Luther's necessarily was, nor is it Hegel's "identity," developed from dialectics. It is something in between: analogy. Man is essentially "God's image." Therefore he can by his own power raise his thoughts to the archetype ... but can approximate it only from a great distance. The various biblical theologies about Christ are merely circling his unattainable image, *ana ton ano Christon.*[32]

The "Gestalt-giving" power of God's Spirit is able to transform historical particularity into a timeless and universal testament about the deep theandric meaning of these events for all peoples everywhere. Here we see that the category of "uniqueness" does not necessarily always mean "idiosyncratic." In theology, as in art, the uniqueness of particularity is far from being an obstacle to universality - it is, in fact, the only way to express it concretely. Christ is *the* "concrete universal" toward which all of history points and in which all of history is fulfilled.[33]   In the

---

[30]*GL I*, 459: "God ... is indeed the "Wholly Other"; but, precisely for this reason, he is also the "Not-Other" (*Non- Aliud*). ... God is able, therefore, to reveal in Christ at once God and man. ... Yet this occurs in such a way that the relativity of the human (as creaturely) does not appear to be oppressed and violated by the simultaneous absoluteness of the divine."

[31]Balthasar, "From the Theology of God to Theology in the Church," *Communio* IX (1982), 195. Balthasar's states: "God speaks in his Son so simply that his words do not grow out of date with the passing of time and do not have to be replaced by others. A shepherd is still a shepherd and always will be, a vineyard is forever a vineyard. A way is a way, truth is truth, and life is life." 214.

[32]Hans Urs Von Balthasar, "Response To My Critics," *Communio* V (1978), 71.

[33]Cf. *"From the Theology of God,"* 216. Balthasar states: "Theology cannot maintain that God's Covenant with Israel was only one of the many ways in which God has had communion with man, for the Covenant with Israel is a unique election which led to the uniqueness of Christ. Theology must sustain the *skandalon* entailed in the truth that Jesus is the concrete universal."

very particularity of Jesus' finitude we encounter the infinite.[34] Indeed, Christ is the center and norm of all history to such an extent that there is nothing in the course of history which has not *already* found its consummation in his life, death and resurrection. As Balthasar puts it: "With the ascension of the Son to the Father, to his throne at the right hand of God, the end is already conceived as present, and all that is still to follow can only be the making known of this end and its establishment in historical time."[35]

Balthasar is critical of the Enlightenment's attempt to ground its notion of "inevitable human progress" in a contrast between the supposedly "linear" nature of biblical time with the "cyclic" nature of time in most other religions. According to Balthasar, even in the Bible time is conceived of as a "falling away" from God and a "return" to God. Thus, all time flows from God and to God and the fundamental "stages" of salvation history (creation-fall, incarnation-redemption, parousia-eschaton) do not contradict this basic pattern.[36] The difference for the Christian is in the radically altered interpretation of the importance of time and "materiality" in light of the Incarnation. Salvation is no longer conceived of as a "flight" from time in order to escape its "illusions" and thereby effect a "return" to the eternal God. Christ has taken time into himself and transformed it from within. Christ is now the "place" where God has "time" for the world.[37] The eternal One is present *now* in Christ and in his Church. Thus, the "return" to God has already been effected by Christ and all that remains is for the reality of this return to be made known through the lives of Christians who share even now in the eternal glory of the Christ who reigns over history.

We can see from the foregoing the heavily patristic flavor of Balthasar's christology: Jesus is the Word of God become flesh - essentially a christology "from above" that accentuates the "Gestalt-giving" power of the divine *kenosis* in

---

[34]*GL I*, 155. Balthasar notes: "Indeed, through the mysterious dialectic whereby Jesus' external, spatially and temporally conditioned finitude is transcended (which is the condition of the coming of the Holy Spirit), ... all that is interior, invisible, spiritual and divine becomes accessible to us."

[35]Cf. *A Theological Anthropology*, 112. Balthasar also notes: "Christ establishes in his earthly life the absolute norm for the world's time." 113.

[36]*A Theological Anthropology*, 110.

[37]Cf. Balthasar, *A Theology of History*, New York: Sheed and Ward, 1963. 34: "Hence the Son, who has time, in the world, for God, is the point at which God has time for the world. Apart from the Son, God has no time for the world, but in him he has **all** time. In him he has time for all men and all creatures: in relation to him it is always Today."

its transformation of historical particularity into a universally valid revelation.[38] All historical events, all of humanity's religious aspirations are, at root, "*logoi spermatikoi*" and, as such, are preparations for the preaching of the gospel.[39] It is easy to see, therefore, why Balthasar wants to establish the importance of historical particularity as an adequate vehicle for a universally *normative* supernatural revelation. And theology deals with the uniqueness of Christian particularity in two basic ways: (1) in the necessary particularity of the historical events of revelation that it reflects upon, and (2) in the uniqueness of God's revelation in Christ precisely as the revelation of an utterly gratuitous divine action. Balthasar underscores the inescapability of this particularity: "An historical event as well as a great 'unique' work of art can be an object of scientific research, and thereby of progressive knowledge as well - without the object ever being really 'worked out', because the character of uniqueness (and, to that extent, incomparability) belongs to its essence." [40]

To downplay the importance of the particularity of God's historical "handing over" of himself in the life of Jesus of Nazareth is to run the risk of robbing God's revelation of its essential gratuity.[41] And it is precisely this gratuity that lends the biblical revelation its particular "weight" or substance. Once this particularity is abandoned the gratuity of the events is sure to follow. Biblical religion then loses its "salt" and is of no interest to anyone. The Enlightenment, according to Balthasar, profoundly misunderstood the particularistic and interpersonal quality of God's gratuitous love (as evidenced in biblical religion) as a form of tribal myth- making among "precritical" peoples. However, to submit the Scriptures to a "demythologizing" process in order to arrive at universal and generic religious truths shared by all religions is nothing less than the destruction of biblical religion at its root. For there is ultimately no way to "justify" the "scandal" of gratuitous, elective love before the bar of Enlightenment rationalism: like Dante's mysterious love for Beatrice, or Kierkegaard's devotion to Regina, the mystery of

---

38 *"From the Theology of God,"* 216. Balthasar states: "Theology cannot maintain that exegesis requires that christology be merely from below. This christology never reaches a christology from above, in which, namely, the Word of God becomes flesh. This view ignores the essential claim which Jesus made, to be himself the Word of God, a claim which we can already ascertain in the synoptics."

39 *"From the Theology of God,"* 215.

40 *Convergences*, 51-52.

41 *Truth is Symphonic*, 44-45.

love's gratuity remains forever opaque to the rationalistic and reductionistic categories of Enlightenment reason.[42] The sheer gratuity and particularity of God's love poured forth in Christ is an unfathomable concept for the "lowest common denominator" rationality of the generic, deistic religious philosophy of the 18th and 19th centuries. Jesus is not rejected out of hand by the deistic thinker, but his life is redefined in nontraditional ways: no longer is his life seen as *the* theandric event *par excellence* which is constitutive of universal salvation as an efficient cause, rather, he is now viewed as one religious "prophet" among many who simply reveals something to us about God's character.[43]

It is here, according to Balthasar, that we see the fateful turn taken by exegesis as a direct result of the Enlightenment's distrust of historical "positivity" as "mythological" and therefore as an unsuitable vehicle for supernatural revelation. Once the uniqueness of Christian particularity is relegated to the periphery of theology (if not simply rejected) as an unimportant "vestigial" myth that may be excised without damage to the overall theological organism, then any hope of developing a truly profound christology crumbles before our eyes. Balthasar summarizes this point as follows in a lengthy quote worthy of repeating in its entirety:

> Through the "demythologizing" examination of Scripture, the figure of Jesus fell apart. Inconsistencies, for example, in the accounts of the resurrection, led to doubt in the attested facts, including the Resurrection itself. The miracles could have been invented or at least strongly exaggerated. The sayings of Jesus may have been stylized and elevated to a greater authority than he himself claimed. The infancy narrative may have been added from legends. The meaning of his death on the Cross and its assessment by Christ himself is uncertain. Similarly uncertain is the exact significance of his words and gestures at the Last Supper. Through such questioning of the texts (contrary to their clear intention - but the text is "conditioned by the times", the enlightener knows better), the figure of Jesus pales to that of the founder of a religion, comparable

---

[42]*A Theological Anthropology*, 187. Balthasar states: "Historically, this absolute election of a single spiritual person takes place only within the sphere of biblical revelation. .... Only from the free uniqueness of God can an 'exclusive' love between persons justify itself before the universal reason: as a decision which is not provisional, but final and irrevocable."

[43]*GL I*, 561. Balthasar sums this up as follows: "The Enlightenment excludes all positivities in rationalistic fashion and its thought aims at universal logical concepts, and the consequence of this is that the Enlightenment likewise subsumes supernatural revelation as a whole under a universal ('natural') conception of revelation which, whether consciously or unconsciously, necessarily dissolves christology itself."

to other founders. His incomparable uniqueness that cannot be mastered by reason disappears. He becomes a perhaps significant moral paradigm in a "religion within the bounds of unaided reason."[44]

The historical origins of the Enlightenment's distrust of "accidental historical truth" as a vehicle for a universally applicable divine revelation cannot be evaluated here in detail, nor its complicated relationship with the Enlightenment's respect for the empirical "fact."[45] Suffice it to say that, despite the respect that the Enlightenment showed for the particular, empirically verifiable "fact," the Christian claim to universality was rendered suspect by the discovery of the new world, as well as post-reformation religious wars and interconfessional condemnations.[46] Furthermore, the Christian narrative is not "empirically verifiable" in its "miraculous" and "supernatural" elements. Thus, these are not "facts" in any meaningful, empirical sense. A universal God must reveal himself universally and, for the Enlightenment intellectual, reason, "unaided" and "unencumbered" by particularistic supernatural revelations, was the doorway to universal religious truth. Revelation is possible, but it must appeal to the certain and universal principles of reason in order to be in any way proportionate to the infinite God who is being revealed. Finite, categorical, historical events are, by definition, not capable of universalization since every historical event is totally conditioned by its cultural time-boundedness. The gospel must then be reinterpreted without its particularistic "supernatural" accretions in order to arrive at its "true," universal meaning. The Bible, therefore, was for Enlightenment thinkers like Lessing religiously "significant" without necessarily being religiously "normative." Thus, as was the case with the project to reinterpret the figure of Jesus, Enlightenment

---

[44]*A Short Primer*, 34-35.

[45]For what follows concerning the historical development of the Enlightenment's approach to scripture I am indebted to Hans Frei, *The Eclipse of Biblical Narrative* (New Haven: Yale University Press, 1974). Frei develops in great detail a coherent analysis of the Enlightenment's approach to exegesis - an analysis which is strikingly similar to Balthasar's concern for the narrative integrity of the biblical texts. I turn to Frei here because he develops in systematic fashion a historical analysis of this period's approach to exegesis with which Balthasar simply assumes the reader is familiar. Balthasar will draw freely from this history, e.g. an analysis of Semler or Reimarus or Bultmann, without ever developing a full-blown "history of exegesis" as such.

[46]*A Short Primer*, 34. Balthasar puts it succinctly: "In great part, the Enlightenment was certainly brought about by the quarreling among Christians. Behind the 'denominations' people sought a position that could neutralize the opposition of denominations by attempting to reduce them to the level of criteria that can stand their ground before human reason. The correlation of the figure of Christ and the faith of the Church ... was broken off."

thinkers did not reject the Bible out of hand - these were, after all, men who thought of themselves as still, in some sense, "Christian." They simply reinterpreted the Bible as "containing" religious truths which are intelligible as examples of generally discernible human religious truths.[47] In other words, the truth or falsehood of biblical claims was now to be determined by their conformity to universally accepted truths of human religious consciousness. The Bible itself, especially in its highly particularistic claims about supernatural revelation, is not the standard of its own credibility; this credibility is now to be sought outside of the Bible within the "truths" established by universalizing Enlightenment reason. It is then a short step to more deistic, theocentric theologies as opposed to salvation-historical, Christ centered theologies.[48] Hans Frei, in a statement that echoes Balthasar's analysis of this era, summarizes this development as follows:

> The religious dispensability of the Bible did not mean that it was meaningless but only that the criterion of its religious significance had to come from somewhere else. The meaningfulness of the Bible depended on a broader religious context than its own specific pronouncements or beliefs. Lessing's plea that the Bible be seen to *contain* religion rather than *define* it was typical of the position that the Bible, though not religiously indispensable, is nonetheless religiously meaningful.[49]

Balthasar sees in the philosophy of Lessing the quintessential expression of this fundamental attitude toward historical positivity. For, according to Lessing, it is not only philosophically dubious, but also personally dangerous, to chance one's eternal salvation based on an allegiance to a "particular" revelation. What if you are wrong? What if it is someone else's revelation that is the "true" one and yours is "wrong?" How can the truth claims of these competing revelations be adjudicated?[50] Out of this confusion Lessing, and most of the Enlightenment as well, reached the understandable conclusion that the "contingent historical truths"

---

[47]*The Eclipse of Biblical Narrative*, 124-125. Frei states: "Everyone who believed that the sense of the gospel narratives is the history of Jesus the Messiah believed also that the notion of historical salvation or revelation is itself meaningful. On the other hand, people who believed that monotheism, immortality, and the realization of man's happiness through altruism are the substance of man's religion, equally available to all men of all times without any special revelation, discerned this as the true sense of the gospel narratives, the messianic history being merely their outward trapping."

[48]*The Eclipse of Biblical Narrative*, 90-124.

[49]*The Eclipse of Biblical Narrative*, 118.

[50]Cf. *GL* V, 186.

upon which "particularistic" revelations are based, could not possibly be a basis for grounding "the necessary truths of reason."[51] Thus begins the modern division between theology (subjective faith) and philosophy ("real" knowledge). Whereas in Aquinas and the scholastics the division is posited as a formal distinction between two related and mutually necessary sciences, it is now seen as a division between two qualitatively different, and somewhat antagonistic, disciplines. Theology deals with non-verifiable and extremely opaque historical facts requiring extremely "subjective" interpretations (faith), while philosophy deals with the "necessary truths of reason" (knowledge) to which all reasonable people of good will can appeal in order to resolve the pressing issues confronting society at large. According to Balthasar, the main goal of Enlightenment theology was to "neutralize" the importance of historical particularity by eroding the sense of historical uniqueness attached to the scriptural events.[52] The road would then be cleared of all the scandalous roadblocks which stand in the way of the development of an "enlightened" theology where Christianity would take its place as an equal among the pantheon of human religions and philosophies. Only thus could theology stand as an equal partner next to the "necessary truths" of philosophical reason. Balthasar outlines and laments this trend toward the "splitting-up" of theology and philosophy as follows:

> The middle of the last century then saw the end of all those great theological systems which still followed the great examples we have cited and clung in spite of all to the model of the ancient unity between philosophy and theology, bypassing the modern understanding of "faith" and "knowledge." .... The distinction is formulated at its deadliest by Lessing, when he says that theology is a science of "accidental historical truths", while philosophy deals with "necessary truths of reason".[53]

Balthasar had little patience for such a distinction between historical events seen as empty contingency devoid of a distinguishable inner *telos* , and the "necessary truths of reason" seen as the real norm of ultimate meaning. For what the Enlightenment began still flourishes today: the subordination of historical

---

[51]*GL V*, 575. Cf. *A Short Primer*, 34.

[52]*GL V*, 560-561. Balthasar concludes: "For, what else did the theology of the Enlightenment hope to achieve but to uproot from scripture and dogma everything considered to be purely positive, or at least to erode it to the point where it would lose its form as 'accidental historical truth'?"

[53]*GL I*, 73-74.

positivity to the idealism of universalizing rationality. And what is vanquished in this idealizing process is precisely the ancient notion that history is a meeting place of various "freedoms": mine and yours, his and hers, theirs and ours, God and humanity's and so forth. What is lost is precisely the category of the personal with its opaque irreducibility. The beauty of this personal dimension of existence, for Balthasar, is "the evidence that here an essential depth has risen up into an appearance, has appeared to *me* , and that I can neither reduce this appearing form theoretically into a mere fact or a ruling principle - and thus gain control over it - , nor can I through my efforts acquire it for personal use."[54] The history of Western philosophy is, therefore, one of an "open readiness, service and submission before 'things', 'reality', and should precisely be defined from that perspective."[55]

Therefore, as soon as we begin to see in the Enlightenment the transformation of the philosophical act from an "understanding" of Being as it freely manifests itself in the world of contingent forms to the *apotheosis* of human *eros* , the handwriting is on the wall.[56] The idealism of the Enlightenment, according to Balthasar, represents a reassertion of the classical pagan temptation to equate the "light of Being" with the inner dynamism of the human spirit as such. When this happens, "particularity" (either that of historical events or that of everyday sensible experience) loses its specific "weight" as an epiphany or self-manifestation from the realm of Absolute Being. Universalizing reason seeks "reality" only in the "necessary truths" of rationality, and the consequence is that universality and particularity now come to be seen as dialectical opposites.[57]

---

[54]*GL I*, 152-153.

[55]*GL IV*, 177.

[56]*GL IV*, 177.

[57]Cf. Peter Gay, *The Enlightenment: An Interpretation. The Rise of Modern Paganism*, (New York: W.W. Norton & Co., 1966). Gay's analysis of the Enlightenment as a reassertion of pagan antiquity underscores Balthasar's approach. Gay, of course, gives a much less negative view of this association between paganism and the Enlightenment than does Balthasar. Balthasar views Christianity as a "superior" synthesis of Judaism and paganism. Christianity is "superior" because it incorporates the best of both worlds and holds them together in a dramatic tension. The historical and "horizontal" nature of Hebrew religion is wedded with the "vertical" desire of the pagan for immediate contact with the divine realm. Furthermore, Christianity achieves this synthesis, not by the clever manipulation of philosophical and religious categories by human thinkers, but through the definitive epiphany of God in the Incarnation. In other words, the "superior" synthesis which Christianity represents is not the product of human religious *eros* , but a truly supernatural integration of the world with God through the kenotic Incarnation of God himself. Human religious *eros* is made use of (including that of paganism) and becomes part of the dynamic "taking up" of the world into God. However, the Enlightenment's attempt, according to Balthasar, to "explain" the Christian synthesis within the usual categories of the "history of

As Balthasar makes clear, Enlightenment idealism is intrinsically related to the naive realism we examined earlier. Either biblical meaning is found in a direct correspondence between narrative and "factual" history, *or* it is found in an idealizing search for generic religious principles of the kind sought after by deistic thinkers.[58] The importance of the gratuitous particularity of God's revelation in Christ, as witnessed to by Scripture, is now eclipsed by the idealist's obsession with human subjectivity as it relates to history: how are the polarities of subject and object reconciled in the knowing subject and how does this relate to our knowledge of past events? Furthermore, given the radical historicity of all particular, historical events, how can anything from the past lay a moral claim upon the present? The Kantian revolution, with its final death-blow to naive epistemological realism, gave birth to the modern concern with historicism, and brings the Enlightenment's flight away from the importance of historical particularity as a vehicle for a universally normative divine revelation to completion. The "catholic" claim to totality, based upon the unique activities of one, particular historical personage, is now viewed as an absurdity.[59]

In contrast to this apotheosis of philosophical *eros* (which Balthasar sees as the chief philosophical characteristic of the post-Kantian Enlightenment), we are given by Balthasar his own theological aesthetic as a corrective. The connection between his theology of revelation and his approach to biblical exegesis is, at this juncture, very clear. Rather than approaching the Scriptures in a quest for "religiously significant" themes which comport well with a generalized analysis of our own dynamic *eros* , he instead emphasizes the "objectivity" of the biblical revelation - an objectivity which bears within itself an inner aesthetic "*Gestalt* " which possesses its own credibility.[60] Exegesis, like the classical Western

---

religions" school, totally misses the point of Christianity's unique character as a definitive synthesis initiated by God himself. That being the case, the Enlightenment cannot be perceived, according to Balthasar, as anything less than the dissolution of the Christian synthesis and as a "regression" into a more polarized way of thinking about God: either human freedom or divine freedom, either the world of matter or the world of spirit, either universality or particularity, and so forth. The result, as in pagan antiquity, is either a retreat into mythological dualism or, once again, a falling into a host of various philosophical monisms. Cf. Balthasar, *A Short Primer for Unsettled Laymen*, 11-46.

[58]*Theo-Drama III*, 59-122.

[59]*Theo-Drama II*, 420-426.

[60] The main point that needs to be emphasized here is Balthasar's insistence that the Bible should be approached on its own terms as a unified communication from God for and to humanity. As such it must contain a discernible "objectivity" distinct from the categories of

philosophical tradition noted above, should be "an open submission before things," and in this case the "things" are the dynamic events of the biblical narrative which must be encountered in the full weight of their particularity in order to be understood. Thus, the "particularity" of biblical events, due to their essentially "aesthetic" and dramatic nature, *is* the medium of divine revelation in Scripture and may not be bypassed -- *das Ganze im Fragment* . To ignore the divine aesthetic/drama at work in the finite particularity of biblical revelation - an "aesthetic" which is the work of the Spirit bearing witness to the Word in a unified and authoritative manner-- is to open oneself to the dead-end that is the realist-idealist dialectic. And this in turn, according to Balthasar, leads to an inevitable dualism between past event and contemporary significance:

> By this tragic dualism Bultmann's methodology remains the perfect expression of Protestant anthropology as such. What the "whore reason" accomplishes apart from faith is both indispensable and unacceptable. In Kantian fashion, Bultmann paves for faith a path whereby it criticizes and limits itself and, thus, admits its inability to come to see the object of faith, namely, an "historical Christ". The dualism that thus arises between history (*Historie*) and contemporaneity (*Geschichte*) is truly tragic. First, it is tragic for theology itself, which is now coming close to giving up altogether the fact of God's Incarnation: henceforth theology can be founded only on the sole absolute remaining to it, namely, faith's self-understanding. And this dualism is also tragic for the Church's proclamation and mission, which cannot interpret such retrogression other than as an act of self-forsaking on the part of Christianity.[61]

Ultimately, for Balthasar, scriptural exegesis must emphasize the centrality of historical particularity because of the one theological assertion which sets Christianity apart as the aesthetic religion *par excellence* : the resurrection of the flesh. The Incarnation and the Resurrection should act as theological correctives against any attempt to downplay the objectivity and positivity of God's revelation in the Scriptures in favor of an exaggerated negative theology. The resurrection of the flesh is the poet's "vindication" and underscores the importance which God grants

---

Kantian subjectivity - an "objectivity" which is borne by the Spirit and which can be universally discerned by human beings in so far as their own inner dynamism has been touched by the same Spirit: *gratia perficit naturam, non supplet* . What is involved here is a kind of sophiology that corresponds to the divine Sophia in the Scriptures. Balthasar states: "the interpreter himself enjoys an inspiration in accordance with the inspiration of his subject, analogous to the way the divine Sophia interprets and praises herself in the Wisdom books." *GL I*, 44.

[61] *GL I*, 534.

to materiality, temporality, positivity and finitude as vehicles of his self-expression. Finitude is not God's enemy nor some impenetrable obstacle to God's will to communicate: finitude is God's creation (indeed, creation is nothing other than God positing finitude) and it is precisely through corporeality that God creates and *is* the aesthetic *"Gestalt* " of revelation. Exegesis which ignores this "aesthetic" quality of revelation will constantly be searching for the kernel of timeless "religious truth" behind the dispensable historical "husk" that houses it.[62] This, was the essential theological mistake in the Enlightenment's flight from the positivity and particularity of revelation into the world of Kantian idealism:

> If there were no such thing as the resurrection of the flesh, then the truth would lie with gnosticism and every form of idealism down to Schopenhauer and Hegel, for whom the finite must literally perish if it is to become spiritual and infinite. But the resurrection of the flesh vindicates the poets in a definitive sense: the aesthetic scheme of things, which allows us to possess the infinite within the finitude of form (however it is seen, understood or grasped spiritually) is right. The decision, therefore, lies between the conflicting parties of myth and revelation.[63]

3. Canonical Unity and Enlightenment Exegesis: Apologetics, Demythologization, and Sophiology.

One of the consequences of the Enlightenment's naive realism and its relativization of historical positivity was the shift in exegesis away from purely intratextual concerns toward a more apologetical approach with correlational concerns. It should come as no surprise, therefore, that these more "correlational" apologetical approaches were not concerned with formulating a completely "airtight" biblical worldview into which the world must somehow "fit". Instead, they sought to establish that the Bible possesses a general religious "meaningfulness" which could then be compared to the general religious aspirations of the rest of humanity. One of the general corollaries of this approach was that

---

[62]*GL I*, 209. Balthasar states: "Whoever dissects the historical aspect of revelation by means of the 'historical-critical' method, in order to be left with the content that fills revelation as sole interior kernel, will in turn have no eyes to perceive the beauty and the evidence peculiar to this form."

[63]*GL I*, 155.

some of the books of the Bible could now be viewed as "more" inspired (or at least, more important) than others depending on how much "religious truth" they were seen to "contain." Even within a single book one part may be more "religiously significant" than another. Indeed, whole sections of the Bible may now be viewed as irrelevant if they are seen to be overly wedded to a mythological narrative for their intelligibility.

This is a fundamentally different outlook from that of someone like Luther who saw different parts of Scripture as more or less normative depending on whether or not they revealed to us something about the mystery of Christ. In Luther's approach the heuristic principle for interpreting Scripture remained fundamentally intra-biblical. However, the general trend of Enlightenment thinking was to locate the credibility of particular texts in such extra-biblical criteria as the compatibility of the biblical text with what is generally viewed as suitable for the spiritual edification of all peoples everywhere.[64] It goes without saying that such a shift was of monumental importance. Instead of the "world" needing to be "assimilated" into the horizon of the biblical narrative, the biblical narrative is now placed in the dock and cross-examined before the bar of human reason.[65] The key difference between the two approaches is that the "assimilationist/canonical" model needs, and seeks to preserve, the theological unity of the biblical narrative in its plain sense, while the latter "Enlightenment/rationalist" model neither needs, nor goes out of its way to prove, such theological unity. For the Enlightenment thinker it is enough to sustain the Bible's "meaningfulness" if it can be shown that some, if not most, of its eclectic texts contain elements of "authentic human religion."

Balthasar is most certainly of the assimilationist/canonical school in his approach to exegesis in so far as he locates the "credibility" of Scripture within the overarching totality or *Gestalt* that the biblical narrative forms. He therefore has sharp criticism for the Enlightenment tradition's search for the "credibility" of biblical texts in extra-biblical sources. For Balthasar, the apologetical motives which caused such an extra-biblical orientation are in themselves laudable.

---

[64]*The Eclipse of Biblical Narrative*, 111. Frei puts it as follows: "Luther had done so in the sixteenth century, but that was a different matter because he had appealed to the Bible itself, its central meaning being Christ, for the basis of the distinction. But Semler appealed to more general criteria, presumably found within and outside scripture, chiefly the spiritual edification of men in all ages."

[65]*The Eclipse of Biblical Narrative*, 3-6.

Furthermore, given the context of the times there was a certain inevitability about the quest for some kind of "certitude" concerning the Bible's reliability as a "religious" document. However, this entirely understandable quest for certitude had almost the opposite result: the search for an extra-biblical warrant for the Bible's credibility gradually led to a loss of focus on the Bible's own internal unity and cohesiveness. It is ultimately only this *inner* unity that can account for the Bible's unique probative force in the hearts and minds of those who have the desire to "see."

Along these same lines Balthasar stresses that one of the chief legacies of the Enlightenment is the erosion of our spiritual senses of seeing and hearing. Once again, we see that the Enlightenment constitutes for Balthasar a kind of vulgarization of theology.[66] Without these "senses" it is impossible to perceive the deep inner unity imparted to the Scriptures by God's Spirit - a unity which runs like a thread throughout the disparate parts and binds them together. And whereas in the past a legitimate "sophiology" had always stressed the development of an inner "sym-pathy" between the exegete and the divine Sophiology contained within the scriptural word, the Enlightenment, with its search for "straightforward intelligibility and utility,"[67] cast a cynical eye on such notions. Enlightenment thinkers, with much justification, saw such "sophiology" as lacking in historical integrity and thereby degenerating, as if by some necessity, into a pathetic array of fanciful allegorizations.[68] Given this view of things it is little wonder that the Enlightenment sought to develop extra-biblical criteria for imparting some semblance of "order" on the eclectic corpus of biblical literature.

Balthasar rejects this characterization of the sophiological tradition of "spiritual" exegesis and offers his own definition of its meaning and importance. First, from a purely historical perspective, it is important to point out that most of the biblical literature was written at a time when "poetry" was still the dominant

---

[66]*GL I*, 33-34. Balthasar conceives of this notion of "spiritual seeing" along the lines of artistic perception in so far as artistic perception requires a certain "cultivated" taste in order to distinguish between the profundity of truly great art and mere *kitsch* . Likewise, in theology, Balthasar states that: "a certain esotericism is unavoidable and the proofs for the truth contemplated necessarily bear the character of a ritual initiation. ... Even so truly a 'church of the people' as the Catholic Church does not abolish genuine esotericism. The secret path of the saints is never denied to one who is really willing to follow it. But who in the crowd troubles himself over such a path?" For Balthasar's description of the "art of total vision" see 509-515.

[67]*Theo-Drama* II, 420.

[68]*GL I*, 44.

form of literary expression. Historical saga, moral instruction, juridical pronouncements, liturgical and credal formulas, all were preserved with a strong poetic flavor due to the mnemotechnical needs of a largely oral culture.[69] One of the consequences of this poetic structure is that there is a strong aesthetic and dramatic quality to much of Scripture. This is as true for the historical books as it is for the psalms; Scripture does not contain history, biography, or even philosophy and theology, in the modern sense of those terms. The aesthetic quality of the Scriptures gave rise, within both the Old and New Testaments, to a form of writing known as "wisdom" literature. Balthasar describes these "writings" as follows:

> In this third group of writings there emerges spontaneously an unmistakable aesthetic element which is not consciously present in the first two groups. But here it emerges in the context of the objective stance of the "wise man" as he meditates on the dramatic religious-political history which the Heptateuch, with its appended books, and also the Prophets -- wholly integrated into the foregoing histories -- unfurl before the beholder.[70]

The inclusion of these later books into the scriptural canon by the Catholic Church means, at least for Catholic theology, that a purely historical explanation for the "poetic" nature of the Scriptures is questionable. In the Wisdom books, "The Holy Spirit of Scripture reflects on himself."[71] In other words, the Wisdom literature represents Scripture's own inspired self-contemplation and self-glorification. This fact is underscored in the Old Testament's statements with regard to the self-praise of the divine *Sophia* in heaven as well as in creation (Prov. 8:12; Sir. 24).[72] One of the purposes of God's activities in Israel's history and in creation is simply the manifestation of the divine glory. Therefore, it should come as no surprise that the Scriptures contain an aesthetic interpretation of Israel's history. The Wisdom books cast an aesthetic eye backwards over the poetic form of the Law and the Prophets and draw out their inherent dramatic and aesthetic meanings. Therefore, rather than being an unnecessary addition to the truly

---

[69]*GL I*, 42.

[70]*GL I*, 42.

[71]*GL I*, 43.

[72]*GL I*, 43: "The self-contemplation of Sophia is 'glorious praise,' and, therefore, in its own way it is just as prophetic and poetical as God's revelation in history, nature, and human life, which she likewise extols. And here the claim that the poetic form of the first two sections of the Old Testament can be explained in purely historical and cultural terms is no longer tenable. The argument now in retrospect becomes questionable."

"important" books of Scripture, the Wisdom books comprise an appropriate self-contemplation of the events of salvation history from within Scripture itself.[73]

None of this is meant to imply that the "aesthetics" of Scripture means the elimination of all historical and literary analysis of the various biblical sources. Indeed, the more we know about the literal, historical context of the various biblical narratives, the more will our appreciation increase for their "aesthetic" meaning. What is important is to pay close attention to the manner in which the Bible itself combines "aesthetics" with "history," and "poetry" with "prose." The peculiar *gnosis* which the biblical world creates and imparts is a unique combination of event and interpretation that often makes it difficult to differentiate the one from the other. The two extremes that are to be avoided in exegesis, therefore, are, on the one hand, a naive, pre-critical romanticism such as is often seen in the allegorizations of the patristic era, and, on the other hand, a reductionistic anti-supernatural historical criticism such as is often seen in modern "scientific" exegesis. The sophiological tradition, far from fleeing into the esoterica of wild allegory, actually offers a far more *biblical* approach to the question of canonical unity than anything the Enlightenment offers us in its place. The sophiological tradition represents the Bible's own *gnosis* and provides a hermeneutic for transcending the above extremes:

> The problem may, indeed, be further sharpened by again relativizing historically the complementarity of biblical sophiology and the sophiology of the Patristic and classical scholastic periods. One would, in this case, relate them both to the common cultural atmosphere of late antiquity, ... and which must be expurgated from both the Bible and the history of theology by means of de-mythologization, in a determined effort to transcend it. But we will ask: Transcend it in favor of what? In favor, perhaps, of a Harnackian "essence of Christianity" or of a Bultmannian "understanding of existence"? But note that from the sophiology of the late Old Testament connecting lines lead directly to Paul, to the author of the Letter to the Hebrews, and to John. ... The two late

---

[73]*GL I*, 43: "The specifically biblical form of inspired contemplation casts an aesthetic light backwards (and also forwards) over salvation-history, a light that allows the unique and supernatural dimensions of the 'Law' and the 'Prophets' to shine forth along with their natural poetic form. We are not dealing here with a feeble, belated, and romantic transfiguration of a long-past and heroic 'golden era.' We are witnessing the radiant drawing out into consciousness of the aesthetic dimension which is inherent in this unique dramatic action, a dimension which is the proper object of a theological aesthetics."

groups in either Testament are in many ways connected by a subterranean bond, a current of biblical "*gnosis* ".[74]

In his theological aesthetic Balthasar is concerned with the overall "form" that revelation assumes in God's historical self-manifestation. Therefore, the main issue that is at stake in his concern for the "poetic" structure of the biblical revelation is whether or not the scriptural authors have imposed a "form" back on to a reality which is, in itself, "formless." Were the events of salvation history simply events like any other historical events which later "religious" reflection transformed, mythologically, into something more than they were? Or were the constitutive events of salvation history truly the result of a spirit-filled providence that imparts to these events a genuine aesthetic/dramatic "form" that later religious reflection, "inspired" by the same providence, is able to discern?[75] This is the real question that is at stake in the debate, spoken of earlier, with regard to a "hermeneutic of suspicion" versus a "hermeneutic of trust." Are there two relatively independent movements within the scriptural record, one called "event" and the other called "interpretation," such that the former can be identified and then isolated from the latter? Does the scriptural record contain a "historical Jesus" that can be disengaged from the "Christ of faith?" Or is there simply one, integral "form" which the scriptural record gives to us that is a divinely inspired witness to a set of providential events -- events which, in themselves, are already teleologically oriented to just such an interpretation? What the sophiological tradition within the Bible points to is the presence of just such a providential, teleological orientation within the events of salvation history themselves. Therefore, "spiritual exegesis," far from being a questionable departure from the more important task of "scientific," historical-critical exegesis, should be seen as a biblically justified aspect of truly theological exegesis. This also sheds light on why Balthasar has little patience for "suspicion" as the primary determinative criterion of one's hermeneutic. The historical-critical method does not necessarily have to be used in conjunction with a hermeneutic of suspicion. Once this method has been liberated from the reductionistic "suspicions" of the Enlightenment, it can be used fruitfully in a theological and spiritual exegesis that accepts the integral image of the scriptural

---

[74]*GL I*, 44-45. Balthasar points out that it is, therefore, decidedly unbiblical to ignore the Bible's own aesthetic self-interpretation within the Wisdom traditions.

[75]*Theo-Drama III*, 64.

record in an attitude of "trust," i.e., the "form" of the scriptural witness (interpretation) accurately reflects the providential, teleological orientation of the original "events."[76]

This sophiological approach to exegesis also addresses the Enlightenment's concern for apologetics by concentrating our focus on the profound theandric milieu which the biblical narrative develops and which is credible in its own right and on its own terms to anyone who has perceived the ultimate futility of human life without God. Either the Bible presents us with a unified, coherent worldview worthy of belief in its own right or it does not. And, according to Balthasar, if it does not, then no amount of "apologetics" that seeks to "justify" the Bible on extra-biblical terms before the bar of skeptical, corrosive modern cynicism will work. This is especially true for the image of Christ presented by the gospels as a harmonious totality. People are not brought to faith because they perceive that the biblical narrative has finally been stripped of its mythological garments and now stands before them in some kind of "essential" purity - a purity which only now makes the Bible "worthy" of belief by a "modern" person who has emerged from the naiveté of pre-critical childhood. Once the biblical narrative has been dissected and "gutted" of its narrative "weight" it no longer possesses any *kerygmatic* warrant for demanding a faith response.[77] For Balthasar, what it finally boils down to is an aesthetic perception (or non-perception) of the "rectitude" (beauty) of the divine-human form placed before us in history and in the Scriptures. The dualistic either/or approach - *either* biblical events are "really" historical *or* they are mythological and should be demythologized- is a false polarity that is ultimately destructive of the integrity of the biblical narrative and which therefore has a hard time finding a sufficient theological warrant for the unity of the canon. And it is precisely because the aesthetic/sophiological approach is able to preserve the theological unity of the biblical canon that it presents us with a credible apologetic - a feat which Enlightenment exegesis, with all of its "skill" and scientific "technique", is unable to match because it is methodologically blinded by its own reductionistic naturalism:

---

[76]*Theo-Drama III*, 63-68.
[77]*GL I*, 536.

The central question of so-called "apologetics" ... is, thus, the question of perceiving form - an aesthetic problem. ... The heart of the matter should be the question: "How does God's revelation confront man in history? How is it perceived?" But under the influence of a modern rationalistic concept of science, the question shifted ever more from its proper center to the margin, to be restated in this manner: "Here we encounter a man who claims to be God, and who, on the basis of this claim, demands that we should believe many truths he utters which cannot be verified by reason. What basis acceptable to reason can we give to his authoritative claims?" Anyone asking the question in this way has really forfeited an answer, because he is at once enmeshed in an insoluble dilemma. ... This is the kind of apologetics that distinguishes between a *content* to be believed which remains opaque to reason and the "*signs* " that plead for the rightness of this content, signs which, alas, prove either too much or too little. How strange it is that such an apologetics does not see the form which God so conspicuously sets before us.[78]

Before we proceed with our analysis of Balthasar's sophiological approach to exegesis we must pause here to point out that Balthasar was not opposed to the use of such "exact" sciences as philology and archaeology in exegesis as long as their subordinate role is kept in view. It must always be remembered that for Balthasar exegesis is a theological activity with a specifically theological method. And for Balthasar exegesis only reaches the level of the specifically theological when it passes beyond the level of the exact sciences - which seeks to establish the "facts" of history - and onto the level of contemplation of the total form which the Spirit imparts. Thus, as Balthasar puts it: "True theology begins only at the point where 'exact historical science' passes over into the science of faith proper - a 'science' which presupposes the act of faith as its locus of understanding."[79] Spirit and letter are not opposed to one another: the exact sciences should not be seen as establishing the only "real" sense of Scripture nor should "what the Holy Spirit wishes to teach" be used as a "*deus ex machina* " for positing meanings which are simply not there. Balthasar is not talking here of an anti-intellectual pietism in a romantic quest to establish canonical unity at all costs. Rather, what he is seeking to establish is the dramatic/aesthetic quality inherent within the past historical events themselves.[80] Thus, the fundamental meaning of any biblical text is "the

---

[78]*GL I*, 173.
[79]*GL I*, 75.
[80]*GL I*, 43.

'historical', the directly human meaning intended by the writer."[81] Furthermore, the "deeper" spiritual meaning of a text is not some "second" meaning which is somehow "hidden" behind the literal sense.[82] The deeper meaning enters in precisely when all the various discrete parts of the Bible are contemplated within the totality of the biblical vision. Only then can inner connections be made which are neither forced nor arbitrarily contrived. But these connections cannot be made if one has assumed *a priori* that such an inner meaning is impossibly subjective and that "inner meanings" are not "scientific" unless they adhere to the canons of rationality put forward by a reductionistic philosophy of science. When this happens it is a clear signal that exegesis has lost its nerve as a *theological* discipline. Balthasar states:

> Few among today's "exact" biblical scholars, however, make any room at all in their biblical science for the *fruitio* of the *sensus spiritualis* , to say nothing of assigning it to the place of honor. I say "place of honor" because this act is the central act of theology as a science. According to an unformulated but generally accepted opinion, this act is either banished from "scientific" theology into the realm of unscientific "spirituality", or it must remain suspended until "exact" research has passed its more or less definitive judgment concerning the historical meanings and contexts of the *littera*.[83]

The sense of Scripture established by exact historical science is not a static meaning closed in upon itself. The historical events described by Scripture are open to the interpretations offered by the creativity of "religious imagination."[84] One has only to look at the "late" sophiological books of both Testaments to understand that this is not "theological revisionism" (in a pejorative sense), but a legitimate attempt to see the guiding hand of God (providence) within the events of salvation history.[85] Balthasar places great emphasis on these "late" books precisely because he sees in them a significant scriptural paradigm for how theology should approach the interpretation of the "facts" of salvation history: since there is no such thing as an "uninterpreted" historical fact, and since all "raw" historical data is polyvalent vis-a-vis the variety of possible interpretive frameworks, then theology

---

[81]*Theo-Drama II*, 113.
[82]*Theo-Drama II*, 113.
[83]*GL I*, 76.
[84]*GL I*, 42.
[85]*GL I*, 43.

175

should not eschew the task of searching for the heuristic *telos* of salvation history.[86]   Indeed, this should be one of the primary tasks of theology. Furthermore, this is not, according to Balthasar, an "eisegesis" where we read into history what the prevailing *Zeitgeist* would like us to see. This is the problem which demythologizing, correlational theologies fall into. They fall into such error precisely because they conceive of the theological task as a demythologizing of the scriptural interpretive framework - which is seen as mythological - and the construction of "new" correlational frameworks into which "we" can now fit the "raw data" of salvation history. Balthasar rejects such attempts, as we have seen, primarily because he sees them as pale "anthropological" creations devoid of lasting significance compared with the "theandric hermeneutical framework" with which the Scriptures provide us.

The late sophiological books of both Testaments, far from being the semi-gnostic musings of ahistorical visionaries, are, in fact, an intra-biblical attempt at an interpretation of salvation history which now becomes part of the revelation event itself and *cannot be separated from it* without doing serious damage to the salvation-historical context of scriptural events.[87]   In other words, there is no such thing as a "pure biblical history" out of which various meanings may be rather arbitrarily "extracted" depending on the context of one's current *Sitz im Leben* . Such approaches run the risk of equating all forms of "interpreting the events" as inherently revisionistic and, therefore, that it makes little theological difference which "revision" one decides to adopt.   The deciding factor is no longer theological/biblical at all but sociological and pragmatic.   Therefore, the only properly theological attitude of the exegete must be one of "receptive contemplative obedience" to the scriptural *Gestalt-telos* which God himself places before us and,

---

[86]Balthasar, "Liberation Theology in the Light of Salvation History," in *Liberation Theology*, James Schall (ed.) (San Francisco: Ignatius Press, 1982) 131-144. Balthasar notes (139-140) that if theology ignores its responsibility to explicate history properly, there is no lack of secular competitors who are more than willing to take up the slack.

[87]*GL I* , 45. Balthasar emphasizes the fact that the *historical* nature of the Bible is hurt when it is treated in a positivistic manner: the Bible recounts a particular kind of historical event which can only be interpreted within the framework of a particular kind of interpretation. It is a document of faith and must be interpreted accordingly. To treat biblical history as if it could be "bracketed" from later interpretations is, in fact, to treat it ahistorically. Balthasar states: "To excise all this [later interpretation] from scriptural revelation would mean abandoning the historical setting of the biblical revelation, and would leave only a certain moralism which was non-historical and, therefore, however existential, ultimately ineffective."

at the same time, gives us the power to understand.[88] The late sophiological books must not be played off of the earlier historical "kernel" as if the former represented a secondary "human" element which can be scraped away in order to get at a historical nucleus - a nucleus which is seen to be closer to some kind of direct divine agency than later "interpretations." For Balthasar *all* of Scripture is a thoroughly theandric entity which bears the final formative "stamp" of God's spirit.

B. "Die Endgestalt ist normative"
1. Old Testament

This "form-giving" influence of the Spirit is what Balthasar means by his often repeated exegetical principle: *"Die Endgestalt ist normative* ."[89] By this principle he is not advocating a naive fundamentalism that adopts an adversarial attitude to historical criticism and seeks to establish the ahistorical nature of Scripture - a view that often sees the Bible as some kind of "divine dictation" devoid of any human influences whatsoever. Ultimately, fundamentalism is just as destructive of biblical unity as was the reductionism of the Enlightenment because it is the other side of the same coin of "naive realism." Rather, Balthasar develops this exegetical principle along three lines: (1) The historical nature of the *Endgestalt* ; (2) God's Word as both that which is attested to and that which "generates" its own interpretive field; and (3) The relationship between "letter" and "spirit."[90]

Let us begin with an examination of the historical nature of the *Endgestalt* . Balthasar makes it quite clear that the Word of God does not find expression in an ahistorical vacuum: the Word "journeys" with history and undergoes a perceptible evolution in both its historico-cultural expression and in the level of understanding

---

[88]Balthasar, *Liberation Theology*, 133. Balthasar states plainly: "But, as a believer, man has to be primarily a hearer of the Word, and he must let this Word finish speaking without abruptly interrupting with his ready-made notions. Man must allow his presuppositions to be criticized and modified by God's Word, in the knowledge that no human thought-model is sufficient to capture the fullness of divine grace and truth."

[89]*Theo-Drama II*, 106: "It is the final form that is normative. Its definite and definitive quality is all of a piece with the decisiveness and resoluteness of God's offer of salvation. And God's last word has not been said until the "word" "resurrection" has been developed and formulated in such a way that its whole range is made visible. God's final word is so vast, however, that it makes room for us to hear his silence too, just as the stars reveal the night sky."

[90]*Theo-Drama II*, 102-115.

it evokes.[91] The scriptural text, during the long centuries of its composition, "is continually being reread and reinterpreted; as its deeper meaning comes to light or its current relevance comes into focus, it is reformulated, interpolated, brought up to date, heedless of anachronisms. ... So ... the most diverse layers of tradition are found in a single text."[92] Thus, there is both "progress" in revelation itself and in the understanding of revelation.

However, we must make a distinction between the Old and New Testaments. We see in the Old Testament a genuine progress in revelation itself. As the Word addressed to the people journeys with them historically, it is embodied in a variety of "forms" or "types" which progress from the henotheistic tribal myths of the patriarchs to the lofty monotheistic religion of the prophets and the "writings."[93] The Old Testament's prohibition against creating "images" of God was, most certainly, an iconoclastic corrective within Hebrew history -- a history replete with examples of Israel's "backsliding" into paganism. However, the iconoclastic element within Israel was not, according to Balthasar, a purely "negative" principle. It had a strong, constructive goal: to clear away the clutter of human idolatry in order to make way for the successive "types" which God's revelation to Israel exhibits.[94] However, these types "progress" in such a way as to mark out a trajectory toward a future eschatological fulfillment of these types within history - a fulfillment which would be initiated from within the divine freedom itself and bring human history to its ultimate completion in God. Israel's history is, therefore, simply generalized human history "contracted" into a categorical specificity. Thus, it is of tremendous exegetical importance to understand the true historical context of this evolution of the Word in Israel's self-consciousness. It is precisely the historical-evolutionary character of the Word in the Old Testament which constitutes its revelational "content": the succession of "types" point beyond themselves and, therefore, knowledge of their historical

---

[91]*Theo-Drama II*, 103.

[92]*Theo-Drama II*, 103-104.

[93]For what follows see, *GL I*, 618-643.

[94]*GL I*, 634-635. Balthasar states this as follows: "There is in all Israel a continual dynamism of transcendence that dissolves images. ... On the other hand, this dynamism is conscious of not dissolving images in a negative, revolutionary sense, ... but that it is, rather, engaged in the positive work of preparing the fragments of an image-to-be."

"progress" can only enhance our appreciation of their plain historical meaning and, thereby, to their inner meaning as "pointers" to an as yet undisclosed future.[95]

The exact relationship between these "types" and the antitype (Christ) must not be cast in an overly "tight" fashion. This was the mistake of the Patristic era where Israel was almost seen as a kind of "wandering *Civitas Dei* on earth, that *Ecclesia ab Abel* which Christ the Bridegroom comes to seek on earth to bring her home to heaven."[96] Likewise, the attempt by the "History of Religions" school to find an exhaustive explanation for the ultimate resolution of Old Testament types within the cultural-religious milieu of Israel's neighbors does not do justice to the unique transformation of its surroundings which Hebrew religion was effecting, however subtly. Neither of these approaches, according to Balthasar, does justice to the truly *figural* dimension of Israel's history - a "dimension that remains itself, indissolubly, in spite of all progress on the part of revelation, in spite of all attempts to take up the old themes of revelation in order to deepen them and bring them closer to the meaning of the Sermon on the Mount."[97]

The "progress" which the Old Testament makes as a "figure" for the New is not linear, i.e., successive figures do not replace older figures as if the older figures now, somehow, lose their quality as a "type." Rather, as Balthasar states, "what is involved is a 'fanning out' (as in the realm of nature) whereby all the forms subsist alongside each other as a qualitative totality. ... Each image brings forth the next, ... [and] each image will in its own place be indispensable for the coming antitype."[98]

This is important because it means that there is an inherently fragmentary and incomplete quality to these Old Testament types which cannot be "unified" except by a leap to a qualitatively higher antitype. There is no inner *eidos* which runs like a recurring theme through every single Old Testament type and which can be used, threadlike, to pull all of the disparate images together into a monolithic unity. For while it is true that each image points beyond itself, nevertheless, it is part of Israel's historical *martyrion* that what each image points to remains opaque prior to the antitype's manifestation:

---

[95]*GL I*, 626.
[96]*GL I*, 627.
[97]*GL I*, 627.
[98]*GL I*, 641.

How could the 'Son of Man' in Daniel at the same time be the son of David? How could the glory of God in Ezekiel, which returns at the time of salvation, be one with the suffering servant of God in the Book of Consolation? How could the *kairos* -theology which the prophets unconditionally demand be one with the contemplation of the wise men, which is wholly divorced from time? And how are we to harmonize Job's dealings with God, the almost Buddhist resignation of Qoheleth, and the ardent eroticism of the Canticle within this total form, which in every direction is pulled apart by intolerable tensions? ... No! The elements that Israel successively bears and gives to the world are, humanly considered, absolutely disparate and demonstrably irreconcilable.[99]

For Balthasar, the Old Testament images cannot be the source of their own unity. Therefore, our choice is a simple one: either the Old Testament is a syncretistic collection of profound, but eclectic, religious writings, or it is a divine pointer to an ever-greater fulfillment in some future, definitive revelation. The question of canonical unity can never be resolved so long as a figural interpretation of the Old Testament is excluded. According to Balthasar, the Old Testament types can only make sense if they are seen as "expanding" our theological categories in order to create a space for the unifying archetype[100] - an archetype which "is to be the absolutely creative unification of what in itself cannot be united."[101] The Old Testament, in so far as it shows us God's Word as a Word that "journey's" with the history of the people of Israel, a Word that evolves and progresses, also shows us a Word that, as yet, remains fragmentary and in the form of an open question. It is a Word that demands a response in the form of an expectation - an expectation that does not know clearly that for which it is waiting. Israel remains a puzzle to herself and a stumbling block for the gentiles. Balthasar states:

> But the essential point is that Israel as a whole and existentially is an image and a figure which cannot interpret itself. It is a sphinx's riddle which cannot be solved without Oedipus. Most recent research on Old Testament messianism tends to confirm this. The

---

[99]*GL I*, 639.

[100]*GL I*, 634. Along these lines Balthasar states: "Israel's history is the upward movement from the level of myth as type to the level of Christ as antitype. ... This transposition, however, can be achieved in no other way than by breaking up and, in fact, shattering the mythical image of totality conceived by this understanding of reality and of the world on behalf of a new totality which lies in the point of convergence in the future. This new totality requires far vaster dimensions than those afforded by myth and, hence, it cannot even be anticipated in terms of the myth."

[101]*GL I*, 634.

'prophetic element' of Israel lies in the fact that Israel, throughout the Old Testament, is at work on an image which, in spite of all borrowings from an historical model of an earlier time, can less and less be interpreted in terms of its earlier history - an image which, by its own internal logic, becomes more and more fractured into elements which can no longer be synthesized, unless it be a fundamentally new level which Israel can only hope for but cannot itself construct.[102]

2. New Testament

In the New Testament-Old Testament combination, however, we find the *Endgestalt* as such. The heuristic antitype through which all of Scripture is to be interpreted and to which all of Scripture points is now manifested. For when the "antitype" (Christ) manifests himself all of the various Old Testament types are transcended and fulfilled in a supereminent manner. The "progress" in revelation which we saw in the Old Testament through a multiformity of successive types now gives way to a final and definitive revelation from God that fulfills all earthly forms in one, divine "superform."[103] Therefore, the only kind of historical "progress" that applies to the New Testament is one of appropriation and understanding. The divine revelation in Christ is complete in itself. However, no single human being or historical era can possibly take in this totality. Indeed, according to Balthasar, the revelation of God in Christ is infinite and can be applied anew in every historical context. Thus, the insistence by Balthasar that revelation is "complete" with Christ in no way implies that a very real "progress" in the subjective unfolding of revelation is impossible. In a very real sense, therefore, we can say that even the New Testament image of Christ undergoes a kind of "progress" as its latent meanings are drawn out by each generation.[104]

One of the corollaries of this principle is that all of the historical "layers" of development are important for our understanding of the total picture. "Earlier"

---

[102]*GL I*, 628.

[103]*GL I*, 646-647.

[104]Balthasar, *Theology of History*, 135-137. We can not deal here with Balthasar's conception of "linear" vs. "cyclic" time nor of the importance he places on the "vertical" nature of our relationship to God in Christ vis-a-vis the "horizontal" nature of that relationship in the Old Testament. Our concern here is simply to explicate Balthasar's theology of revelation as it applies to the search for canonical unity in scripture.

strands of the biblical witness should not be played off of "later" developments as if the former are somehow closer to the truth than the latter. Indeed, for Balthasar, later developments like the gospel of John, precisely because of their longer period of theological reflection may tap into real historical remembrances of Jesus which may have been ignored by the Synoptics as incomprehensible.[105] This flies in the face of conventional Scripture scholarship's reconstructed historical Jesus who, it would seem, would not be at home in the linguistic world of John's gospel. However, for Balthasar, such "conventional" reconstructions are only true if one has already presumed that only the Synoptics are to be normative in such endeavors. Balthasar is not claiming that John's gospel was written by an eyewitness to Jesus or that it contains the very words of Jesus.[106] Rather, what he is attempting to establish is the *objectivity* and trustworthiness of the vantage point which faith brings: far from "distorting" the historical Jesus in the "bias" of its subjectivity, faith, in so far as it is the theological faith imparted by the Spirit, gives us the only real "subjectivity" that does justice to the historical Jesus.[107]

Therefore, it is not as simple as it at first appears when reductionistic forms of exegesis simply presume that "earlier," more "historical" layers can form a "canon within the canon" and that "later" books, though normative as pedagogical paradigms, can be "bracketed" with regard to the theological interpretations they contain.[108] Canonical unity can only be achieved if one asserts the trustworthy nature of faith's subjectivity and the total *Gestalt* which its inspired vision imparts. Only the eyes of faith, i.e., someone who "sees" from within the vantage point of

---

[105]*Theo-Drama* II, 104: "Indeed, we may wonder whether the radiance of Easter, shining on past events, did not shed light preeminently on those words and deeds of Jesus that the disciples had not understood and which stuck in their memories as such. This could explain, in part, the problem of the difference between the Synoptic and the Johannine picture of Jesus: the mind of the Fourth Evangelist, with his deeper grasp, retained things that the others largely missed. No one has yet explained the source of the 'meteor from the Johannine heaven' in Matthew and Luke, which does not appear in the same form in John (Mt. 11:24ff; Lk 10:12ff.). It argues for the historicity of an entire layer, which otherwise is only spotlighted with the same explicitness in John."

[106]*Theo-Drama II*, 105: "The final redaction of scripture does not need to coincide absolutely, in a *material* sense, with the actual spoken words of Jesus, with the actual shape of his deeds and movements."

[107]*GL I*, 491: "The dimension extending from the Jesus of history to the Christ of the *kerygma* of faith and of the written Gospel is the dimension of objectivization by the testimony of the Spirit."

[108]*GL I*, 542.

the resurrection, can see the true inner significance of the historical Jesus.[109] John's gospel is just as normative in its own way as Mark's is in its because the false polarities of naked fact and distorting tradition have been overcome in the "objectivity" of the Holy Spirit's "subjectivity."

The Spirit's testimony to Jesus, as it takes shape in the Scriptures, "is not external to the events, insofar as the latter are themselves understood, in biblical terms, as 'words', 'utterances', 'judgments' of God."[110] God's Word is dialogical and seeks to create the ability to "hear" and to "answer" in the dialogue partner. In other words, God's Word already contains within itself the form and the possibility of an answer. We see this pattern throughout the Scriptures which accounts for the extreme difficulty in differentiating between God's Word spoken to Israel and the reflective response of Israel to that Word. There is a free-flowing ease with which the Scriptures move from one to the other, such that the two almost meld into one, creating a single unified scriptural *Gestalt* : no event in biblical history goes uninterpreted, and every event becomes inextricably "entangled" in the great net of Israel's inspired self-interpretation.[111]

We should not be tempted by this close identification of Word and answer to reduce the mystery of scriptural inspiration to an anthropological monism and to thereby miss the profoundly theandric character of the biblical witness. Canonical unity is the product of a divinely initiated confluence of human and divine freedoms whereby God's Word establishes its own field of interpretation precisely through its dialogical encounter with human agency. Canonical unity is, therefore, a necessarily ecclesial achievement born at that precise moment when the Spirit bears fruit in the hearts of believers.[112] The "form" of the originating Christ-event is

---

[109]*GL I*, 538-539. Balthasar summarizes this as follows: "And it is also correct to say that only the Church's faith in the Resurrection - faith *in* the Resurrection and faith *as* resurrection - possesses the adequate 'eyes of faith' that can read accurately the legible form that began to take shape during Jesus' time on earth: This can occur only in the light of that total form which was already intended from the beginning and which was to unfold fully only in the medium of the Church's faith. But for this very same reason, however, it is not true to say that what are involved here are subjective projections of the later stage back onto the earlier stage; this is not true because the outlines of Jesus' earthly form could not have been filled out and completed in any way other than in the fully realized form of the Christ of faith."

[110]*Theo-Drama* II, 106.

[111]*Theo-Drama II*, 107-109.

[112]*GL I*, 542-543: "Scripture is indeed a sign of the 'conclusion' in the developing revelation, but only in the sense that, being henceforth the canonical image of revelation, scripture makes possible and guarantees the uninterrupted birth of the Church, the continuing impregnations

mediated accurately in the "form" of the scriptural witness because it is the same movement of the same Spirit that is at work in both. The Christ-event, precisely as an historical event, demands interpretation and appropriation. And in order to accomplish this necessary interpretation the Christ-event posits its own "interpretive field" (Scripture) as part of its own inner orientation. Thus, even though we must distinguish between the originating events and their subsequent scriptural mediation, nevertheless, both event and witness to the event must be viewed as part of the same, integral movement of the self-revelation of God.

Here, the truly aesthetic/dramatic nature of exegesis is once again underscored. Canonical unity will never be perceived if one does not appreciate and grasp the full length and breadth of the divine image which revelation places before us. Obedient contemplation in faith of the divine form allows one to enter into the subjectivity of the Spirit and to plumb the depths of revelation. According to Balthasar, neither reductionistic Enlightenment exegesis, nor the exegesis of those who, possessing faith, nevertheless engage in a "hermeneutic of suspicion," will be able to perceive this unity.[113] And it is aesthetic/dramatic precisely because it is not an appeal to pietistic fideism: there is a *real* disclosive power in the objectively revealed divine form which can only be perceived if it is "performed" and entered into existentially. For Balthasar, "obedient contemplation" is not some starry-eyed Gnostic "wisdom" unavailable to the common people, but a real moral, existential and subjective response to the divine disclosive power which the *kerygma bears within itself.* [114] As Balthasar puts it: "The claim of this Word as a claim of the historical Jesus and of the Christ of faith today is always one and the

---

of the souls of believers by the Logos. Scripture and Sacrament belong together and constitute the continual and unattenuated presence of revelation in the Church's every age."

[113]*GL I*, 486-488.

[114]The question arises with regard to how Balthasar can reconcile the "availability" of the basic meaning of Scripture to the common person, with the earlier observation concerning the unavoidable "esotericism" of spiritual exegesis. Balthasar would argue that there is nothing inherently "mysterious" or "hidden" about the meaning of the Scriptures such that only an "expert" can understand them. However, that is not to say that the Scriptures are easily understood by just anybody -- what is required is the "discernment of spirits" that only comes with a sincere, lived-out faith. The "difficulty" in approaching the Scriptures is, therefore, analogous to the "difficulty" involved in living out a life of faith: it is available equally to all, but is actually chosen by only a few. Along these lines, Balthasar is quick to point out that the life of the saint is, in some sense, a mysterious "secret," and yet, is a way of life to which all are actually called. Cf. *GL I*, 34.

same claim. It is the same 'eyes like flames of fire', the same 'voice like the roar of mighty waters'."[115]

This disclosive power is polyvalent and therefore allows for a legitimate perspectivism and prevents us from viewing Scripture in either a fundamentalistic or static manner. The "closing" of revelation at the end of the apostolic era is a "closing" only in so far as the object of that revelation is final and definitive and cannot be surpassed.[116] However, for that very reason it is, at the same time, an infinite "opening" to the world and to all of the multifaceted ways in which this "final" revelation awaits intellectual appropriation and existential application.[117] Balthasar appeals to the Alexandrian development of the *corpus triforme* to make it clear that the Scriptures are not, by themselves, to be monistically equated with "revelation." The Word of God is "enfleshed" in a threefold way: (1) the Incarnation itself; (2) the "letter" of the written word; and (3) the faith of the eucharistic Church.[118] Thus, even though the scriptural witness forms an indissoluble unity with the Word/events of salvation history, nevertheless, the witness is not the original event nor does it exhaust the length and breadth of revelation. Scripture itself hints at this on more than one occasion (Jn. 20:30; 21:25).[119] For Balthasar, Scripture is not to be "hypostasized" and turned into a quasi-revelation which stands over and against the revelation of God in the Christ-event. Rather, Scripture is part of that "field of interpretation" which the Word itself posits in the form of a dialogical encounter with human agency. Therefore, it is an intrinsic part of the Christ-event and is a part of revelation. Balthasar summarizes this as follows:

> As we have already said on several occasions Scripture does not stand over against this form of revelation by way of imitation as a second, autonomous form, complete in itself: for Scripture itself belongs to the sphere of revelation and, being the normative testimony, it is itself a part of revelation. ... Scripture's form is

---

[115]*GL I*, 495.

[116]*GL I*, 552: "The canonical image of revelation is 'closed' because an intensification of God's gift of himself to the world beyond that given in Jesus Christ is an intrinsic impossibility. But, precisely because of this divine unsurpassability, the image of this reality remains for all historical time open to ever deeper comprehension and penetration."

[117]*Theo-Drama* II, 105.
[118]*GL I*, 529.
[119]*Theo-Drama* II, 108.

authentic precisely in so far as it is the measure of the historical order of salvation.[120]

Historical critical exegesis, by "loosening up" our precritical and naive identity of event and witness, reminds us that the revelation of God in Jesus is always bigger than the scriptural vessel.[121] To monistically equate, in a relationship of strict identity, the Word of God in Christ and this Word's normative scriptural attestation, is, ironically, the very process whereby we turn the Bible into a "dead letter" that kills: either, on the one hand, we engage in a stultifying legalism that imprisons the Word in propositional dogmatisms or, on the other hand, we see in Scripture "something like a magic and sacramental icon within which the thing - grace itself - lies substantially hidden and imprisoned."[122] This latter approach is the other side of a legalism that can no longer stand its own smallness and resorts to all manner of "secret" interpretations and codes which are somehow "hidden" in the words and in need of careful "deciphering." And it is precisely this static, exhaustive equating of the written word with revelation that Paul opposes in Romans: the "Law", for Paul, represents the dead letter of the Old Testament "types" when they are ossified into ends in themselves and no longer contain the life-giving Spirit that points to their fulfillment.[123] The "words" of Scripture have become "dead" because they are no longer allowed to transcend themselves into the Word that is their very inspiration and which alone assures their fecundity precisely *as* words. And for Paul, as for Balthasar, this fulfillment must be Christologically grounded. Notice that Paul is not saying that the written word is unimportant or opposed to the Spirit - far from it. Rather, he is simply stressing the same central point which Balthasar has repeated again and again: all of Scripture is a dead letter that kills unless it is interpreted from within the liberating faith of the Church - a faith which points to and derives from an Incarnation event which has been borne by the Spirit from the beginning.[124] Therefore, the transition from "letter" to "spirit" has its paradigm in the transition from the Old Testament to the New. Not,

---

[120]*GL I*, 546.

[121]*GL I*, 542: "The 'loosening up' of the text by means of the critical method has in general brought with it an invaluable theological gain since, with the heightened perspectivism that is its result, wholly new dimensions for the theological perception of the object are opened up in the drapery of Scripture's garment, as it were."

[122]*GL I*, 542.

[123]*Theo-Drama* II, 109-115.

[124]*GL I*, 548.

as is often supposed, in the sense of dead legalism evolving into a formless "charismaticism," but rather, in the sense that all "flesh" has been assumed, in a positive manner, into God's eternity by means of Christ's salvific actions. Balthasar puts it as follows:

> What is involved ... is that radically new re-creation of all meaning through the death of God's Logos. In so far as Scripture is the 'body of the Logos' and not only the unparticipating testimony to his death and resurrection, the transition in Scripture from the littera to the spiritus is a participation in the event of salvation. ... For here 'spirit' refers not to some kind of abstraction, but rather to that universalization of past history by means of a positive assumption of time up into God's eternity whereby the Incarnate Logos wholly becomes Pneuma.[125]

The Incarnation, the scriptural witness and the eucharistic faith of the Church form a total unity. However, the Incarnation is the "primal revelation" from which the other two flow and to which they point.[126] In essence what Balthasar is saying is that the Incarnation acts as a kind of "final cause" drawing the apostolic witness into its ambit and imprinting the various "layers" of the apostolic witness with an overall unity. Therefore, the entire transposition from "letter" to "spirit" must be christologically/pneumatically grounded. From beginning to end the formation of the biblical canon is a slow, Spirit-led process that refers everything back to a christological center. The process is not simply the accidental end result of historical happenstance but a thoroughly theandric process that is at once flexibly open-ended (since it involves human freedom and idiosyncrasy), as well as teleologically oriented to its christological foundations. Therefore, none of the components can be "reduced" to the others.

The Enlightenment's attempt to "reduce" exegesis to the "rediscovery" of the historical Jesus is mistaken because it does not do justice to the apostolic and ecclesial theologies which "share" through an inner "engraced" participation in the Incarnation event itself. However, equally to be avoided is the reduction of revelation to either its scriptural or ecclesial witnesses. Neither the

---

[125]*GL I*, 549.

[126]Hans Urs von Balthasar, *Love Alone: The Way of Revelation*, 47. For Balthasar, the "primal authority" is not possessed by the Bible, the *kerygma*, nor by Church office. The primal authority is the Son interpreting the Father through the Holy Spirit as divine love. Balthasar states: "All an authoritative call to submissive faith in revelation can do is to prepare men to see the love of God made manifest, and help them to value that love fittingly."

"hypostasization" of Scripture nor the over-sacralization of Church authority is a substitute for the Incarnation itself.[127] Both the *sola scriptura* of the Reformers and the ultramontanism of decadent Catholic scholasticism are to be avoided. Therefore, according to Balthasar, the historical critical method is properly used when it helps us to keep these three interrelated components from collapsing into either a scriptural or ecclesiastical monism. That same method is abused, however, when it attempts to "dislodge" the Incarnation from its later interpretations in order to "recover" its true "historical" meaning in some kind of purity. For Balthasar, only a transposition from "letter" to "spirit" that keeps in mind the total unity-intension of Incarnation, scriptural witness and ecclesial *kerygma* will do justice to the *theological* nature of biblical exegesis.

The establishment of a biblical canon was not simply a "late" ecclesial "freezing" of certain traditions vis-a-vis other traditions (the "losers" having simply somehow "lost" in the battle for ideological consideration), but a real theological process which had begun with the birth of the Church in Mary's *fiat* and now culminates in an ecclesial *anamnesis* . Exegesis must be a theological/canonical reflection on the Christ-event that takes seriously the total unity of the Christ-form imparted by the Spirit - -a unity which is dependent upon the historical antecedents of its "parts" and which, at the same time, transcends the parts into a revelation which has an universal as well as a local, "occasional" meaning. In other words, the mere fact that the various strands of the scriptural tradition have an "occasional" nature does not mean that any search for canonical unity is an artificial, ecclesiastical anachronism. The "eyes of faith" can detect the movement of the Spirit in the development of the biblical canon. And it is not just any "Spirit" who is detected - it is Christ's Spirit. Balthasar summarizes as follows:

> If we let the "gramma/pneuma" antithesis stand in all its radical contrast, as the watershed between the old and the new aeon, it is clear that the only really Christian interpretation of Scripture is a pneumatic one, that is, one which reads the (ancient) Scripture ... with a view to the Incarnation of the entire divine Word and all subsequent Scripture in the light of the Incarnation; furthermore, it will seek to interpret what it reads by the Pneuma of Christ.

---

[127]We will not discuss here the difference between the positive innerancy of scripture vis-a-vis the purely negative "infallibility" of *de fide* Church pronouncements. All that is attempted here is to establish that Balthasar's development of the "unity" of the canon is based on the overall "movement" of the Incarnation from original event to ecclesial witness.

However, insofar as Scripture as a whole is only one aspect of the Word's total Incarnation event, not separable from the others, Scripture shares in the theodramatic character of this totality.[128]

In summary, then, we can say that the Christ-event creates an "interpretive field" within which the Scriptures are to be located. The inner spiritual *telos* of the Christ-event itself demands just such an interpretation and creates the conditions necessary for its execution. Thus, the *Gestalt* of revelation does not end with the Christ event, but includes its various mediations as well in an integral union of event and interpretation. Balthasar draws upon the patristic tradition of the *corpus triforme* to illuminate his basic point. The main image here is that of the "body" of Christ. Christ's "body" includes not only his actual historical body (Jesus of Nazareth), but also the "body" that is Scripture and the "body" that is Church. The Word is "enfleshed" in the words of Scripture and in the historicity of sacrament and Church life. That is not to imply that the latter two enfleshments represent "new" incarnations, or "new" hypostatic unions. They are the providential, spiritual "extensions" of the originating event into history. Thus does the originating event become contemporaneous with the believer. It is the task of theology to contemplate the "form" of revelation as an integral aesthetic unity of the originating Christ-event and its "extensions" into Scripture and Church.

What remains is an examination of Balthasar's development of the ecclesial mediation of the form of revelation. Chapter six will continue the examination of Balthasar's use of the patristic concept of the *corpus triforme* as it applies to the Church. It will be shown how Balthasar once again draws upon the image of the "body of Christ" as his primary metaphor for discussing the relationship between the form of the Christ-event and its ecclesial mediation. It will be shown that the scriptural and ecclesial mediations are intrinsically oriented to one another by virtue of their primary grounding in the originating Christ-event. The close connection that Balthasar draws between the Christ-event and its mediations leads him to the inevitable conclusion that Christian theology is, by nature, "ecclesial theology," i.e., it must be a theology with a contemplative/aesthetic orientation to the *Endgestalt* of revelation as presented to the believer in the Church.

---

[128]*Theo-Drama* II, 113-114.

Chapter Six:
The Ecclesial Mediation of the Form of Revelation

We must now examine the second great mediation of the form of God's revelation in the Christ-event. Once again, the chief question that is being asked is how revelation can be considered "contemporaneous" to the believer? How can a past revelatory event be present now in its original purity and form when it must be mediated to the believer through the filter of history? We saw that Balthasar appeals to the patristic doctrine of the *corpus triforme* in an attempt to show the deep theological connection between the originating revelation and the "interpretive field" it posits as its mediation. We saw with the mediation of this revelation in Scripture that this deep theological connection cannot be perceived if one approaches the Scriptures from within purely intramundane categories. The same is true of the mediation of the form in the Church. The Church's true inner essence as a mediation of the Christ-form will be lost if one does not approach the Church as a genuinely theological reality.

The mystery of the Church's inner essence cannot be analyzed from within sociological, historical, or psychological categories in a reductionistic fashion. To do so is to prejudice the analysis in an anti-theological nature from the outset. For if the Church is who and what she claims to be, then she cannot be understood if one ignores the profound theological reality that makes up her inner essence and orientation. Many modern ecclesiologies, preoccupied with the legitimate socio-political problems of our time, engage in a largely "historical-critical" approach to the Church as an institutional reality. This is a necessary enterprise for a variety of reasons. However, such a focus upon the Church from within largely sociological categories can easily lead to an overall diminution of our sense of the Church's inner theological essence.

In contrast, Balthasar approaches the Church as a deeply theandric reality grounded in the union of God and man in the Incarnation. The Church, like Jesus, brings together the divine and human realms through the agency of a spiritual subjectivity. Thus, the question for Balthasar is not "what is the Church?", but rather, "who is the Church?" This personalistic foundation is what gives the Church its theological and historical concreteness and is the theological reason why the Church's inner reality cannot be predicated upon sociological, psychological, or ideological abstractions. Furthermore, this personalistic/christological approach does justice to a "communio" ecclesiology that can balance the Church's institutional, historical "visibility" with its inner spiritual core. Finally, Balthasar's theological elaboration of the Church's christological subjectivity provides us with a useful model for situating the proper theological role of Mary within the economy of salvation. Therefore, in what follows I will attempt to develop the manner in which Balthasar analyzes the unique christological (theandric) "subjectivity" of the Church. Only then can we hope to understand how it can mediate the form of God's revelation in Christ.

A. The Church as the "Body" of Christ.

Balthasar is explicit in his affirmation that the primary theological task of the Church is to mediate Christ to the world.[1] From a theological perspective there is but one function for the Church: to act as the mediator of the Christ-event. What this means is that the "form of the Church is a relative form, whose function it is to point to Christ who is the supreme form of revelation."[2] However, Balthasar's use of the term "relative" here, does not mean that the "form" of the Church is of only passing importance when compared to the form of Christ. Rather, he means that the only legitimacy that the Church has as a "form" is precisely as the mirror image

---

[1] Balthasar, *GL 1, 556-557* : "In what now follows we will discuss the Church only in so far as she can be and intends to be a medium of God's form of revelation in Christ. This is probably to pose the decisive question beyond which there is theologically speaking probably nothing more that can be asked of the Church."

[2] *GL 1, 557.*

192

of the Ur-form in the Christ-event. Balthasar acknowledges that here the analogy between a divine, theological aesthetic and a worldly aesthetics breaks down. In "worldly" aesthetics the product of the artist's creativity can take on a life of its own and transcend the vision of the artist. The result is that the work itself becomes polyvalent in its possible meanings in a manner that can surpass the originating artist's wildest expectations or motivations. However, this does not apply to the relationship between the "relative" form of the Church and the Christ-form. The Church springs from the very being of Christ and flows from him in a relationship of total dependence. The Church, therefore, is not simply a piece of divine handiwork such that it now possesses a form of its own that can grow beyond the original intent of its creator. The Church has but one proper inner orientation: to be as transparent a vessel as possible for the Christ-form.[3] The Church has no theological ground of possibility other than its relationship of complete dependence on the Christ-event. Therefore, in her essential reality she is the very "body" of the risen Lord. This, then, is the "bedrock" theological principle upon which Balthasar will build his entire ecclesiology: the Church owes everything to Christ and possesses no autonomous form of her own.[4]

The ground of possibility for this christological form of the Church is the bringing together of the divine and the worldly in the Incarnation. The Church mediates and bears the form of Christ and, therefore, shares in his role as a mediator between God and the world. Furthermore, just as the form of Christ is "transparent" and allows the Father to "shine through" to humanity, so too the Church must be transparent and allow God to shine through. It is in this "transparency" to God that the credibility of the Church resides. The Church has no credibility in herself and always fails to "impress" humanity when it seeks to champion herself through an appeal to "worldly" principles of prestige, honor, and success. Unless the Church is christologically grounded, its true inner vitality will remain opaque to the world and will fade with the passing fortunes of time. Thus, for the Church to be "transparent" and to allow God to shine through, it must obediently bow before Christ and allow itself to be shaped in his image. Therefore,

---

[3] *GL I*, 557.

[4] *GL I*, 558. "It follows from this that the Church cannot claim for herself an autonomous form, even if she can be distinguished from Christ by analogy with the wife's distinction from her husband."

all historical positivity in the Church, insofar as it is to become transparent as a vehicle of the divine, should strive to ground itself in its christological archetype.

However, the "transparency" of the Church does not end with the divine pole of the Incarnation. The humanity of Christ and of the Church is also the place where the world becomes "visible" for God. For in such a grounding, the Church's historical positivity achieves a degree of inner "necessity" that is analogous to the aesthetic necessity of a work of art. No single element, taken by itself, has the quality of "necessity" attached to it, and can even appear as utterly accidental. However, when that same single element becomes a part of a synthesizing whole, then it attains to the level of necessity in virtue of its participation in this "whole." Similarly, in the Church, as with Christ, there is a union between that which is fortuitous, and that which is utterly necessary.[5] The Church is not "transparent" because one "sees through" the worldly dross to the essential divine core. The human, or "worldly," element in Christ and in the Church is part of a larger theandric whole that imparts to each of the constitutive elements an aesthetic necessity. The necessity spoken of here is referred to as "aesthetic" because this "theandric" whole is more than a simple juxtaposition of ill-assorted fragments. The integration between the divine and human realms achieved by the Incarnation means that it is precisely in the humanity of Jesus, lived to its fullest, that the divinity of Jesus is manifested. Likewise, it is precisely in the openness of his humanity to be the vehicle for the divine epiphany ("God with us") that we see the real humanity of Jesus manifested.[6] In other words, we see God in virtue of Jesus' humanity, and we see the true dimensions of what it means to be human in Jesus' divinity. Neither pole can be separated from the other -- their unity is complete and without the slightest hint of "tension" between the divine and human realms. Divinity is revealed in humanity and humanity is revealed in divinity. The image of Christ presented to us is concrete and will not suffer any

---

[5]*GL I*, 560: "This means that in the Church, as with Christ himself, all historical positivity can and must lose its fortuitous character for the world (just as a work of art justifies itself in spite of its fortuitous uniqueness by appealing to its aesthetic necessity) by virtue of the fact that this positivity is made credible as the plausible expression of the God who reveals himself in Christ."

[6]*GL I*, 560: "Christ's Incarnation goes to the limits of realism, to the point that no one other than Christ can represent man and display man's being so well before God. ... Man reveals himself by responding to God through the Church and through Christ."

"rationalistic dissolution" of its theandric form; one cannot "get to" the divinity of Jesus by seeking the "meaning" of his life behind all of the historical "accidents."[7]

This pattern holds true for the Church as well. Balthasar refers to the dual manifestation of divinity and humanity within the one man, Jesus, as a kind of "double visibleness." Christ is the primary instance of this double visibility. The Church, by extension, is the secondary instance of this double visibility. Everything that Christ manifests to the world can also be manifested by the Church. However, the Church can only manifest this visibility of Christ if she is, in fact, what she was intended to be: "The imprint of Christ's form in the medium of those who have followed after him and whom he has called his own."[8] Balthasar asserts that it is in virtue of the power of the Spirit that the Church is able to bear and to mediate this "visibility" of Christ. Wherever this Christ-form is imprinted into the lives of men and women, there is the power of the Spirit. This "creative" movement of the Spirit in the Church is not a "separate" action of the Spirit such that it can be differentiated from the action of the Spirit in the Christ-event itself. The dual movement of the Spirit in Christ and in the Church has, as its underlying ground of possibility, the same divine initiative: the revelation of the trinitarian life of God within history, in order to "elevate" the world into that same divine life. In other words, "revelation" is not a static term denoting an event that happened once and is now forever locked into the past.[9] Revelation comprises the originating Ur-event, as well as the "field of interpretation" (Scripture and Church) that this event posits as its own most proper historical fulfillment. This is what Balthasar means when he says that the "double visibility" of the Church is only a "secondary" instance of this visibility when compared to Christ's primary visibility. The Church

---

[7]*GL I*, 561. Balthasar states: "Only the whole can be understood in all its profound significance by aesthetic-theological contemplation. Christ is the *Ecce homo* as he is, namely, as the one who came to be from the Holy Spirit and from Mary and as the one who was subject to the actions of men; and, in thus being the *Ecce homo*, he is also the *Ecce Deus* . The analysis of the Christ-form and, therefore, by extension, of the form of the Church in their relations to God and the world is not, therefore, meant as a rationalistic dissolution which would destroy the form, rendering it superfluous as soon as one has arrived at the concept which the form expresses in images. Rather, it is solely in this image and form that the "concept" of God and of man becomes truly concrete for us; the idea becomes radiant only in this *conversio ad phantasma*, in this turning to the image which is Christ."

[8]*GL I.*, 562.

[9]*GL I*, 562: "If the form presented by Christ can be grasped by analysis and synthesis, then that form must also be able to be grasped wherever it is impressed on other men by Christ and his Spirit by virtue of the power of the same divine revelation."

is "less" than Christ in the sense that any image is "less" than its archetype, or that an "interpretation" is "less" than the original event.[10] But the spirit-filled union of Christ and Church is such that the Church can claim no other image as its own other than that of Christ. And this "claiming" of the image of Christ on the Church's part is not simply a "moral" claim, but an ontological claim as well; the inner orientation and essence of the Church is the very being and substance of Christ himself. Therefore, the Church is, in a very real sense, the "body" of Christ.

And just as the body of Christ is not amorphous, so too the ecclesial mode of Christ's bodiliness is not without a "form." Just as, according to Balthasar, the Incarnation has as one of its chief aims the "visibility" of divine life, so too the Church's visibility as a "form" is part of its inner constitution as Christ's body. Here, as elsewhere, Balthasar's insistence upon the visibility and "form" of revelation leads directly into an aesthetic analysis of the act of faith: the Church mediates the Christ-form to the believer insofar as her "form," filled with the creative power of the Spirit, "bears" the Christ-form and elicits from the Spirit-filled individual an act of "theological recognition."[11] There is in revelation an "ecstatic" movement of God toward the believer through the media of Scripture and Church, as well as an "ecstatic" movement of the believer toward God. And both of these ecstatic movements are carried within the same movement of the Spirit and converge upon the central form of Christ.[12]

---

[10]This is precisely why, according to Balthasar, "historical criticism" of Church proclamation and of scripture remains valid despite his insistence upon the integrity of the *Endgestalt* of the Christ-form. The union between Christ and the Church must not be conceived of along monistic lines. Balthasar is not asserting here a christomonism. There is a distinction to be made between Christ and Church. Thus, in Balthasar's use of the patristic doctrine of the *corpus triforme*, care must be taken not to equate all three "enfleshments" of the Word as equals. The priority resides with the originating historical events. Thus, historical criticism is a valuable tool in reminding us that we must not falsely "hypostasize" scripture and/or over sacralize the Church.

[11]*GL I*, 216-217: "The God who becomes man in order to die and rise is the only glory of God's that is manifested in the world: Christ is God's total *doxa*, which dwells within him 'corporeally,' and from Christ's indissoluble form his glory sheds its light on the cosmos. Thus, this radiance must be, inseparably, both a spiritual light and a structured form: inseparably, Holy Spirit and ecclesial norm. Both of these, in their unity, mediate Christ, who mediates God; but no one of these three centers can, for all that, be regarded as the 'intermediary' in a legal sense; for the Spirit is Christ's and the Father's in unity, and the Church is Christ's body in unity, and Christ himself is one in essence with the Father. [And] where, for other unenlightened eyes, there seem to stand intermediary figures as obstacles, there precisely it is that faith perceives its own light within the form of revelation."

[12]*GL I*, 604.

B. The Church as the Bride of Christ

Several questions are raised by this emphasis on the close identity between Christ and his Church. First and foremost is the question of the Church's identity. Is the Church to be strictly identified with Christ such that the Church has no specific essence of its own? And does not such an identity reduce all of the problems associated with the God-world relationship to a simplistic christomonism? Do individual human beings have anything at all to contribute to the salvific work of the humanity of Jesus? If they do, what does that mean for the Church, seen as the community of those gathered in response to divine revelation? Furthermore, how does the "fallible" and sinful humanity of the Church fit into Balthasar's aesthetic analysis of the Church's form as the mediation of the Christ-form?

Balthasar attempts an answer to these questions by appealing to personalistic categories. The central question is not "'what' is the Church?", but rather, "'who' is the Church?" Balthasar notes that in the very asking of such a question one is presupposing that the Church is, in some sense, a "person."[13] But what could such an assertion possibly mean? Does not personhood imply a conscious subjectivity that is the active agent of a whole range of "acts" attributable to that subjectivity as to a single entity? Or does it mean something less literal and more metaphoric along the lines of a "collective" personality? This latter usage of the word "person" has precedents in the family, the race, and in humankind in general. It would seem, therefore, that the "personification" of the Church presents us with mutually incompatible options. Furthermore, neither option seems to do justice to the theological reality that the Church represents and is.

Balthasar begins his approach to these questions by first making clear that the "subjectivity" of the Church is Christ, i.e., the "subject" of the Church is that of the Incarnate divine Logos. This is in line with the "body" of Christ imagery used before; Christ and Church comprise one fundamental reality with Christ as the "head" and the Church as the various "members" of the "body."[14] The "subject" of

---

[13]*Explorations in Theology, II : Spouse of the Word* , "Who is the Church?" (San Francisco: Ignatius Press, 1991): 143.

[14]*Explorations II*, 144: "This Head is the glorified Christ, his Person transcendent over the whole Church, sovereign and unaccountable. For him it is no sort of hubris but a simple statement of fact to make the equation: *L'Eglise, c'est moi.* ... This means, if we allow its full range of meaning, that the Church, in regard to her Head, is not a person on her own, a new and second one. The 'body,' ... is a person only 'by grace' of the 'Head.'"

the Church is, simply, Christ. It is Christ who "posits" the Church's acts and forms the foundation for that long-standing ecclesial awareness that it is not the individual believer or priest who baptizes, confirms, forgives sins, and so forth, but Christ. Balthasar sees in this awareness on the part of the Church the primary reason why the Church cannot be seen as a "collective" personality. At the heart of the Church's reality there is the singularity of the "acting" Christ. Thus, sociological descriptions of the Church as a mere "aggregate" of like-minded individuals falls far short of the Church's theological-christological reality.

At this juncture, however, Balthasar points out that just as the Incarnation forges a union between the divine Logos and human nature without violating the integrity of either, so too the Church does not simply "collapse" into complete identity with its divine center. The humanity of the Church does, in some sense, comprise a "partner" for Christ in the divine drama of salvation. Balthasar sees in St. Paul's development of the bridal imagery for the Church, a vague inkling of this mysterious "partnership" between Christ and his Church. In Ephesians Paul combines the "body" and "bridal" imagery by seeing in Christ's "headship" over the Church an analogy to the "headship" of the man over the woman in marriage. "The comparison," states Balthasar, "between husband and wife on the one hand and Christ and the Church on the other obliges us to take the image of head and body in a nuptial and personal sense."[15] Furthermore, the Johannine image of the Church's "birth" from the wounded side of Christ on the cross evokes the image of the creation of Eve from the side of Adam. The Church is the "New Eve," the "spotless bride" without "blemish or "wrinkle."[16]

However, the unique union of "body" and "bridal" imagery means that all of the "bridal" imagery for the Church must not be pushed to the level of an independent principle in competition with the concept of the Church as "body." The analogy with worldly marriage breaks down at the point where the marriage partners are conceived of as two distinct persons entering into a moral union.[17] Christ's relationship to the Church is not that of a moral union between two autonomous parties. The marriage analogy does help to preserve us from a

---

[15]*Explorations II*, "Who is the Church?," 147. The question of the "patriarchal" nature of such an analysis cannot be dealt with here. The question of how Balthasar utilizes "masculine" and "feminine" archetypes is too complex to deal with in the current context.

[16]Explorations II, 146.

[17]*GL I* , 558.

christomonism where the Church loses any identity of her own and is simply viewed as one of Christ's "modalities." What this conjunction of images points to, according to Balthasar, is that the Church, paradoxically, is both "body" and "bride," both "one" with Christ and "distinct" from Christ.[18]

This paradoxical conjunction of images provokes a further question: did the Church "begin" with Christ's death on the cross or did it, in some sense, "preexist" as a "partner" waiting for her beloved? The image of the Church as Christ's "body," born from the very being of Christ, gives the impression that the Church began only after Christ had completed his earthly mission and had then "commissioned" the Church, in the Spirit, to continue that mission. The bridal imagery caused many a Church father to speak of the Church as sojourning invisibly in the Old Testament -- a view that led many fathers to wild allegorizations in their Old Testament exegesis.[19] Balthasar states that these differing ecclesiologies can lead to two basic misunderstandings in our development of the Church's "subjectivity." First, the "body" imagery for the Church can lead to the mistaken assertion that the Church's subjectivity is but a different modality of the subsistence of Christ's personality. "Taken to its logical conclusion," states Balthasar, "the idea leads either to a pure *anhypostasis* of the Church (Karl Barth) or to the identification of the Christian Church as such with Christ."[20] The bridal imagery of the Church, with its implication of the Church's preexistence and its emphasis on the Church's distinction from Christ, can lead us into the opposite extreme: a "Gnostic" personalizing of the Church into a distinct cosmic principle of its own. This Gnostic personalizing usually utilizes the same masculine/feminine archetypes as Paul uses in his bridal imagery, but with much more elaborate mythological garb.[21]

The question that was asked at the beginning of this section, therefore, remains without an adequate answer: what do we mean when we say that the Church is a "Who" rather than a "What"? The Church has no other subject than the singularity of the subject of the Incarnate Christ, and yet the Church is not to be simply reduced to Christ in a relationship of strict identity. The Church is not a

---

[18]*Explorations II*, "Who is the Church?": 148.

[19]*Theo-Drama : Theological Dramatic Theory: III. Dramatis Personae: Persons in Christ* (San Francisco: Ignatius Press, 1992): 344.

[20]*Theo-Drama III*, 343.

[21]*Theo-Drama III*, 344.

singular "person" (in the Gnostic sense described above) distinct from Christ, nor is it simply a different "modality" for Christ. Furthermore, the concept of the Church as a "collective" personality is drawn more from sociology, according to Balthasar, than from theology. The juxtaposition of "body" and "bridal" imagery within the New Testament attempts an answer to the problem, but these images, taken by themselves, are not entirely satisfying. The answer, according to Balthasar, must be approached from within a christological theology of "mission" as this applies to each and every believer. This "theology of mission" includes Balthasar's development of the role of Mary in the Church, as well as the relationship between the external "institutional" elements of the Church and the internal "spiritual" core of the Church.

C. Christological Theology of Mission and the Concept of "Person"

Balthasar makes a distinction in his analysis of human "personhood" between what he refers to as a "spiritual subject," and a more theological understanding of "person." "Spiritual subject" refers to the self-aware subjectivity of all human beings. All human persons have a spiritual nature that allows them to know and to will. These aspects of human subjectivity are, therefore, universal and shared by all. However, in Balthasar's theological development of the concept of person, a limitation is introduced that accounts for the element of the unique and unrepeatable in each and every human being. Personhood is distinct from mere self-aware "subjectivity" insofar as each human being has been given a specific "mission" or vocation from God. Every human person, therefore, exists in the order of grace as "one who is sent" by God with a specific "task."[22] In other words, no human being is merely an "individual" concretion of a generic spiritual "nature" shared by all. This might be a philosophically adequate way of viewing human individuality, but it does not suffice for Christian theology. It does not do justice to the question of the inner orientation of the human person: is "my" personhood a radically plastic thing capable of genuine "fulfillment" in whatever avenue "I" find subjectively "pleasing," or is "my" personhood founded upon a deeper spiritual reality that points to a more particular fulfillment that makes a moral

---

[22]For a complete exposition of Balthasar's theology of mission see: *Theo-Drama III* : 149-282; *The Christian State of Life* (San Francisco: Ignatius Press, 1983): 72-83.

demand upon me? The view of human subjectivity that sees it simply as an individual example of a more generic "nature" is, according to Balthasar, partially correct. However, it does not go far enough in pointing out what is most truly unique and unrepeatable within human personhood. Thus, even though "individuality" is a necessary prerequisite for personhood -- and, therefore, has a certain dignity -- it is, nonetheless, not a completely sufficient explanation of personhood:

> Jacques Maritain, and not he alone, always held to the principle, "The individual exists for the society, but society exists for the person." Herein lies implicit a first decision: if one distinguishes between *individual* and *person*, then a special dignity is ascribed to the person, which the individual as such does not possess. We see this in the animal kingdom where there are many individuals but no persons. Carrying the distinction over into the realm of human beings, we will speak in the same sense of "individuals" when primarily concerned with the identity of human nature, to which, of course, a certain dignity cannot be denied insofar as all human beings are spiritual subjects. We will speak of a "person," however, when considering the uniqueness, the incomparability and therefore irreplaceability of the individual.[23]

The "I" of the human being is unique, not because it is simply a discrete individual example of human nature different from all other individuals, but because God has given it a "mission" that no other person has been given.[24] Furthermore, the theological nature of this concept of personhood is incomplete, according to

---

[23]Balthasar, "On the Concept of Person," *Communio* (Spring, 1986): 18. The question of the relationship between the philosophical concept of person and the theological concept of person need not be dealt with here. For the present purpose of this essay it is sufficient to note that Balthasar sees no contradiction between the two approaches to personhood. Indeed, as elsewhere in his theology, Balthasar sees the theological concept as fulfilling the philosophical concept from within, while not destroying the true inner integrity of philosophy. Balthasar states: "The unique trinitarian or christological content that the concept acquires in theology casts its light back upon the general (or philosophical) understanding without the latter having, therefore, to leave the realm of what is generally human. If this is the case, then it can be asserted from the outset and still without proof that the word 'person' in the sense of a human being, and in contradistinction to mere individuality, receives its special dignity in history when it is illuminated by the unique theological meaning. When this is not the case, however, the human person sinks back into the sphere of mere individuality." 19.

[24]*The Christian State of Life* : 72: "Rooted in service to the calling originally prescribed for him by God, namely, love of God and neighbor, man's fundamental state of life is none other than the 'state of grace' in which God established him and in which he is expected to remain. Corresponding to this state, which is common to all men, is each individual's personal state of life -- the unique state that determines his existence, that has been assigned to him by God, and that gives his life its true content, its *raison d' etre* . This state is determined by the *grace of personal mission* ."

Balthasar, unless it is traced back to its ultimate christological roots. The "mission" that has been granted to each individual human person has its ground of possibility in the "mission" which Christ had from the Father. Christ exists as "he who is sent" from the Father to the world. Balthasar sees it as essential, therefore, that the man, Jesus, was aware of being "sent" from God in a manner that transcended the "sending" of the prophets. Jesus was aware of his special relationship with the Father and he knew, according to Balthasar, that his "mission" was the result of a special divine "sending." He was aware that his "mission" was a "sending" from within the very essence of God's intradivine life.[25] Herein lies the connection between Balthasar's trinitarian theology of the divine "processions" and his christology based on the concept of "mission." The "mission" that is Christ's "sending" has its ground of possibility in that eternal, infinite pattern of "sending and return" that constitutes the divine *perichoresis* of "persons" within the Trinity. Thus, in Balthasar's terminology, the "mission" of Jesus is rooted in the "procession," from all eternity, of the Son from the Father in the Spirit.[26]

The theological concept of person, therefore, must not get caught up in static concepts of "individuality," but should revolve around a dialogical and kenotic concept that has its foundation in the trinitarian relations. Indeed, with regard to trinitarian theology, to conceive of "person" as an isolated individual would be the first step toward tritheism. Here Balthasar finds affinities between the Christian doctrine of the "nonindividual person" in the Trinity, with the Buddhist concept of the "selfless self": "If one takes the Christian doctrine of the Trinity seriously," states Balthasar, "then the divine persons Father, Son, and Spirit appear, if one wants to hold on to the unity of God, to be constituted in nothing

---

[25]*GL I*: 328: "As a man assumed into God, Christ necessarily participates in the self-consciousness of the eternal Son in his eternal procession from the Father and his return to him, and this becomes reflected in the human self-consciousness of Christ to the extent that he experiences this self-consciousness of the Son *interius intimo suo* and that he possesses it by opening himself to it."

[26]"On the Concept of Person," 25: "'As the Father has sent me, so I send you,' Christ says. Here we can presuppose, with St. Thomas, that in a trinitarian sense *missio* is the economic form of the eternal *processio* that constitutes the persons of the Son and of the Spirit in God. Participation in the mission of Christ (or that which in the building up of the Church Paul calls 'charisma' and which is given to each as his eternal idea with God and his social task) -- that would be the actual core of the reality of the person. The world situation today shows clearly enough that whoever discards this Christian view ... must in one way or another find in a personless collectivism or individualism (which converge upon one another) his downfall."

other than pure love or selflessness."[27] This does not mean that the "self" dissolves itself in a frenzy of self-abnegation in order to "make room" for the other. What it does point to is the mysterious nature of the trinitarian *perichoresis* . The Father does not "add" to his essential nature the generation of the Son and Spirit, but rather, he is the pure act of generating the Son and Spirit as such.[28]

Likewise, human personhood, though essentially linked to the principle of individuation, is also internally oriented to the "other" in such a way as to find its truest inner fulfillment in the kenotic gift of self to the other. Thus, there exists in the realm of human personhood something analogous to the *perichoresis* of the intradivine, trinitarian relations. The "mission" which each individual person receives from God is essentially and socially oriented to all of the other "missions" of all other human beings. Humanity is not simply an aggregate of individuals, nor simply a beehive-like collective person. The Christian vision sees in the mission of Christ a universality that sums up and grounds within itself all of human personhood and the various "missions" of all people. Unlike the rest of humanity, the humanity of Christ alone has the nature of an "assumed humanity."[29] It was noted earlier that the "mission" given to each individual person is what "specifies" this individual member of the species as something special and unique (and thus, "personal"). However, in the case of Christ's humanity, because it is "assumed" by the divine person of the eternal Logos, the mission it has received is capable of a universal significance and openness. In short, Jesus was the only human being whose "mission" was not "de-limiting," but universal in a truly theological and ontological manner.[30] Therefore, insofar as the individual person's "mission" finds its proper fulfillment in Christ, it too transcends the barriers of time and space and is spiritually connected to the missions, both hidden and visible, of all other

---

[27]"On the Concept of Person," 26.

[28]"On the Concept of Person," 26: "What is discernible here at least from a distance is the dialogue with Buddhism with all its forms, for which the 'tiny I' (roughly, the person in the definition of Boethius) must disappear for the sake of something that is inexpressible that one can describe paradoxically as the selfless self. As long as we do not see our I and our person in a trinitarian light but cling to a fundamental and lasting 'independence,' every encounter with the Asiatic search for selflessness is futile."

[29]*GL I* , 328.

[30]*GL I*, "The God-Man's experience as creature is, as such, an expression and function of his trinitarian experience. In other words, his experience of distance from God, which in him constitutes the archetypal *fides*, is as such the expression of God's experience of himself within the Trinity in the distance of distinction between Person and Person."

people. Furthermore, just as the humanity of Jesus through the person of the Logos was united, in some mysterious fashion, to the *perichoresis* of the Trinity, so too do all human beings find their deepest personal fulfillment in the incorporation of their "mission" into Jesus' trinitarian orientation.[31]

D. The Subjectivity of the Church

An answer can now be attempted with regard to the "subjectivity" of the Church. Christ's "subjectivity" finds its proper realization in the Church in the various subjects that make up the Church:

> We are obliged to affirm that, if there is to be a nuptial (and so some kind of personal) contradistinction between Christ and the Church -- however this may be subsequently determined -- the basis of it lies, indeed, in God's life imparted but no less essentially in the subjectivity and personality of the real subjects who form the Church.[32]

This anthropological grounding assures us that the concept of the Church as Christ's "body" and "bride" will not be construed in a mythological manner. Insofar as each and every member of the Church is a "Christ-bearer," and seeks, through the fulfillment of his or her individual mission, to bring Christ's salvific presence into the world, we can say that Christ becomes the "subject" of the Church. The emphasis, therefore, is not on a romantic, triumphalistic vision of the Church, but on the responsibility of each and every human being to respond to the kerygmatic force of the gospel and to make Christ present to the world through engraced ethical/spiritual living. This ethical/spiritual *perichoresis* of missions within the Church, insofar as they are within the realm of grace, are "taken up" into the *perichoresis* of the Trinity itself and given a "collective" reality. This collective reality is different from "worldly" analogies because it is patterned on the model of "collectivity" represented by the life of the Trinity. Thus, the "communion of saints" within the Church means more than a large aggregate of "holy people" under one roof. Insofar as their holiness is rooted in the realm of grace, they can be said to be present to one another in the Spirit in a manner that is truly real. The

---

[31] *Explorations in Theology, II*, "Who is the Church?": 179.

[32] *Explorations II*, 156-157.

"mission" of the most obscure and hidden person is, therefore, "present" in the mission of a more "public" person and vice versa. The reality of God's love "spreads out" from the christological center and brings to light how the various strands of the tapestry fit together into a coherent pattern. *Perichoresis*, according to Balthasar, represents more than a mere metaphor, and the "collective" nature of the Church is more than a merely "figurative" use of language. *Perichoresis* as a model for engraced human consciousness in the communion of saints is an analogical reality with its ontological roots deeply imbedded in a theological trinitarian paradigm.[33] The subject of the Church is Christ, but Christ as he has become present in the engraced response of individual subjectivities linked together by the same Spirit that is the expression of the trinitarian "We." Balthasar summarizes as follows:

> This is in fact, the image of the Church already adopted once one takes seriously the question "Who is the Church?" For the only satisfactory answer is that she consists of real subjects. She is not a mere collectivity that, in comparison with the real interconnection between one generation and another of mankind as a whole, always has something fictitious and accidental about it. Real subjects, then, but only such as participate through divine grace in a normative subject and its consciousness. ... This grace ... makes all spirits, in all their personal varieties of missions and spiritual ways, converge in a single consciousness, opening in Mary to Christ, and through Christ to the Holy Spirit of the three-personal God, who in the beginning overshadowed Mary and, since Easter and Pentecost, dwells in the Church.[34]

The mutual "indwelling" of the various missions within the Church leads to a new "ecclesiasticizing" of the individual conscience.[35] The highly individualistic and atomistic conception of the "I" of the "old man," is replaced by the ecclesial consciousness of the "new man" who has "put on the mind of Christ." Balthasar refers to this new consciousness of the believer as the *anima ecclesiastica* . St. Paul

---

[33]*Explorations II*, 171: "The mysteries of the *communio sanctorum*, the degree of the mutual circumincession of the members, their mutual power of representation before God, their community of goods even of the most inward, the monadic power of love to draw everything on itself and into itself and, as a result, to extend itself over everything and, while remaining a single heart, to become one *cor mundi* : these mysteries cannot be adequately mastered by means of purely philosophical distinctions ('*entitative* singular, *intentionaliter* universal'). The theological paradoxes are sharper, and it is simply a question of preserving their sharpness and not reducing one side to the other."

[34]*Explorations II*, 179-180.

[35]*Explorations II*, 166.

is a perfect example of this new consciousness. Paul frequently uses the pronouns "I" and "we" in his admonitions, but rarely do they have the connotation of a personal command that comes from Paul as an isolated individual. Paul is acutely aware of the source of his authority and is at pains to establish the credentials of his own mission as "one sent" from Christ himself. Thus, Paul's letters frequently betray his profound consciousness of speaking, not on his own authority, but with the full authority of the Church and, therefore, of Christ. Just as the "I" of Christ is part of the circumincession of the trinitarian "We," so too the "I" of the individual believer is not negated in the new ecclesial consciousness, but is raised to a new level through participation in the "we" of the Church with its "constellation" of missions.[36] Thus, it is fruitless to try and write a "psychology of Paul" that begins by ignoring the force of this new spiritual reality in transforming Paul's personality. "The personal reality," states Balthasar, "that drives forward with such impetus cannot, by its very nature, be contained in these [psychological] categories, although it does not destroy them but makes sovereign use of them."[37] Paul's personal "I" has not been destroyed, but transformed into the new *anima ecclesiastica*.

The question, therefore, that was asked at the outset -- "who is the Church?" -- has now been given a partial answer. The subject of the Church is Christ, but Christ now made present in the personal "missions" of the individual subjects in the Church united in the Spirit. However, the answer is only "partial" because Balthasar is not content to speak in vague terms about the Church's "collective" personality. Just as Christ represents a "single consciousness," the consciousness of the Church must also reflect something of this "singularity" and concreteness if it is to be taken seriously as a "form" that can reflect and mediate the originating Christ-form. Since the ultimate question which is being discussed here is the precise manner in which the "form" of the Church mediates the form of Christ, then it will be necessary to relate the foregoing discussion of the "subject" of the Church to this question of mediation. All of these issues, according to Balthasar, converge in the figure of Mary and the exact relationship she bears to the Church and its various offices. The christological theology of mission finds its deepest expression in Mary and, therefore, the exact nature of the new

---

[36]*Explorations II*, 168.
[37]*Explorations II*.

"ecclesiastical consciousness" can best be outlined by turning to an analysis of Balthasar's development of the role of Mary in the Church.

E. Mary, "Mission," and the "Holiness" of the Church.

In the "external" structures of the Church there is what Balthasar refers to as an "objective spirit" or an "objective holiness" that is not dependent upon the individual faith of the priest or other sacramental minister. This is what has been traditionally referred to as the *ex opere operato* nature of the sacraments. The efficaciousness of the Church's various sacraments and offices is not dependent upon the subjective faith or holiness of the minister. What this means, according to Balthasar, is that the "objective spirit" that governs the operations of the sacraments is none other than the subjectivity of God, since God alone fully understands the "scope and range" of the realm of grace. In other words, God alone fully "grasps" the meaning of the Word which the apostles preach, and God alone fully "perceives" the grace that is imparted in the sacraments which the apostles administer. But this "objective spirit" necessarily implies that there is a "subjective spirit" within the Church capable of receiving it.[38] However, who in the Church is capable of integrating the two into a single identity? The new Testament makes it quite clear that the sinfulness of the apostles (e.g., Peter) means that they are not capable of bringing together into unity the "objective holiness" of their office and their own subjective holiness. Christ alone, in his role as the high priest, brings the two together into an identity of objective office and subjective holiness. However, precisely for this reason, according to Balthasar, the Church too must reproduce in its "body" this same fusion of objective and subjective holiness. Christ desires that his Church be a glorious "bride" that is worthy of him. Herein lies the important role of Mary. Mary's subjectivity becomes the center of the Church's faith response to the overtures of the Word:

> Mary is the subjectivity that, in its womanly and receptive manner, is enabled fully to correspond to the masculine subjectivity of Christ, through God's grace and the overshadowing of his Spirit. The Church flowing forth from Christ finds her personal center in Mary as well as the full realization of her idea as Church. ... She is

---

[38]*Explorations II*, 160.

not the Word but the adequate response awaited by God from the created sphere and produced in it by his grace through the Word.[39]

Balthasar frequently makes use of masculine/feminine archetypes in his description of the relationship between Christ and the Church, Christ and Mary, and between the "objective" and "subjective" holiness in the Church. The masculine principle is represented in the "objective" structures in the Church and in Christ himself. The subjective, "receptive" side of the Church is portrayed as feminine. Mary's *fiat* is the locus, according to Balthasar, of that perfect "feminine" subjectivity that forms the core of the Church's faith response and, therefore, the Church's subjectivity. The "receptivity" of this feminine act of faith is not "passive" or "servile" in its openness, but rather, is characterized by an active fecundity. Mary's perfect act of faith is what opens the door to the Incarnation of the Word in her fruitful womb -- a paradigm that holds true for all believers who must "give birth" to Christ in the womb of their own hearts through faith. Mary's subjective act of faith becomes, therefore, the ground for the subjective act of the Church as such, as well as the ground for each individual act of faith.[40]

This brings into focus Balthasar's development of the "necessity" of a perfect "subjective" holiness in the Church that acts as the recipient of the "objective holiness." Without the role of Mary, the empirical nature of the subjective holiness of the Church could be called into question. Such "holiness" would remain an abstraction to be sought after and would always seem unreal in the face of the overwhelming sinfulness of the members of the Church. Balthasar's approach to the role of Mary addresses this problem by emphasizing that what Mary represents is much more than a figurative theological abstraction, but a concrete, historical reality. The holiness of the Church does not, according to Balthasar, exist simply as a Platonic ideal in the heavenly realm. Nor is the Church's holiness completely explained by the "objective" efficacy of grace in the sacraments. The holiness of the Church finds its ground and personal center in Mary's immaculate conception and perfect act of faith.[41]

---

[39]*Explorations II*, 161.

[40]*Explorations II*, 165: "The act of Mary [is] seen, absolutely, as the basic subjective act of the Church. ... The subjective act of the Church, even in its perfect fullness in that of Mary, is always one of womanly surrender." Once again, the question of the alleged patriarchal nature of such imagery is beyond the scope of the current work.

[41]*Explorations II*, 177.

Does the Church, therefore, have two "subjects," one represented by Mary and the other by Christ? This is a difficult issue to judge in Balthasar's theology since his use of masculine/feminine archetypes as an explanation for the relationship between the "objective" and "subjective" holiness of the Church could easily lead one to posit two subjectivities in the Church. However, according to Balthasar, there is but a single consciousness that grounds the Church's holiness, and that consciousness is Christ's. There can be no question here of establishing Mary's fecundity for the Church on the basis of some "power" which she herself possesses. Mary's faith is prototypical for the Church and, therefore, she is the "mother" of all believers, but she is not to be seen as an autonomous "goddess of fertility."[42] In a sense, one can say that insofar as the Church is the body of Christ, then he is the subjectivity of the Church. However, insofar as the Church is a "response" to Christ, as a bride to her bridegroom, then Mary is the Church's subjectivity. But since one cannot "carve up" the movement of grace in this manner, one must say that grace "opens up" the believer to Christ through Mary. The relationship between Christ and Mary becomes paradigmatic for the Church as a whole: the grace of Christ, predicated upon the model of the Incarnation with its "union" of "unmixed" natures, creates a union between the believer and Christ that does no violence to the inner integrity of the response of the believer. In other words, Mary's faith, though totally dependent upon the grace of Christ, is, nevertheless, a genuine response of her own. Thus, Mary's perfect act of faith can be seen as the center of the Church's subjectivity, insofar as the Church's response to Christ is genuinely its own. What this dual emphasis on Mary and Christ represents, therefore, is the concrete "personifying" in real subjects of an abstract theological principle: that the Church is both totally dependent on Christ and identified with Christ as his very "body," yet, at the same time, distinct from Christ.[43] What is involved is not a philosophical contradiction, but a theological

---

[42]*Explorations II*, 165: "Mary is the prototype of the Church, not only because of her virginal faith but also equally because of her fruitfulness. This is, indeed, not autonomous (as that of the goddess of fertility), but wholly ancillary, since it is Christ, not Mary, who brought the Church into being by his Passion."

[43]This process of "personalizing" and "making concrete" of what is, at first glance, a theological abstraction, is a direct result of Balthasar's fusing of personalistic and aesthetic categories. This is a constant theme in Balthasar's protological and eschatological theologies and draws heavily upon the philosophical theology of Romano Guardini. Guardini, like Balthasar, sees a danger to Christian theology whenever the dialogical and personalistic nature of the ground of Being is forgotten. God is not an abstraction, but a "Thou" who encounters the human "I" in

paradox involving the complex and mysterious relationship between grace and "nature."

What this means with regard to the personalizing mission of each individual believer is that Mary "stands behind" each person as the "ground' in which their imperfect act of faith is taken up into hers and made available to Christ. The ultimate goal of each and every mission in the Church is the glorification of God. This glorification takes place as each individual's mission is "molded" into a christological form, i.e., the believer must "give birth" to Christ by opening himself or herself to an ever-greater vessel of Christ's grace.[44] This is accomplished with Mary's help as her universal *fiat* is "used" by Christ to give birth to himself again and again in the various missions of each individual:

> [Mary] took part, as an intermediary, in the creation [of the Church] by the universality and unrestrictedness of her *Fiat*, which the Son is able to use as an infinitely plastic medium to bring forth from it new believers, those born again. Her presence with him at the Cross, her eternal role as the woman in labor (Rev 12), show how fully her self-surrender is universalized to become the common source, the productive womb, of all Christian grace.[45]

Wherever, therefore, there is faith, love, and hope, there is the Church in its function of drawing all of humanity into a unified, christological glorification of God. Furthermore, it is essential that this spiritual "core" of the Church be seen as

---

the very depths of the latter's being. If the universe is, in fact, tending toward some kind of theological/cosmological "omega point" (to use a Teilhardian phrase), then it must not be forgotten that what awaits us is not a "what" but a "who," not an impersonal light, but a "face." This protological/eschatological personalism finds a reflection in Balthasar's ecclesiology and Mariology as well: the rejection of the Protestant "either-or" for the Catholic "both-and." The philosophical "tension" created by the more inclusionistic Catholic model is overcome by positing the ground of possibility for all of these tensions within the "difference within unity" of the Incarnation and the Trinity. But these too are personalistic in some sense: the hypostatic union is only possible because of the integrating power of the "person" of the "Logos," and the trinitarian plurality is made possible within the unitary consciousness of God. In ecclesiology, therefore, all apparent dichotomies find their "resolution" in engraced personalistic categories as well, e.g., both collegial authority in the Church and its concretization in the one, Petrine office, both universal presence of God's grace and its particular presence in the christologically grounded sacraments, both subjective holiness of all believers and its concretization in the one subjectivity of Mary. In all of these cases, what is most theologically abstract and universal finds its ultimate resolution in that which is concrete, particular, and personalistic. Cf. Balthasar, *The Theology of Karl Barth* (San Francisco: Ignatius, 1992): 326-363; Romano Guardini, *The World and the Person* (Chicago: Henry Regnery Company, 1965).

[44]*Theo-Drama III* : 353: "Together with Mary, the Church brings Christ into the world in the shape of its members; and the individual Christian, insofar as he is *anima ecclesiastica* , enters into the mystery of Christmas and repeats it in his heart."

[45]*Explorations in Theology, II*, "Who is the Church?": 165-166.

the primary reality around which the Church is constituted. The "external" or "objective" side of the Church is only a means to this "spiritual" end. The institutional aspects of the Church flow out of the Church's spiritual core and have no other function than creating the conditions necessary for the flourishing of the Spirit.[46]

What all of this points to, according to Balthasar, is the impossibility of driving an artificial wedge between the "life" of the Church and the "form" of the Church. Balthasar draws upon analogies from the natural world and states that things as simple as protozoa "have their inner law of form, and the higher the level of conscious life, the higher is the complexity of the structure that supports it."[47] The institutional and spiritual dimensions of the Church may be formally, and even sometimes materially, distinct from one another, but they may never be seen as "contrary" to one another as if they comprised opposing principles. Even though a simplistic "phenomenology" of the Church might be tempted to see the Church's spiritual side as coming directly from Christ, while the institutional side is seen as something "artificial," nevertheless, a more profound theology recognizes that it is only the Church's office, in the sacraments, that guarantees the presence of Christ "the bridegroom," for his Church, "the bride." It is the institutional side of the Church which renders it historically visible and concrete, and guarantees the contemporaneousness of Christ for the believer. It is office and sacrament that "feeds" the spiritual side of the Church by making Christ truly present in a physical, tangible, and visibly historical manner:

> Far from being the antithesis of the nuptial "event," the institution actually makes it possible for this event to be a here-and-now reality at every point through history. The institution guarantees the perpetual presence of Christ the Bridegroom for the Church his Bride. So it is entrusted to men who, though they belong to the overall feminine modality of the Church, are selected from her and remain in her to exercise their office; their function is to embody Christ, who comes to the Church to make her fruitful.[48]

---

[46]*Explorations II*, 158.

[47]*Theo-Drama III* : 355.

[48]*Theo-Drama III*, 354. Balthasar brings the point home by reiterating: "The abiding structure of offices in the Church (the 'institution') means that we are guaranteed the possibility of participating in the original event at any and every time."

This brings us back to the central question asked at the beginning of this essay: how does the "form" of the Church mediate the form of Christ? What we see in all of the foregoing is a return to Balthasar's fundamental assertion that the material world is an adequate vehicle for "bearing" God's revelation. What the "criteria of adequacy" might be is a different subject, but it is absolutely certain, according to Balthasar, that we simply cannot dismiss, in principle, the adequacy of the material world as a vehicle for revelation. That would be anti-incarnational and would establish a false polarity between spirit and matter that would render any Christian theology of revelation impossible on *a priori* methodological grounds. Therefore, the Church, although sinful, is nevertheless "taken up" into the dynamic movement of the Spirit in God's overall economy of salvation. The Church cannot be viewed as a purely human institution that is "isolated" from the overall movement of God's revelation. The Church, especially in the Eucharist and in the various "missions," is part of the overall revelatory process of "enfleshment" that Balthasar sees as so central to Christianity. The Ur-Word that is Christ, the inspired witness to the Word that is Scripture, and the Eucharistic embodiment of the Word in Church, are all integrally related by the Holy Spirit to one another.[49] Thus, the sinful Church, although it can obscure the form of Christ, is still able to mediate that form in all of its integrity because of the presence of the Spirit that constantly "lifts" the individual believer into con-formity with the mind of God.[50] But this conformity arises, not by a direct ascent out of the "world" into the heavenly realm, but precisely through an encounter with the Word which the Church mediates in Scripture, sacrament, doctrine, and proclamation. The Spirit imparts to the believer new "spiritual eyes" with which to pierce through the veil of "flesh" and to see the divine element that is both inseparable from the flesh and yet infinitely transcends it. The aesthetic "form" of revelation is an integrated spiritual "dialogue" between Word, Scripture, and Church, that can only be perceived by eyes that have been given a connatural internal "form" that allows the believer to recognize Christ in the midst of an all-too sinful Church.[51]

---

[49] *Explorations in Theology, I: The Word Made Flesh* , "The Word, Scripture and Tradition" (San Francisco: Ignatius, 1989): 15-16.

[50] *Explorations I*, 21.

[51] Balthasar, *New Elucidations* (San Francisco: Ignatius, 1986): 18-19.

There is here an unapologetic "supernaturalism" in all of Balthasar's theology that is, nevertheless, not anti-worldly or anti-material. It is the spirit of John's gospel where the "flesh" plays such an important role, but is seen as "nothing" without the spirit that animates it.[52] It represents a simple rejection of the basic objections of the radical historicist. Balthasar answers radical historicism by largely rejecting its basic assumptions, and favors instead a strongly supernatural, "transhistoricalism" that emphasizes the power of God's revelatory communicability within the structures of creation. Balthasar acknowledges that all knowledge is "time-conditioned." However, only a simplistic epistemological cynicism, according to Balthasar, would radicalize this insight into an absolute negation of any kind of transhistorical knowledge whatsoever. This is especially true of what Balthasar would characterize as "spiritual knowledge" of a past theological event that has been made "contemporaneous" to the believer through word and sacrament.

The experiential and existential nature of this kind of knowledge is more of a direct participation in a past event made present (*anamnesis*), than it is a "straining" after knowledge of a past event that has long since faded into the mist of time. If the Church were simply a pietistical institution committed to the increasingly vague memory of a dead person, then it would certainly have no claim to be mediating anything of an absolute nature. Furthermore, if the Church were simply committed to the presentation of a figure who had once done something for us, but that we do not need to participate in now, then, again, the Church would have no claim to being an ontological mediation of the form of that event. The "event" which the Church mediates through word and sacrament evokes an existential, experiential knowledge which is the result of the risen Lord being truly present here and now through faith.[53] It is this "supernatural" element in the

---

[52]*Explorations I,* "The Place of Theology," 149; *GL I* , 597.

[53]Balthasar, *In the Fullness of Faith* (San Francisco: Ignatius, 1988): 100-101: "Nothing is plainer, nothing is more evident, than that in the Catholic realm the authority exercised in the Church of the Word and Sacrament is both form and content. ... Were this not the case, there would be an alienating gulf between the proclaimed content and the proclaiming Church. Either it would mean that what is proclaimed is a historical, objectivized, archaeological fact people can 'hold to be true' without inwardly participating in it, such that his obedience long ago makes us 'free Christian men' today. Or it means that we imagine ourselves (in a Pietistic sense) to be sharing directly in the event of the cross, and so reduce the primal act of Christian obedience to the minuscule proportions of an anthropological 'honesty' that 'does justice to the facts.'"

Church that allows her to mediate the Christ-event to the "eyes" of the believer, who can now "see" with a new "supernatural" vision granted by the internal movement of the Holy Spirit. In other words, if the Church and the Scriptures are merely human creations then they would certainly be opaque and unreliable mediations of the Christ-event. However, if they are a genuine work of God, then it is at least possible that the Christ-form is able to forge a supernatural unity with the form of the Church.[54]

---

[54]*GL I*, 603-604. Balthasar states: "In the Church ... the form of Christ, which in itself is hidden from the world, can become so dazzling in the testimony of Christians that its beauty and rightness will be visible and evident. ... Beneath the double servant form of a Church that is herself truly sinful and is darkened by sinners there shines the glory of Christ's love, not only like a little dot of love representing an individual man, but in such a way that Christ's love, starting from this point, moves out to justify the whole, including the Scripture and including the Church in her institutional form."

Chapter Seven:
Evaluation and Critique: Final Thoughts

This concluding chapter has two chief goals. First, to offer an evaluation and critique of Balthasar's theology of revelation as it has been here presented. Second, to offer some insights into where Balthasar's theology might be developed in the future. It is, of course, difficult to "narrow down" the range of options in any attempt to evaluate such a complex theology as Balthasar's.   Furthermore, there is certainly no pretense here of offering an "exhaustive" critique of such a richly textured theological landscape. However, it is possible to pick out a few central themes and to comment upon them. To that end, the remarks that follow will be given with the following goals in mind: 1) an evaluation of some of the positive contributions of Balthasar's theology of revelation; 2) a critique of some problems which arise within his theology; and 3) an evaluation of where these various strengths and weaknesses might be built upon, or corrected, in the future.

A. A Critique of Balthasar's Theology of Revelation.

The first thing that strikes one regarding Balthasar's theology is simply the sheer scope of the project itself. In an age when few theologians dare attempt anything close to a complete synthesizing of the Christian intellectual heritage, Balthasar's "encyclopedic" efforts can seem overwhelming. The key factor, however, is that Balthasar's knowledge of both the Christian and the Western intellectual tradition is astounding. His knowledge of theology, music, literature, philosophy, theater, visual art and history, form the foundation of a mind that moves fluidly from within one discipline to another. One cannot help but see a certain autobiographical flourish in Balthasar's statement that many of the great theologies of the Church have frequently been characterized by a certain "amateurish" flavor.[1] No doubt, he was referring, not just to the often "passionate" nature of such theologies, but also to the fact that they frequently evince a certain "dilettantish" quality with respect to their wide-ranging scope. Balthasar's theology certainly cannot escape the charge of falling prey now and again to the temptation of the dilettante, but such lapses are inevitable in an otherwise laudable attempt to relate theology to the wider world of "letters."

This knowledge of the Western and Christian intellectual traditions does not lead Balthasar to a dry, academic relationship with the Church. There is no arid intellectualism in anything that Balthasar writes, even when he is, at times, repetitious and tedious. Most of what Balthasar writes, like all great theologies, is merely a "variation on a theme." Therefore, Balthasar's theology frequently seems repetitious as it "circles" its object, first from one angle, then from another.[2] But throughout it all, the christocentric center emerges from within his theology like a flame rising up that consumes everything in its path. It is within this christological flame that Balthasar's entire theology is immersed, and it shows most clearly in his passionate explication of the implications of the Christ-event. This leads Balthasar into a complete immersion into the life of the Church. Balthasar is, first and foremost, a *believer*, and his theology is written from within that perspective for those who share that perspective. He is an unapologetically "joyful" Christian who begins his theology, not with "methodic doubt" in order to establish some "neutral" foundation for faith, but with the assumption that faith is still "good news," with the inner power to captivate even the most modern cynic.[3]

Balthasar, of course, could ignore the "apologetic" concerns of the academy because his theology was never produced in such a setting. Associated as he was

---

[1]*Explorations in Theology I*, "Theology and Sanctity," 207.

[2]This "circling" of the object is by design. One of the central thrusts of Balthasar's theology is the recovery of philosophical and theological wonder at "Being." To that end, he organizes his theology of the "glory" of revelation around the convertible "transcendentals" of Being. There can be no analysis of the "True" that does not have reference to the "Good" and the "Beautiful" and the "One." Thus, the same object of revelation can be viewed from a variety of different transcendental angles.

[3]*Explorations in Theology I*, "The Place of Theology," 160: "We need individuals who devote their lives to the glory of theology, that fierce fire burning in the dark night of adoration and obedience, whose abysses it illuminates."

with the secular institute he co-founded with Adrienne von Speyr, his primary concern was with the relationship between theology as an explication of revelation, and the engendering of sanctity in the Church.[4] Thus, in this respect, his theology bears a resemblance to many strands of liberation theology with their emphasis on a theology that leads to *praxis* . The particular kind of *praxis* that Balthasar favors certainly has a far less "political" tone than that of liberation theology. However, the two approaches are similar in their critique of the abstract intellectualism of much of "academic theology."[5]

The problem with such approaches, including that of Balthasar, is that they run the risk of being somewhat disingenuous. Theology is an exercise in some kind of "rationality." Therefore, the fact that one's concerns are not strictly "academic" does not eliminate the burden of needing to offer some kind of rational justification for one's project. Balthasar's theology is filled with rational argumentation and is suitable, almost in its entirety, for discussion in an academic environment. The proper interpretation, therefore, for Balthasar's frequent assaults upon the arid skepticism of the academy, is that his theology is offered as a corrective against the claims of an all-encompassing rationality that threatens to disallow any paradigm for theology that is not "demythologizing." Balthasar's criticism of the academy is not a blanket condemnation of modernity, nor of the attempt to apply modern scientific reasoning to revelation. It is, rather, a condemnation of the materialistic reductionism that has gained ascendancy in the academy since the Enlightenment.[6]

This critique of the Enlightenment leads Balthasar to one of the central insights of his theology: the aesthetic dimensions of revelation and the supremacy of the concrete, the historical, and the personal, over the abstract, the generic, and the impersonal. Balthasar fears what C.S. Lewis has referred to as "the abolition of man," in a slow descent into the brave new world of technological impersonalism.[7] There is an element of the existentialist's rage against "mass society" in Balthasar's

---

[4]Cf. *First Glance at Adrienne von Speyr*, 13.

[5]Cf. Gustavo Gutierrez, *A Theology of Liberation*, (Maryknoll, New York: Orbis, 1973), 3-19; Jon Sobrino, *The True Church and the Poor*, (Maryknoll, New York: Orbis, 1984). 7-38; Juan Luis Segundo, *The Historical Jesus of the Synoptics, II*, (Maryknoll, New York: Orbis, 1985), 3-39.

[6]*Theo-Drama II*, 420-429; *GL I*, 533-534.

[7]C.S. Lewis, *The Abolition of Man*, (New York: Macmillan, 1943).

aesthetic, as he attempts to ground Christian theology in a christological/trinitarian personalism that would rather flirt with the mythological than dance with any kind of Deistic abstraction.[8] The fundamental premise of his theological aesthetic -- that God not only wills to communicate to humanity through the finite forms of this world, but has in fact done so -- forms a basic methodological barrier against all forms of hyper-abstraction and rationalization within Christian theology. Therefore, Balthasar's development of his aesthetic as a direct contradiction to the legacy of the Enlightenment, acts, once again, as a corrective against any tendency in modern Christian theology to veer too far in the direction of a Deistic unitarianism.

There is, perhaps, an element of attacking "straw men" in such a critique of the Enlightenment, since very few Christian theologians would present their more "theocentric" approaches as a simple appeal to the Deism of the Enlightenment.[9] Furthermore, the "bracketing" of historical particularity can serve a legitimate theological and apologetical purpose, especially in the atmosphere of the academy with its demands for evidentiary exposition. This kind of theological "bracketing" of the particularity of revelation has a purely formal methodological purpose. Balthasar's development of a theological aesthetic that calls attention to the "beauty" or "radiance" of the finite vessel of revelation, serves as a reminder that we should not be so quick to dismiss the "evidentiary" force within the simple events of revelation themselves. Theology must guard against becoming jaded by overexposure to its object of inquiry. Biblical religion, in the simplicity and power of its design, still has the power to instill faith and inspire the nations, and theology must live off of a constant return to its most proper sources. Thus, one of the most urgent tasks of the theologian should be the "repristination" of the original "beauty" of biblical revelation. Theology must seek to recapture the reasons why revelation was so captivating in the first place, and to pursue it with the assumption that first

---

[8]Cf. *GL I*, 155; Gabriel Marcel, *Man Against Mass Society*, (South Bend, Indiana: Gateway, 1978).

[9]Cf. David Tracy, *The Analogical Imagination* , 51. Tracy's theocentrism, for example, is fairly representative of those modern theologies that seek a dialogue with nonchristian religions by asserting the common emphasis on God as the center of theology. Tracy's thought might contain elements of Deistic thinking, but his theology does represent a serious attempt to develop a specifically Christian theology. Thus, Tracy's theology, and others like it, do not necessarily represent an attempt at a Deistic reductionism of all particularity into more general universal truths.

century Jews and Gentiles were not so different from twentieth century skeptics. Therefore, although the "bracketing" of particular truth claims within Christianity has a necessary methodological function, the purely "formal" nature of such "bracketing" must not be forgotten. Balthasar's theological aesthetic reminds us of the concrete character of "truth" in Christianity and the necessity of returning everything to its christological center.[10] The ability of his aesthetic to act as a corrective "moment" within other theologies may prove to be one of its lasting contributions to the theology of the "academy."

This is true also for ecumenical discussions with nonchristian religions. Even if, as many are now proposing, the absolute metaphysical claims for Jesus made in the New Testament are largely hyperbolic and, therefore, the status of Jesus *vis-a-vis* other "savior figures" is an open question, it does not necessarily follow from this that the revelation of God in Jesus is a "species" within a larger "genus."[11] Jesus might be one savior figure among many, but it does violence to the fundamental thrust of New Testament religion to transpose its christocentric categories into more "generic" theocentric categories. The universalism that is the central mark of monotheism finds its place in the New Testament precisely in the latter's theology of the universal significance of Christ's redemptive work. The evangelical thrust in the victory of the mission to the gentiles over the objections of those who insisted upon the Judaic character of the Church, clearly shows the Church's early awareness of the universality of the salvation brought by Christ. [12] The absolute claims for Jesus might be hyperbolic, but the fundamental awareness of the first Christians, clearly witnessed to in the New Testament, that somehow the

---

[10]Cf. Balthasar, *The Theology of Karl Barth*, 326-363.

[11]Cf. John Hick and Paul Knitter, eds., *The Myth of Christian Uniqueness*, (Maryknoll, New York: Orbis, 1987); Gavin D'Costa, ed. *Christian Uniqueness Reconsidered: The Myth of a Pluralistic Theology of Religions*, (Maryknoll, New York: Orbis, 1990).

[12]Cf. Pheme Perkins, "Christianity and World Religions: New Testament Questions," *Interpretation*, (October, 1986), 367-378. Perkins states: "[The] New Testament suggests that there are fundamental issues of Christian identity and belief bound up with the conviction that the Christian mission to the world is a summons to conversion. Christianity cannot do justice to its fundamental perceptions about salvation by simply stepping to the place of a reconstructed 'historical Jesus,' the eschatological prophet of God's in-breaking rule, even if such a move would smooth the way for a more accomodating religious pluralism. Christianity's claim is that the creative and saving power of God is embodied in 'the Lord' who calls into being a community which is always trying to live out the implications of the divine refusal to accept cultural, ethnic, political, or other boundaries. ... It may be impossible for us to remember that all these visions of Christianity were not spoken by persons with the effective worldly power to impose them on others but by those who could only suffer patiently when they met with rejection." 378.

universalism of monotheism has now been transferred to the work of Jesus, must be dealt with honestly. Biblical religion makes very exclusive claims for itself. Theology, therefore, should avoid the dual errors of either rejecting such claims outright, or absolutizing such claims beyond even what the Bible demands.[13]

The life of Jesus in particular must be seen as having fundamental revelatory value for the Christian theologian. Anything less than this would be unecumenical, because what the theologian would be offering the dialogue partner would not be an analysis of the ecumenical implications of biblical religion, but a condescending "philosophy of religion" that seeks a "high ground" above both religions, judging both, and insulting both.[14] In such cases the theologian is often simply replacing one particularism with another -- the particularism of biblical religion is simply replaced with the particularism of "my" theory of religion. The aesthetic categories of Balthasar's theology, once again, remind the theologian that the best way to build a religious view of universal significance is often to delve ever more deeply

---

[13]Cf. Pheme Perkins, *Reading The New Testament*, (New York: Paulist, 1988). Also, Hans Kung, *Theology for the Third Millennium*, 251.

[14]Hans Kung, *Theology for the Third Millennium*, 227-256: "In the search for the true religion no one may simply abstract from his own life history and experience. There is no such thing as a theologian nor a student of religion, neither a religious nor a political authority, that stands so far above all religions as to be able judge it 'objectively,' from above. Anyone who thinks he can stand in a 'neutral' position above all traditions, will get nothing done in any of them." Kung goes on to develop an approach to dialogue among the various religions that stresses a threefold criteria for truth in religion: 1) ethical criteria that judge a religion based on its humanistic impact; 2) general religious criteria that seek the manner in which a religion manifests some aspect of the Absolute; and 3) an internal or "intratextual" criterion that judges a religion based on its living up to its own normative traditions. To these three criteria Kung adds a fourth for the Christian: a religion is good and true insofar "as it allows us to perceive the spirit of Jesus Christ in its theory and practice." 248. This is different from Rahner's "anonymous Christian" since Kung is not claiming that other religions are true only insofar as they are secretly "Christian." Christianity is "true" for the Christian just as Islam is "true" for the Muslim. No theologian can prescind from the truth claim inherent in the act of trust which is placed in this particular religion. Thus, it is not arrogance to pursue inter-religious dialogue as a mutually enriching encounter between two religions that both embody religious truth and yet seek to convince others of the truth of their particular religion. It is in this sense that Kung can state: "Jesus Christ is for Christians the deciding regulative factor." 251. What is unclear in Kung's approach is the extent to which Absolute ontological claims can be made by the Christian with regard to the status of other religions and their metaphysical relationship to the universal salvation brought by Christ. Balthasar's approach to inter-religious dialogue is a combination of Barth's condemnation of all religion as idolatry and Rahner's christological inclusivism. It is this combination of seemingly contradictory positions that leads to much of the ambiguity in Balthasar's approach to nonchristian religions. In many ways Balthasar would agree with Kung's rejection of "anonymous Christians" as an insult to both Christians and nonchristians. However, insofar as Kung is not clear as to the ultimate ontological status of Jesus, Balthasar would tend to disagree and to inch back toward a more Rahnerian position.

into the revelatory power, the aesthetic "necessity," of the particular form of God's revelation in Christ.

However, Balthasar's development of his theological aesthetic is not without its problems. The major difficulty lies in the fact that a very large theological edifice is constructed upon a very minimal theoretical apparatus.[15] Balthasar states that he purposefully does not develop a sophisticated aesthetic theory because he does not want to prejudice the theology that is to be built upon it by trying to fit it into too neat of a theoretical straight jacket.[16] Laudable as this might be, it is nevertheless frustrating when one attempts to find justification in Balthasar's aesthetic for many of his theological assertions. There is an apodictic quality in much of Balthasar's theology that is predicated upon principles which are not always as self-evident to the reader as they are to Balthasar. His frequent assertions of the self-evident "beauty" and aesthetic perfection of revelation often resort to a line of argumentation that seems to be only slightly removed from the "either you see it or you don't" school of thought.

Furthermore, his appeal to the necessity of the indwelling of the Spirit in order to impart the "spiritual eyes" required to see this perfection of the form, is a legitimate extension of the "wisdom" tradition within theology into the realm of dogmatics. As such, it represents a significant effort to reunite theology and "spirituality." However, it comes dangerously close at times to a solipsistic argument that closes off further discussion by appealing to some privileged "vantage point." Perhaps he is correct in this approach, but the lack of a strongly dialectical moment within his theology leaves him open to the charge that his theology is perhaps too dependent upon mystical charisms to which he alone is privy -- either his own or those of Adrienne von Speyr -- charisms which may be valid in themselves, but have the flavor of a kind of Gnostic esotericism when translated into dogmatic theology without sufficient explanation.

What this points to is that the final assessment of Balthasar's aesthetic will not be complete until a more sophisticated theoretical apparatus is developed to help his theology bridge the gap between fundamental insight and theological

---

[15]Cf. Frank Burch Brown, *Religious Aesthetics*, (Princeton: Princeton University Press, 1989) 18-20.

[16]*GL I*, 117: "Our point of departure was very much a layman's insight into the beautiful. ... It would be incorrect for us to go beyond this unreflected concept lest we should prejudice our inquiry either philosophically or theologically."

conclusion. Balthasar's theological aesthetic begins with an analysis of how the aesthetic element was lost in the history of theology. It concludes with an effort to reconstruct that lost element. What is often missing is the theoretical "middle step" that bridges the two. The nagging aesthetic question of how a single, finite human being -- Jesus -- could possibly be an aesthetic form with an infinite range of possible "applications" has to be answered. The assertion that this is accomplished by "the Spirit" may offer an indication of which direction the answer may be in, but it does little to assuage the reader's suspicion that this seems to beg the essential question of how the "Spirit" builds on "nature" in order to do this. What is its "ground of possibility?" Balthasar's response that this is accomplished through an analogy with the power of the "expressive form" even in the finite realm, and of our experience of *kenosis* within love, does not completely address the issue of how this can be a vehicle for the specifically infinite in a manner that is absolute and unsurpassable. The basic insight of his aesthetic -- the ability and the will of God to communicate with humanity through the finite forms of creation -- seems to be sound and full of theological promise. However, the issue of how this translates into a unique, infinite, unrepeatable, absolute, and unsurpassable revelation remains open. It remains open insofar as the theoretical apparatus underpinning his aesthetic is never developed enough to offer such an explanation. Thus, Balthasar's aesthetic should be judged a successful first step in the direction of restoring aesthetics to its proper place within dogmatic theology. However, the sheer scope and size of his theology should not lead one to the false conclusion that Balthasar has achieved any kind of definitive "last word" on the subject. The road is now open for other theologians to complete the task that Balthasar has so ably begun.

Perhaps one reason that Balthasar's aesthetic does not contain an elaborate theoretical superstructure in the area of an "aesthetic theory" as such, could be that the specifically theological nature of his aesthetic points to another discipline as its ground of possibility: metaphysics. Two salient facts should not be overlooked here. First, Balthasar's development of his metaphysic takes place within the overall development of his aesthetic. Balthasar sees metaphysics as the necessary theoretical underpinning for his aesthetic, and states that metaphysics begins with "philosophical awe" in the face of the "radiance" of Being.[17]   This leads to the second important fact. Balthasar sees in the biblical concept of "glory" the primary aesthetic moment within theology. The "radiance" of Being is the earthly analogue to this "glory." The extent to which the "glory" of God can be reflected in the "radiance" of Being comprises the metaphysical "ground of possibility" for Balthasar's aesthetic. However, at the very point where Balthasar is pressed to describe the dynamic of this relationship within revelation, he falls back on specifically "aesthetic" arguments once again. He speaks of "form" and "splendor" intersecting in the "radiance" of Being.[18] But he does not offer a detailed enough account of how these basic metaphysical insights into the "beauty" of Being are elucidated by an appeal to aesthetics. Thus, although his metaphysic does provide a much clearer foundation for the theological aspects of his aesthetic, it is still no substitute for a well worked out aesthetic theory.

This fact should not be allowed to obscure the significant contribution that his metaphysic represents. In many ways it is one of the most original aspects of his theology, especially in its relationship with his trinitarian theology. The strongly relational model he draws for the "persons" within the Trinity forms a solid foundation for the "dialogical" metaphysical paradigm he seeks to develop. His analysis of the dialogical character of myth, and its inherent tension with the generalizing universalisms of philosophy, lays the groundwork for a trinitarian christology that transcends this tension and points metaphysics toward a theological resolution of its inner ambiguity. This is Balthasar at his best and at his most frustrating. His emphasis on the ambiguous nature of the human metaphysical and religious quest is a compelling preparation for his development of the clear, radiant light of Christ. It is almost as if one of the "Fathers" of the Church -- Justin, perhaps -- has arisen to remind us that everything that is good and noble and true finds its ground and resolution in Christ. Indeed, Balthasar frequently appeals to the patristic doctrine of the *logos spermatikos* as a reminder of the Christian obligation to "restore all things in Christ."[19]

One other problem that emerges in Balthasar's aesthetic is that it seems to compel him to seek an aesthetic "wholeness" in various aspects of the Christian

---

[17]*GL IV*, 11-39.

[18]*GL I*, 20.

[19]"From the Theology of God to Theology in the Church," 215.

tradition that the tradition itself does not always justify. That is not to say that Balthasar may not use his aesthetic insights to forge a new understanding of ancient texts. However, a caution must be raised against a tendency to "force" aspects of the tradition into a preconceived aesthetic pattern. For example, in his theology of "Holy Saturday" there appear to be two main areas in which Balthasar goes beyond the tradition in order to bring the "wholeness" of the Christ-form to metaphysical completion.

First, Balthasar develops his "theology of Holy Saturday," with its emphasis on the "descent" of Christ into hell, in the light of his trinitarian metaphysic.[20] Christ "restores" all things, even hell, because he has gone to the furthest limits of human experience, to the utmost dregs of human perdition, in order to "retrieve" creation for the Father. However, several questions arise about Balthasar's development of the doctrine of the "descent" into hell. The first question deals with the nature of the Church's doctrine itself. Balthasar seems to be investing this teaching of the Church with far more meaning than it has traditionally contained. Nowhere in the Roman Catholic tradition is there an emphasis on Christ's descent into hell in order that he might "experience the full limits" of the punishment due to sin.[21] At most it is a simple statement of the Church's belief that the Cross works retroactively, as well as in the future. Balthasar may be engaging in a legitimate theological development of the tradition here, but the relationship between this development and the tradition needs to be made clearer.

---

[20]*Mysterium Paschale*, 148-188.

[21]There is an emphasis within certain segments of the Protestant tradition on Christ's "becoming sin for our sakes," in a very literal sense. The strong Lutheran dialectic between sin and grace, law and gospel, pushes Christ to the outer limits of estrangement from God in order to undergo the full consequences of sin. Balthasar also emphasizes a substitutionary theology of the atonement that takes very seriously the Pauline statement that Christ became sin for our sakes. However, Balthasar does not affirm Christ's descent into hell as the result of a strongly dialectical moment in his theology of grace. Rather, he does so out of a more metaphysical concern for the reconciliation of the world, i.e., the realm of "not God," with God. What Balthasar seeks is a soteriology that goes beyond a simple concern for sin toward a deeper metaphysical concern for the "taking up" of creation into the divine life of the Trinity. The cross and the descent into hell become the "condition of possibility" for the absolute inclusiveness of the world - - including reconciled sinfulness - - into the realm of God. This pushes Balthasar in the direction of affirming at least the possibility that all people may eventually be saved. What is of central importance here is the manner in which Balthasar's concern for the metaphysical, aesthetic "completeness" of God's revelation in the Christform pushes him in the direction of departing somewhat from the tradition. However, the question of whether or not this constitutes a legitimate development of the Christian tradition is not of concern here.

The second question revolves around one's definition of hell. If hell is defined as a place of isolation from God on account of one's opposition to God, then it is hard to see how Jesus could have "experienced hell." The traditional doctrine of the descent into hell was developed, it must not be forgotten, within the context of an older theology of atonement that stressed the difference between satisfaction for sin and the punishment due sin. Christ's suffering constitutes a "satisfaction" for sins, but Christ in his person was in no way deserving of the punishment of hell. The historical context for the original doctrinal development of the "descent," therefore, is somewhat different from Balthasar's and needs some explaining.

Balthasar acknowledges these problems by adopting the mythical image of "sheol" as a metaphor for death.[22] Prior to Christ's salvific work ("prior" in a formal sense) there is no heaven or hell, only the mysterious "descent" into the mute condition of death which the Old Testament describes so well. This is what Christ experiences -- the mute "obedience of the corpse." Therefore, the theological development of the tradition that Balthasar seems to be engaging in should not be confused at all with *apokatastasis* or with a simplistic assertion that Christ "experienced" the punishment of damnation. The doctrine of Christ's descent into hell, according to Balthasar, is primarily a statement of the Church's belief in the christological grounding of both heaven and hell. Christ represents the definitive eschatological irruption of God into history. As such, Christ does not simply announce, but *is* the locus of every individual's decision for or against God. Christ "provokes" a definitive decision on the part of every individual merely by his presence. This is illustrated in the New Testament in the many encounters between Jesus and the demonic, where the "demons" seem compelled to address Jesus as if provoked by some inner necessity borne of "recognition." It is illustrated still further in the frequent biblical motif that stresses the "division" which Christ brings to the world --- sheep and goats, good and evil, heaven and hell. Thus, Christ is the ground of possibility of heaven and hell -- without Christ heaven and hell as theological categories have no existential or anthropological meaning. And insofar as Christ is the teleological orientation of all inner decisions for or against God, it can be said that Christ is the very possibility of heaven and hell.[23]

---

[22]*Mysterium Paschale*, 39-75.

[23]*Mysterium Paschale*, 189-280.

What comes through quite clearly in this christological theology of heaven and hell is Balthasar's tendency toward "aesthetic" resolution within his metaphysic. The "distance within unity" of the trinitarian relations comprises the ground of possibility for the distance within unity in the God-world relationship. In the "theology of Holy Saturday" Balthasar is extending the integrating power of the trinitarian ground of possibility into the very depths of human sinfulness itself. The "spaciousness" that exists within the "distance" of the trinitarian relations "has room" to reconcile not simply God and that which is not God, but also, God and that which is anti-God. It is precisely here that Balthasar sees the importance of Christ as a bridge between the metaphysics of antiquity (with its God-world, matter-spirit dualism) and the Old Testament (with its "estrangement" of humanity from God due to sin). Christ represents the absolute synthesis of all conflict and tension within his person and work. In Christ, all of the world's "loose ends" are tied together in a perfect and masterful divine work of art.[24] The inner logic of Balthasar's position would seem to push one in the direction of saying that a final decision against God is impossible, because no matter how far "from God" a sinner went, he or she would already find Christ there with the resolution of all estrangement in hand. Balthasar seems to sacrifice something of the Church's traditional emphasis on the existential seriousness of all human self-determination -- a self-determination that even God respects -- for an emphasis on the aesthetic "wholeness" of Christ's "form" -- a form which must now "stretch" to include even that which is utterly contrary to God.

The second major problem associated with the development of Balthasar's metaphysic is that Balthasar frequently leaves one wondering as to the theological status of the various nonchristian religions. The demands of Balthasar's aesthetic seem to conflict somewhat here with those of his trinitarian metaphysic. In the aesthetic, Balthasar reiterates that God wills to be known through the concrete, the tangible, and the finite. This is shown most clearly, according to Balthasar, in the example of the Incarnation itself. However, Balthasar also affirms the teaching of Vatican II that nonchristians can have "salvific faith," and that their religions can, in some sense, mediate this faith to them. But the emphasis in Balthasar's metaphysic on the ambiguity of the religious quest outside of Christ puts his theology in tension

---

[24]*GL I*, 124.

at this point; the demand that salvific faith come through a mediation of grace through an encounter with a concrete "form," suddenly becomes an abstract searching for Christ "behind" the "distortions" that these forms introduce.[25] Grace, suddenly, becomes much more of an"internal light" resembling Rahner's supernatural existential -- an ironic fact considering Balthasar's criticism of its extension in the notion of the "anonymous Christian."[26]

Balthasar, of course, cannot be judged too harshly for this tension, since the issue of the relationship between nonchristian religions and the absolute claims of Christianity is far from resolved in the theological world in general. The various attempts at a resolution still seem far from satisfying in any definitive sense. Thus, one of the greatest areas for a future development of Balthasar's theology is in the area of ecumenical dialogue with nonchristian religions. A beginning could be made in this regard by extending Balthasar's aesthetic beyond the purely cultic and iconographic element of nonchristian religions, and into the realm of the ethical. Balthasar's emphasis on the concrete nature of truth could shift from an analysis of how "revelation" might be taking place in the various holy books, worship, and beliefs of a religion, and toward an analysis of how this "particularity" of truth might be manifested in the categorical nature of moral obligation. The heroic, kenotic form of love exemplified by Christ, finds an earthly echo in the self-sacrificing love of parents for their children, of spouses for one another, and of neighbor for neighbor. Who would dare say that the almost daily examples of love in the face of inhuman conditions and the horrors of poverty are not "bathed" in the "radiance" of grace? Could it not be said, using an older terminology, that such acts of love are the "ordinary" means of salvation for most people, including many Christians, and that "religion" represents the "extraordinary" means?

It is perhaps here that Balthasar's bringing together of theological aesthetics and theological "biography" might bear the most ecumenical fruit. The Christian's metaphysical claims for the "absolute" nature of Christ's salvific action would also then be translated from an ahistorical cosmology with no possibility of evidentiary rebuttal, into a claim for the absolute identity in Christ between his person and his "doctrine." This is underscored by Balthasar's insistence that the "objective" quality in revelation has but one goal: the internal movement of the person toward a

---

[25]*GL I*, 123.
[26]"From the Theology of God to Theology in the Church," 215.

greater participation in the love that is from God. The point to ecumenical dialogue, therefore, would be the attempt to shed light on the many common ways in which all religions move us toward the *unum necessarium* of the gospel. Furthermore, in ecumenical dialogue, this emphasis on the "one thing necessary" would become the "canon within the canon" for Christians that would judge all of the various forms of their own religion as well.

All of the foregoing underscores yet another dimension of Balthasar's theology: the necessary connection between theology and holiness. Balthasar's situating of theology within an ecclesial context is marked by a strong concern for the integrity of revelation as it has been received and "passed on" by the Church. What Balthasar wants to avoid is an image of the theologian as the "expert" who alone can unlock the "true" meaning of revelation -- a meaning that is viewed as obscured by the distortions of the later biases of "faith." This conjures up an image of the theologian as a lone intellectual hero "tilting at the ecclesial windmill" in order to "liberate" revelation from the reactionary shackles of the "institution." This view, according to Balthasar, "atomizes" the theologian and alienates him or her from the Church. Against this view, which Balthasar sees as "dissecting" the *Gestalt* of revelation, he proposes an image of the theologian whose formal stance before revelation is no different from that of any believer. Faith and personal holiness are the only legitimate starting points for any theology that seeks to be "adequate" to its supernatural object.[27]

The strength of this approach is that it reasserts the importance of the Church in the ongoing drama of salvation history. It questions the rather superficial opposition between "revelation as it really was," and "revelation as it has been mediated." Balthasar too draws such a distinction, but only to later reintegrate the form of the Christ-event with its "later" mediations. Balthasar sees much of modern theology as engaging in an unhealthy emulation of the reductionistic method of the "hard sciences," with their materialistic assumption that the whole is not greater than the sum of its parts. This destroys any aesthetic awareness within theology of the marvelous manner in which God's providence works immanently in history to weave together the great tapestry of revelation. Reductionistic theological methods never seem able to detect such providence, and end up in an elusive quest

---

[27]*Explorations in Theology I*, "Theology and Sanctity," 207-209.

to peel back the layers of the historical onion in order to get at the real object of revelation.[28] These approaches, born out of the Enlightenment, ultimately rest on a dualism of body and spirit that destroys their ontological compatibility and, therefore, the aesthetic *Gestalt* that their union brings about. Insofar as theology is infected with such a dualistic view, Balthasar would seem justified in his contention that the Enlightenment is to be viewed as a neo-pagan reassertion of the dual realities of myth and philosophy against the integrating authority of Christian revelation.

This critique of the Enlightenment becomes especially clear in Balthasar's treatment of biblical exegesis. Balthasar's critique of the reductionistic approach of many modern exegetes is a powerful reminder not to let the quest for the "historical Jesus" obscure the basic theological truth that all of Scripture is inspired. Given that fact, any exegesis which tries to drive an oppositional wedge between revelation "contained" in the Bible, and the "later" biblical theology that develops around it, is doomed to miss the overall aesthetic force of the total biblical *Gestalt* . Balthasar's theology of revelation -- the constant referring of all "parts" to their place in the larger "whole," -- is a more effective tool for preserving the unity of the biblical canon than the "scissors and paste" approach of so much "scientific" exegesis.[29] The assumption that the "neutral" exegete is more capable of retrieving the real historical Jesus, is simply a prejudice born out of the anti-supernatural bias of the Enlightenment. If the "real" Jesus was and is God incarnate, then, in fact, the believer has a better methodological starting point than does the neutral exegete. The assumption of modernity since the Enlightenment that faith represents a "biased" unsubstantiated worldview, is itself the product of a biased unsubstantiated worldview.[30]

Thus, Balthasar's critique of the Enlightenment, though often polemical, and frequently attacking "straw men," is, nevertheless, one of the strongest and most compelling aspects of his theology. The emphasis on the "objectivity" of the perspective of faith is a strong methodological reaffirmation of the reliability of the witness of Scripture and of the Church. The ecclesial nature of theology, therefore,

---

[28]*GL I*, 467-480.

[29]*GL I*, 466.

[30]Roch Kereszty, "Historical Research, Theological Inquiry, and the Reality of Jesus: Reflections on the Method of J.P. Meier," *Communio*, (Winter, 1992), 576-600.

should not be seen as a curtailment of the theologian's "academic freedom." It is instead a reaffirmation of the only real limb that the theologian has to stand on: the objectivity, reliability, and intellectual integrity of the "knowledge" that faith brings. Balthasar's assertion that it is the task of the theologian to render *pistis* into *gnosis* is a needed reminder that "faith" is not something the theologian should be "suspicious" of, but rather, is the only standpoint that gives theology any validity at all.[31]

This strong emphasis in Balthasar's method on the ecclesial (faith) dimension of theology leads us to another area that is both promising and problematical: the use of sexual archetypes in his ecclesiology. Balthasar's use of sexual archetypes is both enlightening and confusing. They are enlightening insofar as they do seem to shed a genuine light on the use of sexual and bridal metaphors within the Scriptures. Balthasar's development of masculine/feminine archetypes as a tool for describing the relationship between Christ and the Church, Christ and Mary, and nature and grace, has the beneficial effect of maintaining a personalistic context for his ecclesiology. It allows Balthasar to view the institutional structures of the Church as both relative and authoritative at the same time. It guards against an overly sociological analysis of the Church as simply one more human institution without any particular supernatural mystery to it. Furthermore, this "mystery" is not viewed as an "occult" knowledge of divine secrets, but as "public" and existential. The personalizing influence of the use of sexual archetypes allows theology to see its task as the reintegration of all things into a divine/human subjectivity, rather than an arid intellectual exercise in dissection. It also allows for a more profoundly ecclesiological and christological mariology.

The use of the sexual archetypes, however, presents a problem when they lose their polyvalent potential and get locked into one particular interpretation. Balthasar's development of the archetypes emphasizes the role of the masculine as that which is "objective," "aggressive," and "initiating," while the feminine is seen as "subjective," "obedient," and "receptive." Balthasar emphasizes that the masculine dimension of the Church is an outgrowth of the feminine and is, in a sense, an "inferior" principle within the Church. Nevertheless, there is a danger

---

[31]*GL I*, 136-141.

here for the masculine, institutional Church to be oversacralized in its pastoral functions. Here, once again, Balthasar's theology cannot be understood without remembering his connection to Adrienne von Speyr and the secular institute with which they were both associated. Balthasar's development of his Jesuit Ignatian spirituality with its emphasis on the development of an "inner indifference" in order to better discern the will of God cannot be overlooked. This partly accounts for his constant affirmations that the believer and the theologian must adopt a similar attitude with regard to revelation.[32] Furthermore, Balthasar's love of Carmelite spirituality with its emphasis on "obedience" further reinforces what Balthasar sees as the need for obedience to revelation. This connection to the kind of "obedience" found in traditional religious life helps to explain Balthasar's strong conviction that the ecclesial office exercises the very authority of Christ in a believer's life. In the traditional theology of the evangelical counsels in religious life, there is often a connection drawn between the will of God and the will of one's religious superiors. The religious is expected to be obedient to the "rule" as if it came from Christ, even if it may occasionally lead to situations which are confusing. The "rule," whose christological authority is embodied in the superior, has a pedagogical value in the spiritual life -- the "soul" is "trained" to "lose" itself in the needs of the community and to grow in humility and self-effacement. Balthasar explicitly refers to the "externalization" of revelation in the Church as representing an "objective rule" with a pedagogical value in training the believer how to be obedient before Christ.[33] However, even though the strong pedagogical role of the magisterium may need reemphasizing in a narcissistic age that insists upon the "right" of the individual to do anything, nevertheless, it does run the risk of oversacralizing the magisterium and cutting-off debate on controversial issues.

Where is the self-correcting mechanism that the "sense of the faithful" brings to the magisterium? Balthasar mentions the necessity of the magisterium to listen to the faithful, and he is certainly not an exponent of a return to an old fashioned ecclesiology that sees the laity as "extensions" of the work of the hierarchy. His theology of "mission," and the various complementary charisms within the one *communio* of Christ's body, precludes any such interpretation. However, his use of sexual archetypes, although helpful in so many ways, must

---

[32]Balthasar, *Elucidations*, (London: S.P.C.K., 1975), 88-90.
[33]*GL I*, 452.

not be misused in order to justify an overbearing magisterium. They must be seen in the total context of his theology with its attempt to reintegrate dogmatics and the spirituality of the evangelical counsels.

Balthasar's use of sexual archetypes also produces a problem with the modern world's legitimate concern for the equality of women in society. The emphasis on the "feminine" obedience of the Church to the masculine Christ sacramentally embodied in Church office, is offensive to many people. Such language could easily be used to legitimate a more traditional position of subservience for women in society and in the Church.[34] Furthermore, modern science can challenge the legitimacy of the stereotypes embodied in Balthasar's use of the archetypes; the "feminine" dimension of our humanity should not be characterized in its essence as "receptive," "obedient," "nurturing," and "immanent," nor should the "masculine" dimension be seen in its essence as "initiating," "outgoing," "transcendent," and "rational."[35] Furthermore, many of Balthasar's statements on this topic only add to his critics' concern that he is not sensitive enough to the problems that his use of sexual archetypes creates. For example, Balthasar stresses that when the Church strives to overcome its "feminine" and "receptive" nature by "grasping" after authority and power in a "masculine" manner, the Church thereby becomes guilty of a kind of "religious homosexuality." This same "religious homosexuality" is present whenever human beings resort to a magical conception of God and seek to "encroach" upon the Deity through manipulation rather than being "receptive" to the divine overtures.[36] Also, Balthasar's use of the dual images of "masculine" penetration and "feminine" receptivity often sounds like what modern readers could only characterize as the language of rape.[37] Thus, Balthasar's use of sexual archetypes, though helpful as

---

[34] Elisabeth Schussler Fiorenza, *In Memory of Her: A Feminist Theological Reconstruction of Christian Origins,* (New York: Crossroad, 1990), 266-270.

[35] Elizabeth A. Johnson, *She Who Is: The Mystery of God in Feminist Theological Discourse,* (New York: Crossroad, 1992), 47-54; 174-175.

[36] Balthasar, *Explorations in Theology II,* 188.

[37] Balthasar's constant reiteration that the proper disposition of the "feminine" Church toward the "masculine" overtures of God is one of complete obedience to the point of a willed servility borders on the language of rape. This is not, of course, what Balthasar means by such language, nor does he develop this concept into anything other than an emphasis on the primacy of grace in the God-world relationship. However, the emphasis on the need for the "feminine" to remain docile before the will and overtures of the "masculine," and of the nature of the "feminine" as that which must "give way" to the "penetration" of the "masculine," is offensive to modern

a tool for understanding some of the scriptural images which draw upon sexual metaphors, nevertheless creates many problems for modern readers who might find such language highly offensive and a stumbling block to further research into Balthasar's theology.

B. The Historical Significance of Balthasar's Theology

It is always difficult to assess the exact significance of any period of history until enough time has passed to see how the various characters and plots play themselves out. What may seem of enormous importance at the time may be scarcely remembered in one hundred years. And what had seemed so trivial as to be barely taken notice of may prove to be the most significant event of all. Such is the situation in the modern world of Catholic theology. So much has happened in the past century, and so much confusion and doubt still remains, that it is difficult to pinpoint with any accuracy those theological currents that are of the most importance. However, it can be said without tremendous fear of contradiction that the Second Vatican Council was certainly one of those watershed moments in the modern history of the Church. That fact alone should provide us with something of a hermeneutical tool for judging the relative importance of various currents of theology within the Church. The following principle could be offered as worthy of consideration: those theologies most directly responsible for making the Council possible by either, a) laying the theological groundwork for the Council, or b) having a direct influence on the Council documents, or c) exercising a pivotal role in the implementation of the Council, could be said to be of seminal and historical importance. This principle is broad enough that it encompasses a wide spectrum of theological opinions, and yet narrow enough to allow judgments to be passed. Furthermore, any theology which fits two or more of the above categories (such as Rahner's theology) should be seen as possessing special importance.

The school of theology known as *ressourcement theologie*, spoken of in chapter one, would certainly fall under at least two of the above categories. It was extremely influential as part of the patristic and liturgical revival during the period

ears. Cf. Hans Urs von Balthasar, *The Von Balthasar Reader*, eds. Medard Kehl and Werner Loser, (New York: Crossroad, 1982), 214-216.

between the two wars, and gained in influence in the immediate aftermath of World War II.[38] The Council documents reflect its concern for a complete reform of theological dogmatics through a return to patristic and biblical sources.[39] The only open question is to what extent this theology has lost its influence in the years following the Council. The rise of political, feminist, and liberation theologies seem to have left the more traditional *ressourcement* theologies behind.[40] The new social awareness of the Church, the growing secularity of traditionally Catholic countries, and the constant assaults on the Church's moral teaching, all point in the direction of a need for a more aggressive, apologetical, fundamental theology that seeks a "common ground" with the world of secular modernity in order to engage it in a meaningful dialogue. The very "churchiness" of the older *ressourcement* theology restricts its audience and limits its apologetical utility. The fact of the matter is that precious few people in today's world care about what Tertullian had to say about the "bridal" character of the Church, or whether Origen elaborated upon Christ's descent into hell.

Theology of any kind, of course, has never been a "popular" pursuit such that its main concerns were also the concerns of the average person. However, insofar as premodern cultures remained within a largely mythopoetic worldview, there was at least a common agreement that an exploration of the main scriptural and ecclesial metaphors for God and Christ had a normative significance and meaning. The situation has changed drastically since the rise of the scientific worldview.[41] The challenge now is to show why traditional Christian ideas about God and world, created as they were within a prescientific worldview, should still be considered normative in any sense for today. There is a common agreement within modern culture that things today are somehow qualitatively "different" and discontinuous with the worldview of the past. There is an attitude, therefore, that past religious truth claims can offer little guidance to the radically new and unique conditions of

---

[38]Cf. Joseph A. Komonchak, "Theology and Culture at Mid-Century: The Example of Henri de Lubac," *Theological Studies*, (December, 1990), 579-602; Aidan Nichols, O.P., *From Newman to Congar: The Idea of Doctrinal Development from the Victorians to the Second Vatican Council*, (Edinburgh: T&T Clark, 1990).

[39]Cf. *Optatam Totius*, 13-18; *Spiritus Domini*, 72-73.

[40]These theologies, of course, also reflect the concern of *ressourcement* theology to develop the tradition. However, they do so with a much more direct eye on changing modern social situations which are marked by injustice. Their hermeneutical stance, therefore, is markedly different from that of the *ressourcement* theologian.

[41]Cf. Hans Kung, *Theology for the Third Millennium*, 123-206.

the present.[42] Fundamental theology, with its concern for the "ground of possibility" for a religious worldview at all, is a much more influential branch of theology in the modern academy. Therefore, almost all of the *ressourcement* theology that was developed before the Council, including Balthasar's theology, despite its important role in the development of the Council, finds that it must rely on the work of the fundamental theologians before it can proceed with an elaboration of Christian doctrine from within the criteria of the tradition itself.

This raises two questions. First, does the relative marginalization of *ressourcement* theology in the modern academy mean that its time has come and gone? Or will its real importance be one day rediscovered by a more contemplative age that seeks a grounding in a less political and more theocentric theology -- what Walter Kasper refers to as "theological theology?"[43] Second, is *ressourcement* theology representative of the fact that all strongly "confessional" theologies will normally be of interest only to those who are trained in theology and have the specific vocation of bringing theology to the Church? I would submit that the answer to both of these sets of questions is "yes." Theologians who engage in the study of the history of doctrine and of the Church's tradition in order to retrieve it for the present, will never be "popular" in the modern sense. Furthermore, even if the particular *ressourcement* theologians who had the most influence in this century are no longer in vogue, it does not mean that the "method" they articulated is lost. There will always be a need to retrieve the Church's tradition, and the necessity of developing a strong biblical theology will always be with the Church. The Church simply cannot long survive if it simply accepts the popular assumption of modernity that the past is of little normative value for the present. For better or for worse, the Church's fate is tied to that of its living tradition. Various *ressourcement* theologians may have their influence "ebb and flow" depending on the current "signs of the times." However, in one fashion or another, the Church will always

---

[42]Cf. William V. Dych, S.J., *A World of Grace: An Introduction to the Themes and Foundations of Karl Rahner's Theology*, Leo J. O'Donovan, ed., "Theology in a New Key," 1-16. Dych points out that the traditional starting points for theology -- scripture, God, Jesus -- are problematical for modern people and are, therefore, unsuitable as a starting point in our dialogue with the world. The answer lies in an "anthropological turn" that seeks a common grounding between theology and secularity in an analysis of the transcendental dynamics of human subjectivity.

[43]Walter Kasper, "Postmodern Dogmatics: Toward a Renewed Discussion of Foundations in North America, *Communio*, (Summer, 1990), 191.

have need of theologians whose primary concern is with the retrieval of the tradition as a service to the teaching function of the Church. Thus, the real historical significance of the *ressourcement* theologians may be as pedagogical guides for the proper way to engage in a theology that has the Church as its primary audience.

This, in turn, has the added advantage of helping us to understand the proper approach to the Council itself. There has been much controversy surrounding the proper implementation of the conciliar decrees; should the letter of the Council be followed as a key to understanding its proper application, or should theologians appeal to the notion of the "spirit" of the Council as a warrant for going further in the reforms than what the Council itself would have dared sanction? The answer lies in an examination of the manner in which the Council engaged in theological reflection. *Ressourcement* theology had helped pave the way for the Council, and its influence can be seen in the way the Council approached theological reform. In both its dogmatic and pastoral constitutions, the Council emphasized a return to a more biblical and patristic grounding for theology. This renewed theology would also have a deeper orientation to "experience" as a primary category, and an eye on influencing the Church's *praxis* . However, once committed to such a program, the Council could not predict what direction reform would take, since it could not, as yet, anticipate all of the fruits that such an approach might yield. Issues such as the ordination of women, the democratization of Church structures, clerical celibacy, and ecumenical relations with other religions, might have been given fairly traditional reaffirmations in the Council. But the theological method followed by the Council leaves open the possibility that such teachings, among others, may not be treated as "sacred cows" just because they appear in the "letter" of the Council in traditional garb. However, the conciliar method also raises a caution against any change that is simply an ill-advised appeasement of the prevailing *Zeitgeist* . All reforms must be theologically rooted in the ongoing and living tradition of the Church. All change must flow from within the Church's deepest and most proper sources. The method of the Council, therefore, is predicated upon the same principle as that of *ressourcement* theology: a profound openness to the Spirit through an ever-deeper immersion in the depths of revelation as mediated through the Church.

Balthasar's theology is significant because of its continuation of this approach to theology in the post-conciliar era. Most of the main ideas of his theology were already contained, at least seminally, in his theological work before the Council. Nevertheless, Balthasar's theological trilogy was written during and after the Council.[44] What Balthasar's later theology represents, therefore, is a post-conciliar attempt at *ressourcement* theology that seems to be slowly growing in its influence. The sheer scope and size of the theological trilogy reminds one of Barth's *Church Dogmatics* ; the breadth of its vision provides an integrating reference point for many modern dogmatic theologians who may disagree with some of Balthasar's particular stands, but admire the overall "context" that his theology can provide for a reform of dogmatics. In an age in which theological specialization and the "contextualization" of political theology have rendered large-scale systematic theologies rare, the appearance of a theology as broad as Balthasar's acts as a corrective against the splintering of dogmatics into a thousand "viewpoints." It also has apologetic value for that same reason as well. It offers the theologian a hermeneutical tool for interpreting the tradition in a synthetic manner. It goes a long way toward answering the objection that the Church's various doctrines represent a set of internally inconsistent assertions. Whether or not one accepts or rejects the claims of Christianity, theologies such as Balthasar's, at the very least, give the Church's teaching an internal consistency and, therefore, a certain measure of credibility.

Finally, the most important aspect of Balthasar's theology may be in his assertion that fundamental and dogmatic theology must coincide with one another, and that the primacy in this relationship resides with dogmatic theology.[45] What Balthasar has attempted to do is to develop a dogmatic theology that is, as such, a fundamental theology. In so doing, he articulates an important methodological point that had always been latent in most *ressourcement* theologies, but had never been made clear. This seems to be one of the most important insights of Balthasar's entire theology: the credibility of revelation must, ultimately, come from within revelation itself. *Ressourcement* theology, therefore, must not be seen as merely a "churchy" theology whose only concern is to make sure that the

---

[44]The development of Balthasar's theological aesthetic is a perfect example of this unbroken continuity between his pre-conciliar and post-conciliar theology. He wrote the seminal essay, "Revelation and the Beautiful," in 1960. By 1965 he had already begun his complete theological aesthetic. Cf. *Verbum Caro (Skizzen zur Theologie I)*, (Einsiedeln: Johannes Verlag, 1960).

[45]*GL I*, 126-127.

Church's teaching is internally credible. Such a narrow view of dogmatic theology turns the theologian into a glorified grammar teacher, and runs the risk of turning the Church's teaching into a beautifully symmetrical solipsism that confuses the elegance of its own jargon with reality. The need to avoid theological solipsism has always been the legitimate insight of fundamental theology, and the fundamental flaw of all purely "intratextual" theologies. Balthasar wishes to extend that insight into dogmatic theology itself, and to turn the explication of revelation from within its own categories into an assertion of universal truth -- an assertion made credible by the existential light that revelation sheds on our existence.

The theologian must not ignore the "signs of the times" or the possible ways in which revelation can be "updated" in order to meet the needs of a changing intelligibility structure in any given culture. Furthermore, Balthasar accepts, to a certain extent, the characterization of modernity as radically different from the premodern. However, he sees this difference, at least in the area of religion, as a largely negative development from an age which still had the ability to "see" spiritual realities, to one that does not.[46] Also, he does not view the spiritual blindness and the anti-supernatural bias of modernity as in any way representing a part of the "natural evolution" of humanity from the pre-critical to the scientific. This evolution from the pre-critical to the scientific was inevitable. However, the anti-supernatural bias that has developed in its wake was not; anti-religious materialism represents a philosophical extension of the "ethos" of the scientific method into an unsubstantiated worldview. The scientific method as such has nothing to say about the existence or nonexistence of a possible supernatural realm. It is, therefore, the task of theology to "unmask" the idolatry of the modern "science myth" by confronting it with an "ethos" (aesthetic) drawn from revelation. Such an approach does not preclude apologetics -- not even an apologetics that must "bracket" the faith from time to time -- but it does point to a definition of apologetics as a subcategory of dogmatics.

Balthasar's theology represents an attempt to make the intelligibility of revelation stand on its own, and to provoke a "decision" from the individual who is confronted with the aesthetic and dramatic force of the Christ-form. This existential quality within revelation to provoke a decision must not be downplayed as one

---

[46]*GL IV*, 17.

analyzes the merits of Balthasar's approach. Latent in Balthasar's assertion that revelation has its own inner, existential, credibility lies an anthropological assumption drawn from theology: human beings are teleologically oriented to grace and, therefore, to faith. Thus, the theologian must never underestimate the simple, but profound, power of revelation to transform lives and to convince "closed" hearts. If that assumption is false, then no amount of frantic "apologetics," secretly convinced that revelation presents us with an untenable position, will ever convince anyone that faith really does represent a fulfilling of human nature. Therefore, the lasting significance of Balthasar's theology of revelation may be in its attempt to unite the concerns of fundamental and intratextual theologies -- from within a strongly contemplative dogmatics there arises the insight that only God's love is credible as the Mystery that explains the question that humanity is to itself.

Bibliography

Balthasar, Hans Urs Von. <u>Christian Meditation</u>. San Francisco: Ignatius Press, 1989.

_____. <u>Credo: Meditations on the Apostles Creed</u>. New York: Crossroad, 1990.

_____. <u>Dare We Hope "That All Men Be Saved"?</u> San Francisco: Ignatius Press, 1988.

_____. <u>The Christian State of Life</u>. San Francisco: Ignatius Press, 1983.

_____. <u>Church and World</u>. New York: Herder and Herder, 1967.

_____. <u>Convergences</u>. San Francisco: Ignatius Press, 1983.

_____. <u>Does Jesus Know Us? Do We Know Him?</u> San Francisco: Ignatius Press, 1983.

_____. <u>Elucidations</u>. London: SPCK, 1975.

_____. <u>Explorations in Theology. Volume One: The Word Made Flesh</u>. San Francisco: Ignatius Press, 1989.

_____. <u>Explorations in Theology. Volume Two: Spouse of the Word</u>. San Francisco: Ignatius Press, 1991.

_____. <u>Explorations in Theology. Volume Three: Creator Spirit</u>. San Francisco: Ignatius Press, 1993.

_____. <u>Explorations in Theology. Volume Four: Spirit and Institution</u>. San Francisco: Ignatius Press, 1995.

_____. <u>First Glance At Adrienne Von Speyr</u>. San Francisco: Ignatius Press, 1981.

_____. <u>In The Fullness of Faith: On the Centrality of the Distinctively Catholic</u>. San Francisco: Ignatius Press, 1988.

_____. <u>The Glory of the Lord: A Theological Aesthetics. Vol. One: Seeing the Form</u>. San Francisco: Ignatius Press, 1982.

_____. <u>The Glory of the Lord: A Theological Aesthetics. Vol. Two: Studies in Theological Style: Clerical Styles.</u> San Francisco: Ignatius Press, 1984.

_____. <u>The Glory of the Lord: A Theological Aesthetics. Vol. Three: Studies in Theological Style: Lay Styles.</u> San Francisco: Ignatius Press, 1986.

_____. <u>The Glory of the Lord: A Theological Aesthetics. Vol. Four: The Realm of Metaphysics in Antiquity</u>. San Francisco: Ignatius Press, 1989.

_____. <u>The Glory of the Lord: A Theological Aesthetics. Vol. Five: The Realm of Metaphysics in the Modern Age</u>. San Francisco: Ignatius Press, 1991.

_____. <u>The Glory of the Lord: A Theological Aesthetics. Vol. Six: Theology: The Old Covenant</u>. San Francisco: Ignatius Press, 1991.

_____. <u>The Glory of the Lord: A Theological Aesthetics. Vol. Seven: Theology: The New Covenant</u>. San Francisco: Ignatius Press, 1989.

_____. <u>Heart of the World</u>. San Francisco: Ignatius Press, 1979.

_____. <u>*Kosmische Liturgie. Hohe und Krise des griechischen Weltbildes bei Maximus Confessor*</u>, Einsiedeln: Johannes-Verlag, 1941.

_____. <u>Love Alone: The Way of Revelation</u>. London: Sheed and Ward, 1970.

_____. <u>The Moment of Christian Witness</u>. New York: Newman Press, 1969.

_____. <u>*Mysterium Paschale.*</u> Edinburgh: T&T Clark, 1990.

_____. New Elucidations. San Francisco: Ignatius Press, 1986.

_____. The Office of Peter and the Structure of the Church. San Francisco: Ignatius Press, 1986.

_____. Prayer. New York: Sheed and Ward, 1968.

_____. *Schleifung der Bastionem*, Einsiedeln: Johannes Verlag, 1952.

_____. A Short Primer for Unsettled Laymen. San Francisco: Ignatius Press, 1985.

_____. Test Everything: Hold Fast to What is Good. An Interview With Hans Urs Von Balthasar by Angelo Scola. San Francisco: Ignatius Press, 1989.

_____. Theo-Drama: Theological Dramatic Theory. Volume One: Prologomena. San Francisco: Ignatius Press, 1988.

_____. Theo-Drama: Theological Dramatic Theory. Volume Two: Dramatis Personae: Man in God. San Francisco: Ignatius Press, 1990.

_____. Theo-Drama: Theological Dramatic Theory. Volume Three: Dramatis Personae: Persons in Christ. San Francisco: Ignatius Press, 1992.

_____. Theo-Drama: Theological Dramatic Theory. Volume Four: The Action. San Francisco: Ignatius Press, 1994.

_____. A Theological Anthropology. New York: Sheed and Ward, 1967.

_____. A Theology of History. New York: Sheed and Ward, 1963.

_____. The Theology of Karl Barth. San Francisco: Ignatius Press, 1992.

_____. The Threefold Garland: The World's Salvation in Mary's Prayer. San Francisco: Ignatius Press, 1982.

_____. Truth is Symphonic: Aspects of Christian Pluralism. San Francisco: Ignatius Press, 1987.

_____. Word and Redemption: Essays in Theology 2. New York: Herder and Herder, 1965.

_____. Word and Revelation: Essays in Theology 1. New York: Herder and Herder, 1964.

Journals

Balthasar, Hans Urs von. "Christian Prayer." Communio: International Catholic Review, (Spring, 1978): 15-22.

_____. "On the Concept of Person." Communio: International Catholic Review, (Spring, 1986): 18-26.

_____. "Creation and Trinity." Communio: International Catholic Review, (Fall, 1988): 285-293.

_____. "Earthly Beauty and Divine Glory." Communio: International Catholic Review, (Fall, 1983): 202-206.

_____. "Ephesians 5:21-33 and Humanae Vitae: A Meditation." Christian Married Love, ed. Raymond Dennehy. San Francisco: Ignatius Press, 1981: 55-73.

_____. "From the Theology of God to Theology in the Church." Communio: International Catholic Review, (Fall, 1982): 195-223.

_____. "God is His Own Exegete." Communio: International Catholic Review, (Winter, 1986): 280-287.

_____ . "The Holy Church and the Eucharistic Sacrifice." Communio: International Catholic Review, (Summer, 1985): 139-145.

_____ . "In Retrospect." Communio: International Catholic Review, (Fall, 1975): 197-220.

_____ . "Jesus and Forgiveness." Communio: International Catholic Review, (Winter, 1984): 322-334.

_____ . "Liberation Theology in the Light of Salvation History." Liberation Theology, ed. James Schall, S.J. San Francisco: Ignatius Press, 1982: 131-146.

_____ . "Life and Institution in the Church." Communio: International Catholic Review, (Spring, 1985): 25-32.

_____ . "Should Faith or Theology be the Basis of Catechesis?" Communio: International Catholic Review, (Spring, 1983): 10-16.

_____ . "Unity and Diversity in New Testament Theology." Communio: International Catholic Review, (Summer, 1983): 106-116.

Secondary Sources: Books

Auerbach, Erich, Mimesis: The Representation of Reality in Western Literature. Princeton: Princeton University Press, 1991.

Berger Peter. The Sacred Canopy: Elements of a Sociological Theory of Religion. Garden City, NY: Doubleday & Company, Inc., 1969.

Brown, Frank Burch. Religious Aesthetics: a Theological Study of Making and Meaning. Princeton: Princeton University Press, 1989.

Congar, Yves, O.P. A History of Theology. Garden City, NY: Doubleday & Company, Inc., 1968.

D'Costa, Gavin, ed. Christian Uniqueness Reconsidered: The Myth of a Pluralistic Theology of Religions. Maryknoll: Orbis, 1990.

Dulles, Avery, S.J. The Craft of Theology: From Symbol to System. New York: Crossroad, 1992.

Eco, Umberto. The Aesthetics of Thomas Aquinas. Cambridge: Harvard University Press, 1988.

Fiorenza, Elizabeth Schussler. In Memory of Her: A Feminist Theological Reconstruction of Christian Origins. New York: Crossroad, 1990.

Frei, Hans. The Eclipse of Biblical Narrative. Yale University Press, 1974.

Gadamer, Hans-Georg. The Relevance of the Beautiful and Other Essays, ed. Robert Bernasconi. Cambridge: Cambridge University Press, 1987.

_____ . Truth and Method. London: Sheed and Ward, 1975.

Gawronski, Raymond, S.J. Word and Silence: Hans Urs Von Balthasar and the Spiritual Encounter between East and West. Edinburgh: T&T Clark, 1995.

Gay, Peter. The Enlightenment: An Interpretation. The Rise of Modern Paganism. New York: W. W. Norton & Company, 1966.

_____ . The Enlightenment: An Interpretation. The Science of Freedom. New York: W. W. Norton & Company, 1969.

Goldberg, Michael. Theology and Narrative: A Critical Introduction. Nashville: Abingdon, 1981.

Guardini, Romano. <u>The World and the Person</u>. Chicago: Henry Regnery Company, 1965.

Gutierrez, Gustavo. <u>A Theology of Liberation</u>. Maryknoll: Orbis, 1985.

James, Jamie. <u>The Music of the Spheres: Music, Science, and the Natural Order of the Universe</u>. New York: Grove Press, 1993.

Johnson, Elizabeth A. <u>She Who Is: The Mystery of God in Feminist Theological Discourse.</u> New York: Crossroad, 1992.

Kasper, Walter. <u>The God of Jesus Christ</u>. New York: Crossroad, 1984.

_____. <u>Theology and Church</u>. New York: Crossroad, 1989.

Kehl, Medard, S.J., and Werner Loser, S.J. eds. <u>The Von Balthasar Reader</u>. New York: Crossroad, 1982.

Kelsey, David. <u>The Uses of Scripture in Recent Theology</u>. Philadelphia: Fortress Press, 1975.

Kung, Hans. <u>Theology for the Third Millennium: An Ecumenical View</u>. trans. by Peter Heinegg, New York: Doubleday, 1988.

Langer, Susanne K. <u>Philosophy in a New Key: A Study in the Symbolism of Reason, Rite, and Art</u>. Cambridge: Harvard University Press, 1957.

Lindbeck, George A. <u>The Nature of Doctrine: Religion and Theology in a Postliberal Age</u>. Philadelphia: The Westminster Press, 1984.

Lonergan, Bernard. <u>Method in Theology</u>. New York: Herder and Herder, 1972.

Murphy, Francesca A. <u>Christ the Form of Beauty: A Study in Theology and Literature</u>. Edinburgh: T&T Clark, 1995.

Nichols, Aidan, O.P. <u>From Newman to Congar: The Idea of Doctrinal Development from the Victorians to the Second Vatican Council</u>. Edinburgh: T & T Clark, 1990.

_____. <u>The Shape of Catholic Theology: An Introduction to its Sources, Principles, and History</u>. Collegeville, MN: The Liturgical Press, 1991.

Palmer, Richard E. <u>Hermeneutics: Interpretation Theory in Schleiermacher, Dilthey, Heidegger, and Gadamer</u>. Evanston: Northwestern University Press, 1969.

Ratzinger, Joseph. <u>Principles of Catholic Theology: Building Stones for a Fundamental Theology</u>. San Francisco: Ignatius Press, 1987.

Oakes, Edward T., S.J. <u>Pattern of Redemption: The Theology of Hans Urs Von Balthasar</u>. New York: Continuum, 1994.

O"Donnell, John J., S.J. <u>Hans Urs Von Balthasar</u>. Collegeville, MN: Liturgical Press, 1992.

_____. <u>The Mystery of the Triune God</u>. Mahwah, New Jersey: Paulist Press, 1989.

_____. <u>Trinity and Temporality: The Christian Doctrine of God in the Light of Process Theology and the Theology of Hope</u>. Oxford: Oxford University Press, 1983.

O'Hanlon, Gerard F. <u>The Immutability of God in the Theology of Hans Urs Von Balthasar</u>. Cambridge: Cambridge University Press, 1990.

Schindler, David L. ed. <u>Hans Urs Von Balthasar: His Life and Work.</u> San Francisco: Ignatius Press, 1991.

Scola, Angelo. <u>Hans Urs Von Balthasar: A Theological Style</u>. Edinburgh: T&T Clark, 1995.

Segundo, Juan Luis. <u>The Historical Jesus of the Synoptics</u>. Maryknoll: Orbis, 1985.

_____. <u>The Liberation of Theology</u>. Maryknoll: Orbis, 1988.

Sobrino, Jon. <u>The True Church and the Poor</u>. Maryknoll: Orbis, 1984.

Speyr, Adrienne von. _Das Johannesevangelium_, Einsiedeln: Johannes Verlag, 1959.

Tracy, David. The Analogical Imagination. Christian Theology and the Culture of Pluralism. New York: Crossroad, 1981.

_____. Blessed Rage For Order. The New Pluralism in Theology. New York: Seabury Press, 1975.

_____. Plurality and Ambiguity. Hermeneutics, Religion, Hope. San Francisco: Harper & Row, 1987.

Secondary Sources: Journals

Dupre, Louis. "Balthasar's Theology of Aesthetic Form." Theological Studies, (June, 1988): 299-318.

_____. "Negative Theology and Affirmation of the Finite." in Experience, Reason, God, ed. Eugene Thomas Long. Washington D.C.: Catholic University Press. 1980: 49-157.

Fiorenza, Francis S. "Theology: Transcendental or Hermeneutical?" Horizons, (Fall, 1989): 329-341.

Kasper, Walter. "Postmodern dogmatics: Toward a renewed discussion of foundations in North America." Communio: International Catholic Review, (Summer, 1990): 181-191.

Komonchak, Joseph A. "Theology and Culture at Mid-Century: The Example of Henri De Lubac." Theological Studies, (December, 1990): 579-602.

Hitchcock, James, ed. "The Achievement of Hans Urs Von Balthasar." Communio: International Catholic Review, (Fall, 1975): 197-319.

Kay, Jeffrey. "Hans Urs von Balthasar: a Post-critical Theologian?" Concilium, No. 141 (1981): 84-89.

Kelley, Anthony J, C.SS.R. "Is Lonergan's Method Adequate to Christian Mystery?" The Thomist, (July, 1975): 437-470.

Lindbeck, George A. "The A Priori in St. Thomas' Theory of Knowledge." in The Heritage of Christian Thought: Essays in Honor of Robert Lowry Calhoun, eds. Robert E. Cushman & Egil Grislis, New York: Harper and Row. (1965): 41-63.

_____. "Fides ex auditu and the Salvation of Non-Christians." in The Gospel and the Ambiguity of the Church, ed. Vilmos Vajta. 92-123. Philadelphia: Fortress Press, 1974.

Lubac, Henri de, S.J. "A Witness of Christ in the Church: Hans Urs von Balthasar." Communio: International Catholic Review, (Fall, 1975): 228-249.

Moltmann, Jurgen. "Christian Hope: Messianic or Transcendent? A Theological Discussion with Joachim of Fiore and Thomas Aquinas." Horizons, Vol. 12 No. 2 (1985): 328-348.

Oakes, Edward T., S.J. "Apologetics and the Pathos of Narrative Theology." The Journal of Religion, 37-58.

_____. "The Usurped Town: The Canon of Scripture in Postmodern Aesthetics." Communio, (Summer, 1990): 261-280.

O'Donnell, John J., S.J. "The Doctrine of the Trinity in Recent German Theology." Heythrop Journal, (April, 1982): 153-167.

_____. "The Trinity as Divine Community." Gregorianum, (1988): 5-34.

245

Olsen, Glenn W. "Hans Urs von Balthasar and the Rehabilitation of St. Anselm's Doctrine of Atonement." Scottish Journal of Theology, (1981): 49-61.

Peelman, Achiel. "The Church in the Light of the Christ Event: a Meditation Based on the Writings of Hans Urs von Balthasar." *Eglise et Theologie* , (1978): 169-207.

Reedy, Gerard. "The Christology of Hans Urs Von Balthasar." Thought, (1970): 470-420.

Riches, John K. "The Theology of Hans Urs von Balthasar: 1." Theology, (November, 1972): 562-570.

Roberts, Louis. "A Critique of the Aesthetic Theology of Hans Urs Von Balthasar." The American Benedictine Review, Vol. 16 (1965): 486-504.

Schindler, David L. "The Life and Work of Hans Urs Von Balthasar." (Thematic issue) ed. David Schindler, Communio: International Catholic Review, (Fall, 1989): 306-490.

Tracy, David. "The Uneasy Alliance Reconceived: Catholic Theological Method, Modernity, and Postmodernity." Theological Studies, (Sept. 1989): 548-570.

Waldstein, Michael. "Hans Urs von Balthasar's Theological Aesthetics." Communio: International Catholic Review, (Spring 1984): 13-27.

Religious homosexuality 232
Repristination of Revelation 218
Ressourcement 10, 11, 13, 19, 233-235, 237
Revelational positivism 107
Rousselot, Pierre 139

Salvific faith 226
Schleiermacher, Friedrich 134
Scholasticism 7, 188
Secular institute 6, 7
Sein 74
Shekinah Yahweh 102
Sheol 225
Socrates 57
Sola scriptura 188
Sophia 170
Sophiological tradition 171, 172
Sophiology 169
Speciosa 117
Spiritual exegesis 154, 172
Spiritual subject 200
Subjective faith 149
Subjective holiness 207, 208
"Subjectivity" of the Church 204
Superform 104, 105
Supernatural 23, 33, 161
Supernatural existential 227
Supernaturalism 213

Technological impersonalism 217
Teleology 154
Telos 119, 137, 154, 163, 176, 189
Tertullian 234
The fourfold distinction (ontological) 77
Theism 34
Theo-drama 133
Theologia crucis 41
Theological aesthetic 9, 13, 29, 37, 99, 100, 115, 122, 135, 218, 219, 222
Theological theology 235
Tillich, Paul 22
Tracy, David 5, 15, 17, 18, 22, 29, 143
Transcendental theology 38
Transhistoricalism 213
Trinity 82, 85, 87, 135, 202, 204, 223

Ultramontanism 188
Universal call to holiness 6
Universalism 219, 223
Universalizing rationality 164
Unum necessarium 228

Vatican II 226
Vergil 67
Vestigia trinitatis 35
Via negativa 18
Via positiva 18
Vision, theory of 135-136
Von Speyr, Adrienne 6, 7, 9, 217, 221, 231

Who is the Church? 192, 197
Williams, Rowan 28
"Wisdom" literature 170
Wrede, W. 153

250